SONOMA COUNTY

WINE LIBRARY

The Grover E. Murray Studies in the American Southwest

THE WINESLINGER CHRONICLES

THE WINE SLINGER CHRONICLES

Texas on the Vine

Russell D. Kane

Foreword by Doug Frost

Texas Tech University Press

This book is typeset in Amasis MT. The paper used in this book meets the minimum requirements of ANSI/NISO Z39.48-1992 (R1997). ∞

Designed by Kasey McBeath

Library of Congress Cataloging-in-Publication Data
Kane, R. D.
    The wineslinger chronicles : Texas on the vine / Russell D. Kane ; foreword by Doug Frost.
        p. cm. — (Grover E. Murray studies in the American Southwest)
    Includes bibliographical references and index.
    Summary: "A chronicle of Texas's emergence as a wine-producing region. Relates the stories of winegrowers, past and present, who have contributed to Texas wine culture"— Provided by publisher.
    ISBN 978-0-89672-738-0 (hardcover : alk. paper) —ISBN 978-0-89672-744-1 (e-book) 1. Wine and wine making—Texas. 2. Vintners—Texas. 3. Viticulture—Texas. I. Title.
    TP557.K35 2012
    641.2'209764—dc23   2011039937

Printed in the United States of America
12 13 14 15 16 17 18 19 20 / 9 8 7 6 5 4 3 2 1

Texas Tech University Press
Box 41037 | Lubbock, Texas 79409-1037 USA
800.832.4042 | ttup@ttu.edu | www.ttupress.org

To Delia
my wife, my partner in life

How much better is thy love than wine!
The Song of Solomon 4:10

Contents

Acknowledgments

I would like to express my gratitude to the many people who saw me through this book project; to all those who provided support, talked things over, read, wrote, offered comments, allowed me to quote their remarks, and assisted in the editing, proofreading, and design.

Charles McKinney for his long hours in telephone conversations so that I might better understand the history and context of the modern wine industry in Texas.

All of the Texas winegrowers and winemakers who took time to talk with me to share their stories and experiences.

Roy Renfro, Bob White, and Grayson County College for hosting my Munson wine tasting and for inviting me to attend the 2010 Texas Wine Quality Boot Camp.

Terry Thompson-Anderson for discussions on Texas's ethnic and regional foods and wine.

The Wine Society of Texas for their scholarship grant award that helped underwrite travel and research expenses.

The Texas Wine and Grape Growers Association for their recognition of my writings on my VintageTexas blog and for presenting me with the 2009 TWGGA Media Award.

The Texas Department of Agriculture for their maps and photographs and for their two media tours of the Texas High Plains.

Guy Stout, Master Sommelier, for many years ago encouraging me to attend and successfully complete the Level 1 Sommelier Course and Exam that furthered my understanding of wines of the world and advanced my wine-tasting abilities.

Todd Staples, Elizabeth Hadley, and Bobby Champion, who gifted me a copy of the book *Deep Roots,* from which I gained greater appreciation of the long-standing agricultural tradition of Texas and the definition of "grit and gumption."

Henry Chappell for his encouragement and advice that helped improve my writing skills.

Scott Tiras for the peace of mind he provided that allowed me to pursue this book project.

My wife, Delia Cuellar, for the hours spent reviewing, proofing, and critically evaluating my manuscript.

My daughter, Caroline Carruba, for rendering the photographs into sketches.

My son, Jacob Vaughan, for his editorial review and advice on everything from word choice to storytelling.

My mother, Beatrice Kane, for instilling in me a love of learning and a quest for knowledge.

My father, Joseph Kane, for showing me how to cook, for it was through my love of food that I found my appreciation for wine.

> " "It was through my love of food that I found my appreciation for wine" "

Just as this book was going to press, Crockett Leyendecker, 81, the acknowledged conversationalist of the "Rolling Hills," passed away on October 20, 2011. Crockett began making wine before he was old enough to drink it legally, and his stories of Texas ethnic winemaking of the past went back still further. Crockett, thank you for sharing your wonderful stories. May they long be remembered and shared by all who savor a glass of Texas wine.

Foreword

Staging a Texas Renaissance

Congratulations. If you picked up this book, you've already demonstrated a keen awareness for the sleeping juggernaut that is Texas wine. Perhaps you're curious about Texas's current role in the wine industry, or at minimum, the evolution and likely future of Texas wines. If so, you've got a remarkably thorough guide in Russell Kane, the man who's been dubbed the "Texas Wineslinger."

Russ could have written authoritatively on a myriad of subjects, but wine—particularly Texas wine—clearly fires his passion. For those of us who are aficionados of America's wine industries, this is an invaluable tome. But here's the thing: that's not why you should buy and devour this book. For one, we can admit that few people outside of the "wine geek" community (you know, hopeful Masters of Wine, Master Sommeliers, Society of Wine Educators, etc.—you know who you are) have waited for someone to unriddle the conundrum of Texas wine. While that's not why this book is important, it certainly provides some serious enlightenment.

Texas wine has been stuck in first gear, or to compare it to the Houston Astros game on my TV screen, it's as if Texas wine has been caught somewhere between first base and second. It hasn't decided whether to go for the steal—hoping to slide in under the throw—or retreat. For too long, the choice has been boringly obvious: safe at first.

How the West Was Won, but Only Briefly

Wine culture came to Texas nearly a century before it made an entry into California, arriving in cuttings brought by Spanish missionaries and the sacramental wines they made. But by the twentieth century, most vines had disappeared from Texas; American wine was synonymous with California. It was only in the 1980s that Texas wine began its rebirth: wine writers started sniffing around; French money launched a new winery in Texas (see chapter 5, Ste. Genevieve Winery). Texans were making good wines and winning medals in major competitions. And they were damned proud of it. Other Texans bought and happily consumed these wines, and, for a time, all was well. Other states such as Virginia and Colorado were inspired by Texas's success. Realizing they had come to the party a bit late, they worked harder. Many of these states were unable to grow classic European vines (e.g., Chardonnay, Cabernet, and others of the grapevine species referred to as *Vitis vinifera*). Without those familiar varieties, their industries had to rely on lesser-known grapes. Indeed, in many states vineyards were possible only through the development of new hybrid varieties (crossings

of vinifera and native American species) or learning how to make good wine from nearly forgotten or disparaged "lesser" hybrids and native grapes.

In the roughly two and a half decades since the *Wine Spectator* featured a Texas wine on its cover, many Lone Star wineries have opened their cellar doors: the number, which varies depending upon how you count, is around two hundred now. But most have continued to rely on grapes such as Chardonnay and Cabernet, varieties that, well known as they may be, are not particularly suited to the climate and conditions in most winegrowing sites around the state.

Perhaps criticism of Texas's efforts with well-known varieties seems misplaced. A business's first concern is to pay the bills, thereby giving its employees a reason to return to work the next day. Chardonnay and Cabernet Sauvignon sell, so what's the harm?

Well, consider this: the wine business is unlike any other. If you have some great ideas on how to make a new wine (one that will build upon past successes and new blends,) you have only one chance each year. Having only one harvest each year limits your ability to experiment. And worst of all, you're not dealing with the *same* growing conditions or yields year in and year out: one year it rains five feet during the growing season (that would be 2004); the next few might be drought years along with a wallop of wildfires (as with 2011). Or something devastating like Pierce's disease comes along, kills your vines, and sends you back to square one—except that now you don't have as much money as you did when you began.

So the opportunities to experiment, to try something new and perhaps light the way forward, are fleeting. In Texas, the issue should be deciding whether Tempranillo, Grenache, Mourvèdre, and Sangiovese can survive and prosper here; understanding how to coax Syrah or Muscat into something delicious; or reaching into the distant past to discover if resurrecting Black Spanish or Lomanto might be the best opportunity of all. Not that these are the grapes that should prevail. That's the point: we don't know.

Yet any step in the wrong direction (I'm looking at you, Chardonnay and Pinot Noir) takes time and energy away from the hard work that needs to be done in the vineyards of the here and now. It's not that tasty versions of Chardonnay and Cabernet aren't grown in the Great State: they are, but there are millions of liters of each grape grown in other places that can be just as tasty (or tastier or more age-worthy) and at prices that make it unlikely that Texas will be growing these two grapes fifty years hence.

If fifty years of experimentation sounds like a long time, please note that fifty years represents only fifty harvests, only fifty chances to figure out what is and isn't working and what direction Texas vineyards should take. Europe has had centuries or more to sort out their choices; it shouldn't be any wonder that they are years ahead of Texas. But time's a-wasting. Texas's best and brightest need to move forward now: is sparkling wine the ticket? Let's encourage lots of people across the state to

work on that. Dessert wines? Well, I've had some absolutely delicious Texas dessert wines. I bet there are more out there.

Somewhere along the way, Texas squandered its lead over most of the other wine-growing states. In truth, I suspect this had as much to do with Texas pride as anything else. Texans love to see Texas brands prevail; they support their own, as well they should. But that tendency allowed many wineries to rest upon their rather wilted laurels instead of pressing forward. Or so it has been until now.

Kane is Able

Now, as you'll read in these pages, there are some dedicated and sometimes just plain crazy folk planting lesser-known vines in places odd or ideal. Russ's book has its fair share of cautionary tales, of "ghost wineries" and of "winegrowers' prayers." But there are so many new vineyards and wineries that diversity is happening, whether or not the collective Texas wine industry has intended to diversify beyond the same ol' Chard and Cab. Texans may have sat back and watched other states' industries slip past them, but this book chronicles a new sense of discovery, energy, and purpose.

And as you'll read here, there are plenty of places left to plant. From kudzu-draped sycamore and scrub pine stands to prickly pear clusters, this state is too big to enjoy only one, two, or even a dozen winegrowing climates. Russ explains that herein. And he tells fascinating stories ranging from Spanish missionary days to the determination of emigrant farmers to bring wine culture to their new Texas homeland. He has looked into the tales of some unlikely vineyards, and Texas tall tales notwithstanding, these are the myths that have launched a lot of vineyards and continue to inspire winegrowers and wine consumers alike.

Why I Care, and Why You Should Too

One of my passions is an American wine competition called the Jefferson Cup. It's been around for more than a decade, and in that time Texas has always held its own against the other states represented amongst the entries. In fact, the problem has never been whether Texas will show well. It's more a matter of whether Texas wineries can afford to hand over some of their precious few bottles for the competition. Texans, as you'll read in these pages, like their wines, so much so that the rest of the country rarely gets to see the best of Texas.

But that's changing. Texan thirst is not sated yet, but Texas wines are again poised to garner national and even international attention. Read on: you'll find out why and how, and you should probably keep a pen and paper handy because you'll find a Texas trail you will want to travel and the wines waiting for you at the end of the road.

Doug Frost
Master Sommelier
Master of Wine

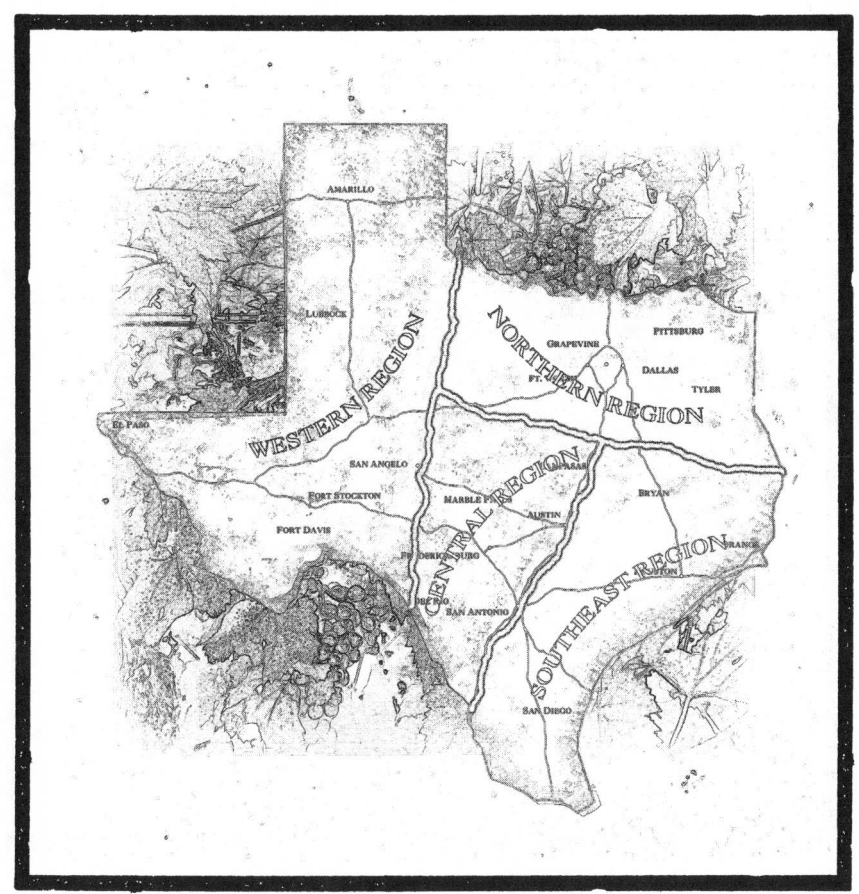

Wine Regions of Texas

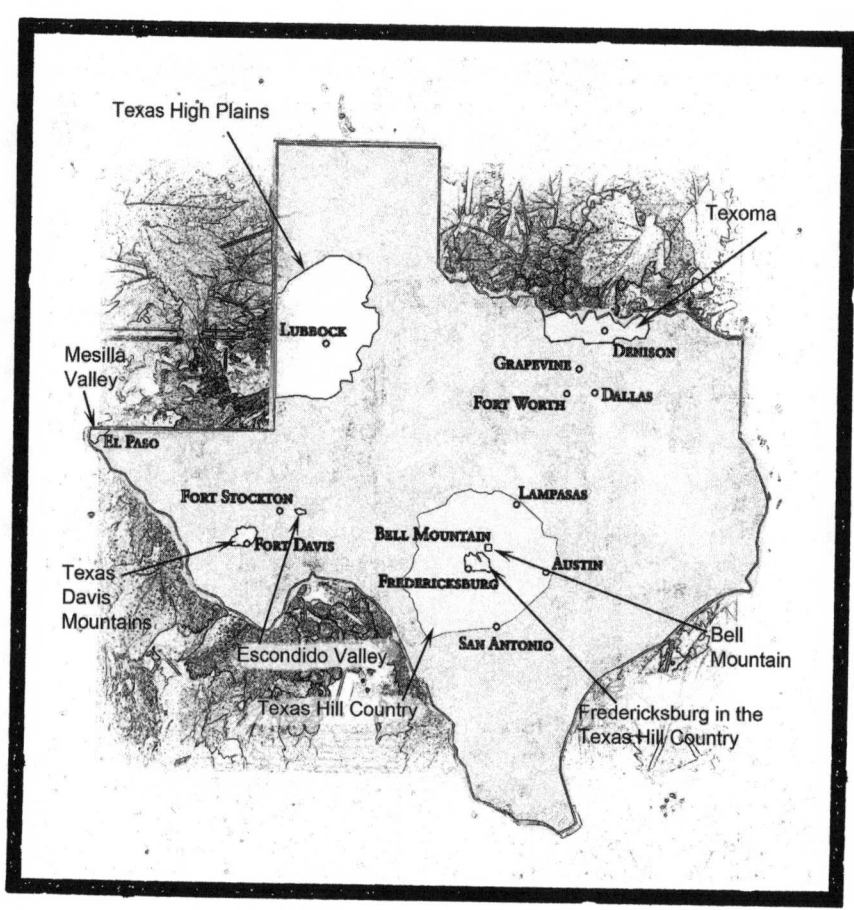

American Viticultural Areas (AVAs) in Texas

Part I

Starting the Journey

A Wineslinger Is Born

I was aware of the expanding Texas wine industry for some time, but I only recently began a journey crisscrossing the state covering all of its known wine-growing regions: western, northern, central, and southeastern. I've experienced all of its American Viticultural Areas (AVAs): Texas High Plains (far northwest near Lubbock), Texas Hill Country (central), Fredericksburg in the Texas Hill Country, Bell Mountain (north of Fredericksburg), Mesilla Valley (near El Paso), Escondido Valley (near Fort Stockton), Texas Davis Mountains (western Texas), Texoma (on the Red River to the north).

In these travels, I've sought out both major and minor places where this western wine culture started, where it was nurtured by the personal touch of man or sustained by more basic elements of nature, and where it's currently stretching out long tendrils into a mainstream industry supported by loyal but increasingly discriminating followers. Figuratively, I've taken pen in hand and started to proclaim what I've discovered, sometimes to interested people and sometimes to those who don't yet understand it but for whom the spirit of discovery enlightens.

In the process, I started a blog (VintageTexas. com), my writing workshop, which some readers call my personal Texas travelogue while others sense in it my deeper quest for knowledge and understanding. A few call my words a beard-growing manifesto. The latter group was most vocal the day I declared myself the Wine Czar of Texas and posted my ten proclamations for the Texas wine industry. I'll admit that it was a bodacious display befitting a Texan, if only a naturalized one.

These blog postings have helped me document and share my quest to define the remarkable and characteristic "sense of place" in Texas, a state where the convergence of land and man spawned a new agricultural revolution. This sense of place is something that wine people recognize and refer to as "Texas terroir."

After one of my initial trips to the Texas High Plains, I came back with what I thought was a rather down-to-earth description of its terroir in a statement from longtime winegrower Neal Newsom, whose high plains Texas Cabernet Sauvignon is winning acclaim in national and international circles. Wines made from his grapes are the foundation of several premium wine programs at wineries around the state.

Neal said, "We have red sandy loam on top of porous caliche limestone, which is a typical soil structure up here on the High Plains. It's a perfect,

disease-resistant soil for grape growing since the red sandy soil has good mineral content and drains rapidly. The underlying caliche allows the roots from the vines to easily penetrate deep underground, where it also holds on to the moisture draining through the topsoil throughout the year, even when the vines are dormant. This gives the vines a source of water that they can use all year long."

Several months after this trip, I was amazed to discover the close comparison between what Neal described and the soil in one of the world's most notable growing regions, the Australian Coonawarra.

One evening, I wrote about this seemingly odd comparison between Texas and southern Australia. Most wine aficionados know the Coonawarra (also known by its terra rossa, or red earth) as the most sought-after vineyard soil in Australia. It too covers bedrock of porous limestone, assisting good drainage but offering summer moisture retention. The terroir of the Coonawarra is one of the renowned regions for growing Cabernet Sauvignon.

My blog post consisted of the following: "Is it any wonder why our very own Texas High Plains 'Tierra Roja' produces rich, full-bodied Cabernets, and now witnesses the emergence of rich red-black Tempranillos and aromatic Viogniers? How these particular soil conditions developed on the Texas High Plains and in the Coonawarra may differ, but the results are undeniably similar. There are now about thirteen thousand acres of vineyards planted on the Australian Terra Rossa, half of them dedicated to Cabernet Sauvignon. We have only about four thousand acres planted in wine grapes in Texas and have a lot more Tierra Roja available for all comers. Now, the task is ours to work with this special soil to expand and optimize vineyard production and bring distinguished Texas wines to play on the world stage."

The following morning after my premise permeated the blogosphere, I found a reply posted on the blog of fellow wine writer Philip White, an Australian located half a world away, but in Internet terms just over my backyard fence. He cited my obvious case of "Coonawarra envy" and questioned my sanity based on a preconceived notion of Texas's affinity to cactus and not winegrowing, chalking up the rest of my argument as a bit of rant and attitude.

"Many know me now as Doc Russ, Texas Wineslinger"

He coined a name for me that incorporates a bit of unique Texas lingo intermixed with its newfound wine culture, its wild and wooly past and its present emergence as a wine-producing region. It appears to have stuck. Many know me now as Doc Russ, Texas Wineslinger.

Giddy up, pardner!

Limestone Ledges and Red Sandy Soil

2

The spring sun warmed my face as I gazed out over freshly greened prominences to the north from a perch high on an eastward-pointing finger of the Edwards Plateau: my personal piece of the Texas Hill Country. I sat there wondering how and where the Texas wine experience all began. As I let my mind override my eyes, I saw the defining moment.

The genesis occurred eons ago in a vast and desolate inland sea predating human consciousness—a wet and hostile place. At an unhurried, nearly unmeasurable pace over millions of years, the shells of countless creatures were deposited on the ocean seabed. Today, their fossil remains cover this countryside. They rest with red sandy minerals brought by estuarial flows from even older continental shores and granite slopes. From time unfathomable, the land of limestone ledges and red sandy soil emerged from the murky depths, pushed by powerful forces within the earth into the light of the Texas sun.

A half a world away on a similar geological

scale, a corresponding process occurred over parts of Europe. The Mediterranean Sea, much larger than its present size, provided its own incubator for geological birth over France.

Then, a millennium ago, the Phoenician Greeks landed on the rocky Mediterranean shore near Marseilles in southern France, bringing civilization, commerce, and their grape-growing expertise. In a flash of time compared to geologic history, Romans, the Catholic clergy, kingdoms, and corporations continued vine cultivation, each seeking the right conditions of soil and climate for what became European grape varieties. For a thousand years of modern history, humans progressed slowly, mostly by trial and error, honing artisanal crafts of grape growing and winemaking into a distinct and definable wine culture. They evolved the land-man conjunction that we know by the French word *terroir* (the sense of place) that describes the local essence of wine.

In 1659, Spanish missionaries and a handful of Christianized native families trekked into uncharted regions northward from Mexico. The Span-ish were driven by the forces of exploration and conquest, overlaid on a foundation of Catholicism that brought waves of Europeans to the Americas. Hot, dusty missionaries arrived with carefully protected vines whose grapes they used to prepare sacramental wine.

These vines and early winemakers, the first traces of what could be called North American wine culture, arrived in Texas over one hundred years before being introduced to California. The epicenter of this movement was El Paso del Norte on the banks of the Rio Grande. This wine culture traveled with Spanish missionaries who cultivated these hearty "Mission" grapevines. Quality and wine appreciation weren't essential in this early wine culture on the Texas frontier. However, wine was an essential ingredient in the Catholic liturgy.

Yet, even before the Europeans arrived, evidence collected from ancient Texas campsites and small villages shows indigenous gatherers of this region harvested the prolific native grapes. This wild fruit provided periodic sustenance for these peoples along with an appealingly sweet opportunity. These were hearty wild grapes, hybridized by nature to withstand local conditions in a wild and then inhospitable land.

This new land called Tejas, a name derived from a local native word for friend, was anything but friendly to missionaries and the settlers that followed. The native tribes were mostly resistant to Spanish conquest. Those that did accept the Spaniards did so to gain protection from enemies or to gain an advantage against adversaries in battle. In like manner, the region's ecosystem and climate were not receptive to the Spanish introduction of non-native grapevines.

Spanish reign over Texas evolved into Mexican sovereignty and continued for a century and a half until, finally, in an unholy union, it was caught in a whirlwind with the westward flow of Anglo American settlers led by men such as land impresario Stephen F. Austin. Austin, who was known for turning a good phrase, reportedly said, "Nature seemed to have intended Texas for a vineyard to supply America with wines."

His words were probably a bit of creative bluster from a speculator looking to draw European settlers to Texas, a venerable land of wine and honey, but, given the abundance of wild grapes, his description was in part true. However, it was not necessarily on the mark when it came to the quality of wines made from native grapes when compared to their European counterparts.

The nineteenth century brought a long, hard fight for the sovereignty of Texas, pitting the Anglo American settlers against their then landlords, the Mexican governors. The Republic of Texas emerged from this brutal conflict, and in another few years the state of Texas was born.

Wine was definitely not the drink of choice for Texans at this time. Something much stronger was needed to remove the sting of hot, dusty days and to calm the nerves after skirmishes with hostile natives.

Wine consumption in Texas increased with the economic development in limited portions of the state. Evidence of this comes from the personal effects of its comfortable citizenry, like the republic's native son and liberator, President Sam Houston. While Houston was best known for his early buckskin attire and affection for stronger beverages, he owned a goodly array of silver wine drinking vessels and goblets used in his later years. Given the scarcity of locally made wine, it is not surprising that manifests from ships arriving to Texas document the importation of French wines, including those from the best French regions of Burgundy, Bordeaux, and Champagne.

By the mid-1800s, California had already progressed through its Spanish missionary period

> ❝ Nature seemed to have intended Texas for a vineyard to supply America with wines ❞

and was spared the ferocity of native Comanche and Kiowa tribes that brought fear, hostilities, and death to Texans for nearly three-quarters of the century. By comparison, the gold rush brought Californians newfound wealth, rapid settlement, and the civility lacking in most parts of Texas. By this time, some well-heeled European settlers found California's sufficiency of water and hospitable climate attractive, thus making grape growing and winemaking a safe and dependable venture. While California flourished, Texas was still involved in countless hostile fights destined to preoccupy its Anglo American settlers as they continued to stream into this vast, varied, and unpredictable land.

Texans were not yet ready for crops of extravagance, instead choosing harvests that provided dependable sustenance or income. Notwithstanding, agricultural surveys of Texas from the 1800s show farmers of the state's south-central and northeastern regions found grapes a useful crop, even attempting limited forays into winemaking using both cultivated and wild grapes. Meanwhile, at this time in its young history, the last stand for domination of Texas was taking place between the zeal of American manifest destiny and the aggressions of increasingly more desperate and hostile native peoples. Encounters with hostile tribes and renegades resulted in death and depredations on both sides and delayed the civility and economic development necessary for expanding wine culture in Texas.

In my search to define Texas terroir, I've often stopped to listen to the voices of the spirits that linger in the rustle of tall grass, the gush of spring water on slab limestone, or the rush of windblown sandy soil. These are the voices that tell of the land's history, its potential, and its past and future trials that test the will of those who try to harvest its bounty. I've also listened to the unspoken words when a grower contemplates the extent of his harvest lost to a late-spring freeze or a summer hailstorm. These are the words that define the grit and gumption of the evolving Texas wine experience.

In the 1860s the Civil War in Texas brought further strife, secession, and outright man-on-man brutality, pitting family against family. Emerging from the war was a state distant from industrial centers, heavily dependent on its agricultural wits for survival. As hostilities ebbed, land was cheap, cotton was king, and hordes of wild cattle were economic opportunities on the hoof for those who had the stomach for hard labor, long hours in the saddle, and a willingness to risk life and limb.

Later in the nineteenth century, Texas became a generally more hospitable place, and technologies like windmill irrigation and barbed wire helped facilitate crop cultivation and diversification in desolate areas. Thomas Volney "T. V." Munson, a Texas transplant, spent years on horseback trekking on dusty trails throughout the state, identifying and categorizing native grape varieties that grew well and survived in harsh areas.

As a horticulturalist living in Denison, Munson also experimented with grape hybridization, crossing French grape varietals with more rugged native varieties. Some say that he traveled over ten thousand miles in Texas alone to complete his research, an amazing physical exploit for a man of his generation. Munson is famously remembered for the rootstock from native Texas grapevines that he sent to France in the late 1800s. They were used in a grafting program to save the French vineyards from widespread devastation from a soil louse named phylloxera. Today, every bottle of French wine has its roots in Texas history and owes its viability to Mr. Munson and the DNA from native Texas grapevines. In 1883, the French minister of agriculture came to Denison, Texas, and conferred the Chevalier du Mérite Agricole (in the French Legion of Honor) on Munson for his work in saving the wine industry in France.

Around Munson's time, two of the most common grapes in Texas were the Mustang, *Vitis mustangensis,* and Muscadine, *Vitis rotundifolia.* These were the grapes of Texas localities like Grape Creek, Grapeland, and Grapevine, able to withstand prolonged periods of hot, dry conditions and grapevine diseases so common in Texas. Immigrant farmers quickly found a recipe for making these grapes into stout, sharp-edged, yet palatable wines by fortifying them with sugar, sugar, and more sugar. With this tradition of sweet wines, it's understandable why some say Texas wine drinkers still have a lingering "sweet tooth."

From Munson's time to the early twentieth century, grape growing for winemaking (winegrowing) evolved into a rural endeavor. According to agricultural surveys in several Texas counties, this business activity reached the point of being commercially viable. The number of Texas wineries grew until 1919, when Texas had over fifty wineries. However, this all came to an abrupt halt with the ratification of the Eighteenth Amendment to the U.S. Constitution, the Volstead Act, also known as National Prohibition.

While Prohibition ended in 1933, it left a complicated and arcane set of laws pertaining to the production and sale of alcoholic beverages and a confounding patchwork of "wet," "dry," and "damp" areas around the state. A brutal fact of life in Texas was that most rural areas were dry, meaning that the production, sale, and consumption of alcoholic beverages of any type were outlawed. Little or no distinction was made between wine, beer, or distilled spirits. During Prohibition, legal alcoholic beverages were simply replaced by homemade distillations of readily available corn, rye, and other grains made in wood-burning stills hidden among tucks of cedar or on remote limestone ledges.

Prohibition so decimated the Texas wine industry that, after its repeal, only one Texas winery remained, Val Verde Winery in Del Rio, Texas (started in 1883 by the Qualia family). Val Verde Winery survived by making sacramental and medicinal wines and selling grapes. In the tradition of the original Spanish missions, Val Verde Winery, on its settlement near the Rio Grande, still operates and is one of the oldest wineries in North America.

It was only in the late 1990s that the number of Texas wineries would finally exceed the pre-Prohibition number. The post-Prohibition maze of state laws governing the production of alcoholic beverages and a monopolistic alcohol distribution system in Texas placed a serious barrier to the development of a commercial wine industry. It was not until decades after the end of Prohibition (in fact, only about thirty years ago) that Texas gave birth to a modern commercial wine industry. It transitioned from native Mustang, Muscadine, and French-American hybrid grape wines and fruit wines made from wild berries, peaches, and melons to growing and making wine from classic European varietals, *Vitis vinifera,* with well-known names like Chardonnay, Riesling, Chenin Blanc, Cabernet Sauvignon, and Merlot.

It's been a slow, hard process to untangle legal obstructions to favor wine production and distribution from the growing number of Texas wineries, and to develop growing techniques here that support the cultivation of classic grape varietals of Europe. Simply put, the "textbook" on Texas grape growing and winemaking is still being written; the ink is still wet, with many pages still blank. Many challenged that wine "grape farming" just could

> **"The modern Texas wine experience is fresh, young, and, in many regards, still rapidly developing"**

not be done in Texas; the heat, humidity, or soil just wasn't right, or there were too many "critters" and diseases that would turn the vines into dry sticks in the hot summer sun.

Today, the good news is that, through the long, hard scrabble, Texas breeds some of the most zealous lovers of its local wines. Texas is now the fourth-largest wine-consuming state in the nation, and Texans drink the vast majority of the premium wine produced in the state. There may be no other state in the Union that so actively supports its own wineries the way Texas now does.

A surprise to many is that Texas ranks behind only California, Washington, New York, and Oregon. If you ask wine friends to name the top five wine-producing states in the United States, they'll undoubtedly ramble through the first four states with little effort. However, when they come to number five, a blank look will overtake them, followed by several wrongly named states.

The modern Texas wine experience is fresh, young, and, in many regards, still rapidly developing, but is overlaid on the spirit of past encounters and challenges and one of the oldest wine cultures in North America. It's being crafted by people with memories of the harsh realities of a sometimes unforgiving land, guided by their vision and sustained by their grit and gumption. Well-deserved thanks go to the many growers and winemakers who have ridden the point on this long, dusty, and at times perilous trail evolving Texas terroir. Equally, encouragement goes to many more who are experimenting with both the present and the future wines of the Lone Star State.

A man who honors me with his friendship, Chesley Sanders, aptly summarized the Texas wine experience when he said this:

"Texas wine is the chill of a blue norther tempered by the fire of the summer sun. It's the fierceness of a spring thunderstorm calmed by an endless sky full of countless stars. It's the stick of a prickly pear cactus soothed by a bluebonnet's kiss."

II
Western Region

A Sip with the Good Friar

 hen we entered the region, we saw grapes growing wild along the rivers of Tejas and they looked like I imagined they did for hundreds of years. The vines were thick, hanging from the trees on the river banks, and sometimes covered rocks and ledges."

This is how Father García de San Francisco y Zúñiga recalled the local landscape in 1659 as he, Father Juan de Salazar, and ten Christianized Indian families made their trek into what was then called Tejas. It was a raw, wild land that harbored Native American tribes. Both land and tribes were unforgiving to trespassers, especially those who were faint of heart or weak in faith.

The group came from Mexico following the bloody defeat of the Spanish missionaries and settlers by the Tewa tribe at a Spanish outpost in Santa Fe. The settlers came to establish a Spanish settlement, a new community outpost on the north bank of the Rio Grande. Earlier that same year, they started a mission on the south bank of the river. It became known as Mission Nuestra Señora de Guadalupe. The mission's location is on what is now the Mexican side of the Rio Grande in the city of Juárez. With time, the nearby settlement on the north riverbank became El Paso del Norte, eventually known as El Paso, Texas.

The day of my arrival in El Paso was a violent one, when over twenty people lost their lives to the gang-related violence in Juárez. This, plus a promise to my wife not to cross the border to find the old Guadalupe mission, made me seek an alternative way to experience a small portion of the wine culture the good padres brought to Texas. First, I had to find an example of the mission wine that Father García and his compatriots first made on the Spanish frontier, something that I could taste and then share with the spirit of the padre that resided in a temporal wrinkle of my brain. This ethereal tasting with Father García took place on a patio just off the plaza near the Guadalupe mission in the shade of a lone live oak tree.

Father García said, "We cultivated the land around the settlement as part of our missionary work. We brought vine cuttings from which we grew grapes to make sacred wines for our masses. Once the vineyard and winery were established, we made sacramental wines for our community and to share with other missions in Tejas and Mexico."

Father García also mentioned that the craft of winemaking in the Americas went back another one hundred years or so before his own viticultural efforts. As best he could find, it started in 1557 and was borne on the "cordon" of a grape variety that arrived from Spain. Known as Criolla, it was a low-grade but hardy vinifera grape with a pinkish skin that took root in South America. The modern-day name of this grape is Mission, in remembrance of its use in the sacramental wines of the Spanish missions. I opened the bottle and then poured two glasses of wine.

Father García, who learned grape growing during his secular life, said, "There was always a debate regarding the lineage of the grapes that we brought to Tejas. Some attributed our grapes to the Argentines, while others implicated the Chileans. I think that the Argentines first cultivated the vines and then the Peruvians as the grape moved farther north. The variety of grapes that we brought to Tejas came from Peru." Father García continued my viticultural lesson as we let the wine breathe in the glass.

"In Peru, the variety was called Pais. I believe that, during its northerly migration, the Criolla grape underwent a change. It likely mutated or crossed with other grapes, yielding a darker color. We liked it because it had better qualities than those available in the wild grapes."

Father García picked up his glass and slowly raised it in anticipation of his first taste of wine in almost three hundred and fifty years. Before tasting, he gave it an appreciative stare and then met me with a questioning gaze.

He said, "This wine is so red, just like the color of the ripe grapes on the vine. As I smell the wine, the aroma is so light and delicate, like I have never experienced in our sacramental wines."

I believe what he was referring to was the ability of modern winemaking and storage techniques to preserve the wine's freshness. Wine in the Spanish missions was often made from near-raisinated grapes, giving the wine a taste more like dried rather than fresh fruit. Additionally, storage of wine wasn't easy in Spanish Mexico in the 1500s. The most likely storage methods were to put the wine in animal skins, clay vessels, or in some cases barrels. Using these methods, wines were susceptible to oxidation that robbed them of their fresh fruitiness.

> **"As I smell the wine, the aroma is so light and delicate"**

As we held our glasses up in a toast to the long history of this grape, the Mission wine caught the sunlight, exposing its red-garnet color and a clarity suggesting its light to medium body. To the nose, the wine showed a light aromatic quality brought about by its high alcohol content. The aroma was that of freshly squeezed red berries.

After the toast, we savored the wine for a moment and then sipped the clear red fluid again. It provided a fresh red cherry flavor and a dry, crisp, and warm finish with a slight woody/metallic note. The overall impression was that of a fresh, light red wine with alcoholic warmth. It was nothing close to the thick, dark, and fruit-driven wines that now occupy our market shelves.

As we tasted, talked, and enjoyed the wholesome fluid, I could see that Father García was starting to relax a bit and leaned back in his chair, his dusty robe hanging to the ground. We were surrounded by near-white midday sunlight that filtered through the oak leaves. It sparkled from the wine as we tasted.

Father García appeared a bit more at ease with his surroundings and comfortable with me, the first person to summon him from the past in what must have seemed like an eternity. I asked him how he'd come to join the order and lead the expedition to the Rio Grande.

He said, "Not many people know this, but I originally came to this new continent not as a priest but in a supporting capacity to help in making arrangements for supplies and to establish new vineyards. The vineyard was always a favorite place for me. I could get my hands in the dirt, give new life to the vines, and train them to produce fruit to be used in the name of God.

"However, the missions were always short of clerics in the new territories. It only became worse after our defeats by the natives at Santa Fe, when some lost faith in our effort. At first, my superiors simply asked me to join their order, but I declined. Then, they became more insistent, and I had to make a hard choice. It would not be easy for me to return to Spain, particularly if I refused the requests of the bishop. So, I decided that I would combine my love for grape growing and working with vines with helping to spread the word of God in Mexico and its frontier region of Tejas."

As our tasting progressed, Father García appeared to become unsettled, as if sensing he would be summoned back to the past before finishing the glass of wine that he was obviously enjoying. He asked me, "Is the wine that we taste from a vineyard nearby in Tejas?"

Alas. I revealed that my search for Mission wine from Texas was unsuccessful. I told him that I had found evidence of Mission wine made in El Paso, Texas, as recently as the 1800s. But because the Mission grape was eventually susceptible to disease along the Rio Grande, they switched to more resistant hybrid grape varieties like Black Spanish (also called Lenoir).

Further, I confessed to Father García that this wine came from California, a region the Spanish settled more than a hundred years after his efforts in El Paso del Norte. The particular Mission wine for this tasting came from Story Winery in the California Shenandoah Valley, which maintains a historical vineyard of Mission vines over one hundred years old. While surprised to hear of the Spanish success in California, the good padre seemed to appreciate the extent to which the Spanish mission culture had grown after his time.

In preparation for my tasting with Father García, I found reports that from 1697 until the 1800s, the Mission grape dominated vineyards in California, as was likely the case in Texas. Some attribute its introduction into the California Territory to Father Juan Ugarte in the 1690s. In 1769, Father Junipero Serra planted Mission grapes in California at Mission San Diego. He also spread vineyards northward in California, establishing eight other missions before his death in 1784.

Father García appeared confused when I tried to describe to him the extent of the recent scientific investigation to determine the actual lineage of the Mission grape. I had forgotten that he came from a much simpler and rugged time. He had little comprehension of the DNA techniques now used to establish familial relationships and lineage. Nevertheless, I told him that researchers recently found an ancestral DNA match for the Mission/Criolla grape. It was in a now little-known Spanish variety called Listan Prieto. While "prieto" means

> **66 Is the wine that we taste from a vineyard nearby in Tejas? 99**

dark, "listan" is a synonym for "palomino," the name of one of the white varieties used in Spain to make sherry.

He was astonished when I told him that Palomino grapes are grown on the high Llano Estacado plains of Texas and blended with Chardonnay, a French grape, and made into a wine produced by Inwood Estates Vineyards. He told me that he'd heard accounts of the Coronado expedition on the Llano Estacado and thought that place too harsh, dry, and desolate for grape growing. After looking around awhile, he acknowledged that many things had probably changed since the days of the Spanish conquests. However, Father García did recognize the grape name, Listan Prieto, from his prior grape-growing experience in Spain. For the next hour, the good padre related his memories of his time in El Paso del Norte.

He said, "Our party arrived at what we called El Paso del Norte, or North Pass, to convert the local Manso and Suma Indians. On December 8, 1659, I held a mass in a newly erected adobe structure that was dedicated to Nuestra Señora de Guadalupe del Paso. In 1662, with the help of the local natives, we began building the mission located around the corner from this patio on what was then just rocky raised ground west of the river. After all these years, I am amazed to see that our mission still stands."

Before we'd covered all the topics I'd hoped to discuss, Father García advised that he'd received a request for his presence and had to depart. He excused himself and said, "You know, a padre's work is never done." In response, I raised my glass to him, and before we took our final taste, I said, *"Gracias, Padre. Adios, y vaya con Dios."*

As he slowly faded back in memory, I thanked him for his dedication and willingness to suffer the hardships and dangers of a new world. I expressed my gratitude to him for bringing the first glimpse of modern civilization and wine culture to this rugged land.

As he vanished like mist in the wind, I thanked him for giving our Texas wine experience its birthright.

Chihuahuan Love

4

As my flight arrived from Houston, a pale orange sunset backlit the hazy blue mountains against the darkening city of El Paso. My pilot seemed to be making his final approach using a ribbon of city lights ahead, the lights that delineated the Rio Grande and the pass it cut between the mountains. Nearly four centuries ago, the Spanish missionaries settled here and named this river valley Paso del Norte.

The following morning as I left the hotel my nostrils were piqued by the smell of "dry." Some might say, Balderdash! Dry doesn't have a smell! Clinically speaking, they may be right; but, coming from Houston, I'm a connoisseur of both wine and air. Most of the year, our air carries an unmistakable moist, dank, earthy scent.

Today, my olfactory nodes sensed the antithesis of my native Houston air. Initially, it had a tactile sensation—a dry prickle in my nose similar to how a spritz of carbonation in wine reacts on the palate. Then, it presented a clean, minerally sensation, what in winespeak might be referred to as "minerality." It was a dry aroma of desiccated rock exuded from the dusty West Texas soil, somewhat akin to the way a fine Chardonnay can express the minerality of a stony French vineyard.

My stop on this trip, over a hundred miles to the east (a mere stone's throw in Texas terms), was Dell City and the Mont Sec Vineyard nearby. This vineyard, first planted over two decades ago and now consisting of over two hundred acres of wine grapes, constitutes the largest private vineyard in Texas, but Texas wine drinkers barely know it exists.

I was prepared to experience a part of west Texas viticulture that's compared to growing grapes on the dark side of the moon: gray and dusty, with lofty peaks that seem to be ever-present on the horizon. While dusty and desolate, this vineyard's Mont Sec name graces bottles of some of the best wines from Lubbock's Llano Estacado Winery. It's said that grapevines need to suffer a bit to make good wine. If this statement is true, I was standing in a wine region that offered them crucifixion.

Leaving El Paso and traveling by car presented a visual geology lesson. To the north, the Franklin Mountains were formed by the heat and forces that thrust Precambrian rocks (formed over five hundred million years ago), along with younger seabed rock, toward the sky. These peaks are over seven thousand feet above sea level, the highest elevation in the state.

The roadbed of Route 180 to Dell City and, in fact, most of the west Texas scenery, was overlaid onto an alluvial mix of sandy limestone gravel nudged from the mountaintops over eons by flowing water. Over the past ten million years this mixture was molded into dunes by the prevailing westerly winds.

The soaring mountain peaks of the Guadalupe Mountains in front of me, for a millennium or more, were the signposts for travelers on their way across this dry and hostile region of Texas. Legends hold that hidden treasure from long-lost Indian tribes and, more recently, buried loot from robberies of the Butterfield Express stagecoaches over a century ago lie secreted away in this range.

When I saw my Dell City turnoff, I was on the

high plain of the Chihuahuan Desert between the garnet Cornudas mounds on my left and the hazy cerulean slopes of the Guadalupe Mountains on my right. In wetter, prehistoric times, I'd be sitting in the middle of prime real estate on the mountain-view shore of an inland lake—now only a dry lakebed. A century ago gunfights were common-place, and the law of the Texas Rangers prevailed to settle the mining rights for its once-valuable salt deposits. Today, as featured on a large billboard, four hundred residents of Dell City find different riches here: cattle, hay, chili peppers, cotton, and grapes.

> ❝It's the late freeze that he calls the 'ten-ton gorilla in the vineyard'❞

At the designated spot, I was met by Llano Estacado Winery's vice president and executive winemaker, Greg Bruni. Greg is the man who, in the early 1990s, relinquished his California winemaking career to become a modern-day pioneer with a vision for improving Texas wines. Since then, Greg's worked with vineyard operators on the Texas High Plains and in this remote desert location. He's particularly proud of what he calls a unique form of Texas desert winegrowing at Mont Sec.

I hopped into Greg's truck, and he drove on to the ranch and navigated through a vast vineyard block. When he stopped, we stepped out onto the windy and waterless terrain as two men watched over the late-winter pruning of the vineyard. They were vineyard manager Robert Carpenter and fel-low Chihuahuan desert grape grower and viticul-turist Paolo D'Andrea, from across the border in Deming, New Mexico. Robert's a longtime west Texas farmer who oversees an agricultural op-eration of over nine thousand acres of hay, alfalfa, chili pep-pers, and the over two hundred acres of wine grapes.

Greg favors this Texas vineyard, just to the Texas side of the southeastern point of New Mexico, partly because of the long-standing grape-growing tradition first es-tablished back in the days of the Spanish missions. As he stood motionless next to rows of countless vines facing the high Guadalupe peaks, Greg had a pensive, look as though in communion with his winemaker brethren of yore.

Although he's spent the last fifteen years in Lubbock, he alluded to another and more practi-cal aspect of why he's partial to this vineyard site. Greg's seen this vineyard location dodge several bullets in the form of late-spring freezes that have wreaked havoc for Texas grape growers elsewhere. Greg feels that all the talk about the Texas heat is overrated; it's the late freeze that he calls the "ten-ton gorilla in the vineyard" that needs everybody's attention.

Despite Mont Sec's appeal, there are other issues to be reckoned with. Greg said, "Out here, when it's hot, it's really hot. When it's wet, the rain comes in torrents, and when the wind blows, it can sandblast the skin right off the vines."

The sun was bright and high overhead, and white wisps of clouds were being buffeted with the stiff and seemingly ever-present wind. After the vineyard tour, we all assembled back at the field house, a low one-story ranch house with a sign over its front door proclaiming it the "Kountry Club."

No sooner did we get into the house than Greg moved to the kitchen and brought out a load of plates and silverware. Like magic, he produced an array of varied wine glasses and a variety of Mediterranean morsels and condiments: first olives, mustard, balsamic vinegar, and olive oil, then plates of cheeses and meats. Greg followed with a selection of his commercial wines from Llano Estacado and several that he described as his "works in progress." The aim of Greg's wine presentation was to highlight the characteristics of wines made from Mont Sec grapes.

As he started to pour, Greg said, "This wine is from grapes that experienced my personal brand of 'Chihuahuan love.'"

We started with an aromatic Chenin Blanc fermented dry and crisp, carrying a green apple flavor and peach aroma. As we sampled, Greg explained his theory that encourages harvesting grapes based on acidity, rather than sugar content alone, to make wines with aromatic characteristics and acidity despite the vineyard's hot summertime temperatures. Greg admitted that this was something that he'd had to learn when he came to Texas. In California, maturity and ripeness come at the same time. However, in a hot, dry area like

this, ripeness oftentimes comes in advance of maturity; if he waits for maturity, he loses the acidity and aromatics.

Particularly intriguing was a wine that Greg called a "bare-naked" Mont Sec Chardonnay, freshly fermented in a tank without oak aging. It gave out tropical notes of coconut and pineapple and the characteristic minerality of Mont Sec wines. As we tasted, munched lunch, and talked, Robert added a farmer's viewpoint to grape growing in Texas.

He said, "The bottom line is that wine growing at Mont Sec appears to make good business sense. In fact, the most labor-intensive times for grape growing are right now in these late-winter months when our other farming operations are mostly quiet. This is when we're planting new vines and pruning the ones we've already got."

After being distracted by a call on his cell phone, Robert continued, "Grape growing also diversifies our farming operations. After making some initial mistakes, perhaps based on knowledge we got from California, we're now improving the vineyard to make it more sustainable and profitable. Greg was a great help, too. I eventually hope to have possibly five hundred acres of wine grapes under cultivation at Mont Sec once our experimentation shows results."

The most amazing part of the Mont Sec tasting was the wines made from aromatic white grapes like Gewürztraminer, Muscat Canelli, and Riesling that normally reside on hillside vineyards in northern Europe, not on the floor of the Chihuahuan

Desert in Texas. Greg poured a tank sample of his premium white-blended wine called Viviana. It featured these grapes and had nose-popping fruit and floral notes that confirmed his theory of Mont Sec winegrowing.

He said, "Some in the wine establishment referred to my Viviana as too unconventional and not in the box. But you know what? Texas *is* outside the box of the conventional wine world and needs to think about how to create something special, something different from what California offers. I think that this is it!"

As we shared the food, wine, and conversation, we addressed the minerally Mont Sec Vineyard soil and its particularly high calcium content. In many regards, it's more like a vineyard in France than one in California.

Greg and Robert agreed that it took about six years starting in the mid-1990s to get this desert vineyard back into line after originally following the advice of some Californians and before Greg experienced Texas grape growing firsthand. Robert said that the conventional thinking in California was to stress the vines by increasing grape yields and reducing irrigation. So that's what he did, but it damn near killed off his vineyard. The improvements in grape quality that Greg is looking for have come with better management of irrigation right up to harvest time and by use of fertilizers and micronutrients that encourage vine growth.

We continued our tasting with a Mediterranean-style dry rosé, followed by its bigger, red-blend brother called Mélange, made with Carignan, Syrah, Grenache, and Mourvèdre. Then, we tasted several of the individual components from this blend.

Paolo, with similar conditions in New Mexico, had success growing varieties of grapes originating from his Italian homeland, which further attests to the versatility of the Chihuahuan Desert vineyards. His grapes include Montepulciano, Aglianico, Barbera, and even the "bad boy" of Italian grapes, Nebbiolo, which rarely grows well outside of northern Italy.

I was glad that Greg had invited Paolo to come across the border to our Texas vineyard gathering and tasting. I learned from Paolo that Mont Sec Vineyard and the vineyards in nearby New Mexico have become some of the most sustainable vineyards in the southwestern United States.

He said, "This sustainability isn't conjecture but proven fact based on both consistent yields at harvest and quality of the grapes."

I definitely experienced the unique world of Mont Sec grape growing. With the vineyard's high-altitude setting and the Guadalupe Mountains as a backdrop, this vineyard reminded me of another well-respected New World wine region on the high, dry Argentine Mendoza plains, backlit with the scenery of the immense Andes Mountains.

We said our good-byes, and, as I walked back to my car, Greg shouted out to me over the drone of the wind, "Hope you had a good time. Let me know when you wanna get a little more Chihuahuan love."

Wine in a Carafe or Barrel

5

It was a Friday evening after a long week of travel and business hassles. I looked forward to winding down as my wife and I walked up our street for dinner with friend and business associate Lars Jorgenson. After my knock, we were whisked through the door and given the usual greeting, "Welcome to Upper Huldy!"

Despite the fact that we live on the same block of Huldy Street, Lars's reference to "Upper Huldy" was meant to highlight the presumed prestigious location of his domicile only about a hundred yards north from ours, a location that he always enjoyed referring to as "Lower Huldy."

After the greeting, Lars led me directly into his tiny white kitchen. On the table before me was a lone carafe of straw-colored wine. We looked at it for a moment in silence, and then Lars said, "Taste this wine and tell me what it is and where it's from."

I recall thinking to myself, Come on. This wine

could be from anywhere, even from Croatia, a place we decided would be a great location to hide if our business venture in Houston took a turn for the worse!

Lars had come to Houston from Denmark. He had developed a distinctly European wine palate and had a penchant for expensive wines from Bordeaux. Later, it was Brunellos from Italy. More recently he started looking elsewhere, with interesting Malbecs from Argentina. When it came to his wines, he was decidedly a man of the world.

> **66 Visually, the wine had a color of light straw, suggesting perhaps a Sauvignon Blanc 99**

When Lars presented me this challenge, I really didn't know where to start except with a good long look, a swirl, and a taste.

As I swirled and sniffed, I started to cast a net around this wine using my eyes, nose, and palate (as my Court of Master Sommelier's training taught me). Visually, the wine had a color of light straw, suggesting perhaps a Sauvignon Blanc. Next, my nose detected aromas of citrus and just a hint of tropical fruit, suggesting a warm growing region where fruit ripeness was unquestionable.

The lack of oak, structure, and earthy characteristics made me veer away from Old World venues. Furthermore, the fruit wasn't as intense as I normally would expect from a New World location like Australia or New Zealand, but more than I ex-

perienced with the white wines of South America. Though I was whirling the complete 360 clicks of the wine world compass, all this actually took only a few seconds. Then, a question struck me: had I actually tasted this wine before? Finally I said, "Is this wine from Texas?" My comment drew a smile from Lars, which exploded into a full-blown laugh.

He said, "Yah, yah, of course it is. It's the Ste. Genevieve Fumé Chardonnay that you told me about. It's the one that won a Silver Medal in your wine competition. I found it at Central Market, and I love this stuff! But, you know, the problem is the big liter-and-a-half bottle. My friends turn up their noses at big-bottle wines, and you know what they say . . . blah, blah, blah! However, when I put it in a carafe, it's different. They love this stuff."

Recounting this story is how my meeting started with Pat Prendergast, owner and president of Ste. Genevieve Winery and Mesa Vineyards.

I'd driven four cold, wintery hours across the barren desert from El Paso to the remote winery about twenty minutes east of Fort Stockton. When I arrived at the meeting location on the south side of the interstate, all I found was a large square corporate building looking a bit worse for wear. The door was locked, but there was a button to push for entry and several signs warning me what not to do. As was obvious, Ste. Genevieve doesn't usually host visitors or specialize in wine country hospitality. They're a no-frills winery that's successfully secured a prominent place in wine stores and grocery shelves alongside well-known wine producers like Concha y Toro, Yellowtail, and all the others that sell in big bottles.

When I finished my Ste. Gen wine-tasting anecdote, Pat leaned back and said, "That's a great story. I certainly like that wine. It's a blend of Sauvignon Blanc and Chardonnay. The Fumé Chardonnay can be a bit harder to find than most of our wines, but it's worth it."

As we talked, Pat discussed the different mindset that's needed in a "big boy" winery like Ste. Genevieve. As the discussion started, we munched Pizza Hut pizza and pasta on paper plates. This seemed like fitting cuisine for a winery that takes great pride in keeping its wine a value in the marketplace, and something that complements everyday cuisine.

How big is Ste. Genevieve, anyway? Well, by far, it's the biggest capacity winery in the state, although Pat doesn't usually talk about these numbers directly. Some estimates batted about indicate that it has over 60 percent of the winemaking capacity in Texas. A quick search before the trip really surprised me. It showed that Ste. Gen was already in the top thirty wineries in the United States in terms of production, about the size of Rodney Strong, La Crema, and Wente in California, but selling 90 percent of that right here in Texas.

In 1983 the Ste. Genevieve winery and its ad-joining vineyard operation was originally set up by an American-French partnership that involved the University of Texas Lands group that's responsible for managing the Permanent University Fund. Their partner in the venture was a French alliance called Gill-Richter-Cordier Inc., a consortium of American and French investors.

Back in the early 1980s, the French part of the partnership, Domaine Cordier, came in and built the winery, something that Pat referred to as an "overbuild." When it started, the winery had seventy thousand square feet of floor space and tiled floors (with the tiles coming all the way from France). It had huge jacketed stainless steel and glass-lined tanks, and a capacity to store a million gallons of wine. Ste. Gen had all this at a time when it didn't even have a brand in the marketplace in Texas, a place that wasn't even known as a wine-producing region. In retrospect, the development of this winery was the equivalent of drilling a Texas wildcat well—a high-risk venture in an unproven area with unlikely odds for success.

Even with what is today a huge facility in the Texas marketplace, Pat laughed when I called his winery big. He said, "If you know my story, you might reconsider that term. I'm a Gallo man and started working in sales while in California. Then, I went back to business school to study marketing and moved into Gallo's international operations and gained experience in Scandinavia, England, and northern Europe. You know, in California, the Gallo winery has a single tank that can hold one million gallons of wine, and that's as much as our total capacity here. Now that's big!" Pat proceeded to tell me how he came to own the operation at Ste. Gen.

After relocating to Texas following his stint with Gallo's European operation, he moved to Austin. Pat remained active brokering wines on the international scene, usually working with companies to expand their foreign markets. Then, one day he got a call from a recruiter who asked if he could help find a CEO/marketing guy for a big winery in Texas.

Pat said, "I thought that was an odd question. Then, they told me that it was French-owned, which piqued my interest even more. I came in to check it out and ended up buying the operation two years later."

I told Pat, "Call me crazy, but I just can't fathom the French wanting to open a winery in, of all places, Texas."

Pat told me what he suspected was the reason. France, at that time, was going through major political unrest. A socialist government was coming into power, and they were looking at nationalizing large independent companies. Domaine Cordier was a large producer of French wines and owner of fine châteaux in Bordeaux and Burgundy, and their management was scared of nationalization. So, they basically needed a way to get money out of France before the government took over their assets and bank accounts. It wasn't about pro-ducing wine in Texas or selling in new markets. Perhaps that's one reason why they obviously overinvested in this place.

Pat said, "For twenty years, this operation felt that pain and had to be reorganized more than once. Finally, Ste. Gen hit a point about seven years ago when it started to make money after a turnaround manager came and cut out a lot of the fat in the operation. It was streamlined with a market focus toward value wines, and a lot of the skeletons hiding in the closet for twenty years were hauled off. At that point, I saw an opportunity for Ste. Genevieve and bought it."

I thought it interesting that we owe it to international politics and financial intrigue for giving a huge boost to the start-up of the Texas wine industry. Pat's comments provided a probable answer to perplexing remarks that I'd heard about Ste. Genevieve. I was told, "If you want to know the real story of Ste. Gen, follow the money!"

We ventured out to tour the vineyard, where Pat introduced me to the two Frenchmen who have been an integral part of the Ste. Genevieve operation for a long time. I have to admit that I just remember them as Michelle and Michelle, or as my notes simply reflected: "MichelleX2." I forgot to get their last names but decided to leave it that way, as this code seemed to fit with the intrigue of the winery's "French connection" start-up scenario.

We walked down the stairs from the executive

offices out into the parking lot. When we opened the door, a gust of bracing cold, moist winter air shot in. The sky was starting to gray over, and without the sun the winter day seemed even colder than when I arrived. We headed out by truck into the vast sleeping winter vineyard with rows of vines that reached to the horizon.

I asked what was so special about the soil here and whether it had similarities to the soil back home in France. Michelle No. 1 said, "This soil is high in calcium. It's similar to some in France, but perhaps overall this place better resembles parts of central Spain."

Pat added, "When they started this operation they had to think scale, and to do that they had to find a place like this one-thousand-acre plot that had a lot of good water and limited exposure to vineyard diseases. To select this site they used data from the early work of Charles McKinney and his University of Texas Lands experimental vineyards. Then, they had to select the right grapes to plant. McKinney's data again helped, but we're still learning about growing grapes here, even after all these years."

As we roamed around the vast vineyard rows and back to the winery, I realized that the biggest surprise of the day was off in the distance, as if staring right at me. Out back of the Ste. Genevieve

winery was a mesa, a flat-topped mountain that looks like a tabletop. This feature dominates the horizon to the south, and the rows of vines in the vineyard provide a perspective relief towards it.

Why was I so surprised with this discovery? Well, it all goes back to the label on a bottle of Ste. Genevieve wine. It shows a picture of the mesa that's actually out behind the Ste. Gen vineyard. It wasn't conceived by the "Mad Men" of Madison Avenue. It's really there!

When I expressed my delight to Pat, he smiled and said, "Yep, that's the one. When I saw that mesa, I knew I was going to call my venture here 'Mesa Vineyards' and I put that mesa in the middle of our label."

> ❝ I wasn't quite prepared for the following winery experience ❞

We returned to the relative warmth of the winery, and, in hindsight, I wasn't quite prepared for the following winery experience. As Pat and I walked into the innards of the winery, it was like turning up the volume on a home dishwasher. There was the polyphonic hum of a large motor overlaid with a whirl of pumps all in surround sound, as if a winery-sized blender had swallowed me.

This wasn't your typical winery tour where they show you hundreds of oak barrels stacked majestically and surrounded by the serenity of cool masonry walls, or where they bring out winemakers to coo about the nuances of French or American oak. When I noted to Pat that I didn't even see a barrel, he corrected me. "We do have *one* barrel here . . . somewhere."

From the cacophony of sounds, I got the sensation of things moving very quickly, but there was very little that I could see actually moving. When I first stepped onto the winery floor, we made our way among a vast array of large floor-to-ceiling tanks, some looming three stories tall. We stepped over a maze of flexible hoses that looked like a tangle of snakes stretching from one tank to another. The only thing that displayed motion was what I could see through the sight glasses near the hose couplings. Some hoses contained an amber froth of moving white wine, while others contained rosy red or purple effervescent liquids.

This was my first visit to a large mechanized winery, and I was in awe. Wineries that I'd visited previously in Texas, California, France, and Italy were generally much smaller and quieter operations. They housed more pastoral trappings where sampling, tasting, slow savoring, and note taking were the norm. We stood in the shadow of Ste. Gen's monster bottling machine that seemed to devour wine as fast as Pat's employees could feed it.

Pat said, "You know, we keep a library of wines as they come off the bottling line, one per hour, and keep them for a year. If there's a problem, we can go back and run tests and check it out." I had to stop and think about what Pat just said and work though the numbers in my head. That's one

bottle per hour. If there are just two eight-hour shifts per day, after one year that turns out to be over 4,000 bottles of wine, or the equivalent of about 350 cases. This is more wine held for quality assurance than in a complete bottling at some of the other Texas wineries.

Before I left the winery, Pat gave a call to Benedicte Rhyne, their French winemaker. Pat, Benedicte, and I tasted through a selection of Mesa Vineyard's premium wine sold under the Peregrine Hill label. This wine is made from Texas grapes and sold at an economical price of around ten dollars a bottle. The Chardonnay showed a ripe, somewhat tropical fruit character that was nicely in balance. Benedicte attested to Pat's comment about having only one barrel in the entire winery, explaining that she used it for her *experiments*. Most of the wines in this winery substitute oak alternatives that can be utilized in stainless steel tanks at a lower cost and with a quicker turnaround, a necessity for Ste. Gen's value-oriented wines.

We ended with two more wines from Peregrine Hill, their Pinot Noir and Cabernet Sauvignon. This Pinot tasting brought back a memory of a wine panel that I attended at the Aspen Food and Wine Festival chaired by wine luminary Joshua Wesson, titled "Warm Weather Pinots." Admittedly, they exhibited different qualities than their classic brethren from cool growing regions. However, as was the case in this Texas Pinot tasting, I found that warm-weather Pinots have a darker berry character and a more rustic style, something more akin to a medium-bodied red Zinfandel. This wine was undeniably not the classic Pinot, but definitely pleasing on the palate.

We finished with the Peregrine Hill Texas Cabernet Sauvignon. This is the wine that came home with a Silver Medal in a recent Lone Star International Wine Competition. It gave aromas and tastes of blackberries, with a punchy note of American oak. My conclusion was that the wines of Ste. Gen were not for those seeking existential nuance. Rather, they are made for value and simple enjoyment, not to be "geeked" to death.

At the end of my whirlwind day at Ste. Gen, I received a bottle of what Benedicte called her "Private Reserve Zinfandel." She's partial to red Zin, having spent time making wine at the Ravenswood Vineyards in California. They're masters at making killer Zins, and I looked forward to this special treat.

As I started to leave, Benedicte said, "I know that Pat told you that we have one oak barrel here. I bet that he doesn't even know where I keep it. Well, this is the only reason why I keep my singular and special oak barrel here . . . so I can make this wine. Enjoy!"

Deep Roots in Texas

6

FOUNDER FRENCESCO ...GLIA

Exiting Big Bend National Park with its high peaks overlooking the flat alabaster surface of the Chihuahuan Desert, I was still almost an hour's ride away from the closest place that could be called a town. The air was hot and desiccating, but as I turned eastward, overhead petite white tufts contrasting on the azure sky grew large and billowy as they met with moisture-laden air from the Gulf of Mexico.

Still farther east, the caliche-white ground, still flat as a tabletop, dropped away at a steady but almost imperceptible rate, signaling the approaching confluence of the Pecos and Rio Grande Rivers. The clouds morphed again from their puffy pallor to sinister gray and yet again to form angry blue-gray monsters that stared at me head-on from the horizon.

Looking out from the road, the isolation in this part of Texas provides little to identify the era. It could be the present day, or just as likely the countryside of the nineteenth century when Frencesco Quaglia and his Italian immigrant countrymen scouted this area. As I slipped into Del Rio from the open highway, the landscape turned to stark urban concrete. After driving through the city center, I exited, like Alice through the looking glass, into a starkly different world. It was one of tall trees, wild green undergrowth, and the lush emerald rows of grapevines that surrounded the Val Verde Winery.

Tommy and Michael Qualia and I sat and shared the cool, subdued light in the original adobe building of Val Verde Winery, its eighteen-inch-thick walls providing a shield from the heat of the day. Their winery, the oldest continuously operated commercial winery in Texas, and one of the oldest in the United States, stands bold and proud against the test of time. Tommy and Michael are father and son, respectively, and also grandson and great-grandson of the winery's founder.

I listened intently to Tommy recount the story of how his grandfather, Frencesco Quaglia (later Americanized to Frank Qualia), and his compatriots left Italy and eventually made their way to Texas. It was easy to sense this family's passion for wine that kept this multigenerational operation going when no other winery in the state could. It survived through the sixteen hard years when the Volstead Act brought a nationwide prohibition on the production and sale of nearly all alcoholic beverages and nearly another fifty years of post-Prohibition wrangling until wine emerged as a national movement and a beverage of choice in Texas.

Tommy said, "My Grandfather Frank came from Castellanza in northern Italy. Del Rio wasn't exactly my grandfather's original destination. He was actually headed for Galveston, then to Mexico City. He signed on with many of his countrymen as part of a Mexican colonization program to bring European agricultural technology to Mexico."

Tommy pointed to the opposite winery wall and drew my attention to a framed certificate. On it was Frank's passport, a legal paper signed by King Umberto (the unifier of modern Italy) that gave him the rights of passage to the New World and a new life.

Tommy continued: "These were agricultural people with expertise on how to drain the wetlands around Mexico City and use them to increase vegetable production for the populace. However, the Mexican government was in turmoil at the time and the Italians were treated more like mere laborers, with little respect for the knowledge and technology they brought. Frank and some of his coworkers wanted a more dignified lot in life."

To escape their dismal experience in Mexico, Frank and some of his friends decided to break with the king's party and purse strings, leaving them with the little money they were able to save from working in the fields.

I started to develop a mental picture of the young Frank Qualia in the New World. He was only eighteen years old but experienced so much so quickly. It was an adventure, the likes of which I really couldn't imagine. He and his colleagues learned fast to adapt to a very different world from the one in which they were raised. They had to search out and take advantage of the new opportunities that lay ahead.

Tommy said, "Most of the men in the party set out for San Antonio, but found that the good irrigable land there was already taken. Two Italian men decided to stay in Mexico, married Mexican women, and, being good grape-loving Italians, opened a winery in Cuatro Ciénegas, Mexico, called the Farrino Winery."

I looked at Tommy sitting in the low light next to the large end-up wine barrel that served as our conference table and at the pictures and awards on the old adobe walls. Then, my eyes glided over to Michael, who at this point had not said a word. He appeared captivated by the unfolding story, listening respectfully to every word that his father said about his family coming to America, knowing that someday he would be the keeper and teller of this story.

Tommy drew back my attention and continued: "After reentering Texas, many of the Italians got jobs on the expanding railroad that was reaching westward from the outskirts of Houston to Victoria and El Paso and would eventually be extended on to the Pacific coast."

Members of Frank's party scouted out along the path of the railroad and found San Felipe del Rio, the point where the tracks were to meet the Rio Grande. Reports sent back from the Italian scouts were almost too good to believe. There was more than ample water, and several thousand acres of land were already in cultivation—some in grapevines. The local settlement was planning to expand as the railroad approached. Best of all, some of Frank's Italian countrymen were already there.

I asked Tommy if the irrigation for the area was from diversion of the waters of the Rio Grande via canals like those built by the Spaniards in old El Paso del Norte two hundred years before. His re-

> **❝ He was only eighteen years old but experienced so much so quickly ❞**

sponse was a short no. Then, he motioned for me to follow him out the back door of the winery and across the street. When we stopped, I looked down into a stone-lined culvert that coursed through the neighborhood. In it I saw the finest, freshest, clearest springwater imaginable.

Since Spanish times, the irrigation water has come from the San Felipe Springs that originate just a few miles east of Del Rio, north of the Rio Grande. I was amazed to learn that for hundreds of years the springs have produced millions of gallons of water a day. In the 1860s, developers acquired thousands of acres of land adjacent to the springs and adjoining creek from the Texas government in exchange for building a canal system, much of which was constructed by the Italian stonemasons. The name San Felipe del Rio was given to the town because local lore said early Spanish explorers offered a Mass at the springs on St. Philip's Day in 1635.

Tommy said, "Frank took the train to what was the end of the line back then in Brackettville, Texas. From there, he and others rode wagons carrying everything they owned."

This was the point in our visit where Tommy's mind's eye worked its way back into his family's history. He talked about how he envisioned Frank forging his way through the flat, parched, white countryside mile after mile by horse-drawn wagon. This was a scene that I easily imagined after my road trip the previous day. According to Tommy, Frank came over a hill just outside Del Rio where the splash of green surrounding the springs came

into view much like it did for me as I crossed what is now the center of town. Tommy referred to what Frank likely saw as "an oasis of green" in the parched countryside. There was plenty of good water and land, and some of his countrymen were here to lend a bit of hometown comfort.

Tommy continued: "Once in Del Rio, things moved pretty fast. Frank met the widow Doña Paula Rivera, who was one of the major landowners and already had a large vineyard in the area. He married Mary Franki, the daughter of one of the party's members, and they started both the Qualia family line and the winery that today holds a special place in Texas history."

Frank owed much to Doña Paula for growing what she called a "Le Noir" grape, which translates from French as "the black." They were grapes with black skins that bled red juice when crushed. Today, this grape variety is referred to as Lenoir or Black Spanish and seems well adapted to Texas, as evidenced by its long history in this region. Frank first leased the land for his vineyard and winery from Doña Paula, but then, with assistance from another farmer, bought the land outright.

While out back of the winery, Tommy pointed to the Black Spanish grapevines, some of which had trunks at least as big around as my forearm. He admitted that he didn't know how old the oldest vines were. However, he knew that some predated him and originated from the early 1900s and those were propagated from cuttings from Frank's original Lenoir vines. These, in turn, were propagated from cuttings originating from Doña

Paula's vineyards that dated back over a hundred and twenty years, and Doña Paula's vineyard derived from cuttings from still older vines that she received from a vineyard near Parras in Mexico. How far back these vines go, no one can tell.

Tommy also mentioned that his father, Louis Qualia, in 1935 brought in cuttings of a grape called Herbemont with a dark reddish-brown skin. Although dark-skinned, it bled amber juice when crushed that they made into a white wine with a decidedly sherry-like taste. He said, "I recall that back then my father was looking for a grape from which to make white wine and corresponded extensively with viticulturists in both Texas and around the United States to find one that would grow here."

Tommy recalled that Herbemont made a decent wine, but was susceptible to chlorosis in their limey vineyard soil and had to be grafted onto wild Mustang grape rootstock to help it survive. Today, the vineyard is almost totally composed of Black Spanish, with only a few sturdy old-looking Herbemont left, mostly for what he admitted was sentimental value, in memory of his father.

Historical work on Black Spanish suggests that it's not related to the original Mission grapes brought from Spain to Texas by the missionaries. It likely came to Texas and the nearby hills of northern Mexico in the late 1700s or early 1800s from the vineyards on the American Atlantic Coast, traveling along the southland and the old Spanish trails. Anecdotal evidence and some chemical analyses suggest that it is the product of an accidental or intentional hybrid of an unnamed European grape variety and a Native American grape.

Evidence also indicates that this grape made its way back to France and the island of Madeira as vine or rootstock after the annihilation of the European vineyards by phylloxera in the late 1800s. The resistance to disease afforded to the Black Spanish grape from its hybrid cross makes it one of the few grapes that can be grown in the hotter and more humid expanses of east and south Texas. This explains why it survives and even flourishes in the vineyards of Del Rio and now all around the Texas Gulf Coast and Hill Country and up into East Texas.

When asked about how Frank's Black Spanish vines were grown and how the wines likely tasted, Tommy took the opportunity to pour me a glass of Val Verde Lenoir (the name Frank preferred to Black Spanish) made on Val Verde Winery's 125th anniversary. The wine was poured from a bottle sporting the dashing image of a young Frencesco Quaglia looking a bit more western than I expected. He sported boots, leather vest, and a turned-up Mexican sombrero under which protruded Frank's long, droopy mustache. It's easy to see that Frank fit in well in his newly adopted Texas.

I raised the glass and could see that the wine was dark, almost black, with a red hue. It had an aroma somewhere between black cherry and mulberry, something uncharacteristic of European vinifera-based wines. As we sat back down, Tommy started to address my questions and said, "Originally, Frank planted his vineyard in an old-fashioned European style."

He pointed me to another framed picture and continued: "The vines were spaced thirty to forty feet apart, something not done today. This allowed him to plant row crops in the area between the rows of vines, which improved the overall economics of his farm. Frank was quite the entrepreneur."

I finally stopped to taste the Lenoir wine in the glass. It was thick yet fresh and crisp, carrying the dark berry experience expected from the wine's nose. We agreed that this was likely not the style of the original wines, as much of the technology in place in the winery today was not available back then. Tommy said that he had initiated a long-standing relationship with Dr. Enrique Ferro, a wine consultant from Temecula, California, another warm growing region like Texas. He helped Val Verde advance the winemaking style evident in this wine.

Next, I received a glass of Val Verde Don Luis Port, a wine made from Lenoir that dates back to a time when Tommy's father, Louis, ran the operation. The wine was dark, nearly brown, and it carried the aromas of its distinctly oxidized style: vanilla, toffee, and coffee. This was followed by alcoholic warmth, a taste heavy on dark fruit overlaid with caramel, and a long sweet finish.

With a wine-induced smile on my face, I asked Tommy about why he thought Val Verde was the only winery in Texas to successfully navigate through Prohibition and the lingering period of malaise in the Texas wine industry that followed for the next fifty years.

He said, "To put it simply, Frank and his son Louis, my father, loved this vineyard and winery as only an Italian would, but they were also successful businessmen. They knew that they had to do whatever it took to keep the operation going. During Prohibition, they made sacramental wine and wine for medicinal purposes. I've seen the old ledgers from back then, and they show who bought what, who paid, and I've even seen prescriptions for wine written by local doctors in Del Rio that the winery had to keep on file."

"Frank and Louis also sold grapes grown in their vineyard and shipped them by train to a lot of people back in and around the Houston area. It was actually a good time for business since all of the other wineries had closed down in Texas."

Back then, there were many Italians living in the city, and many bought grapes. Perhaps some ate the grapes, but my bet is that, being Italian, most people made wine for their own consumption

> **" "Originally, Frank planted his vineyard in an old-fashioned European style " "**

and for family and friends in spite of Prohibition. Wine was part of their Old World traditions and family life, and it was served with nearly every meal. Tommy made it known that being Italian, they weren't going to stop drinking wine just because somebody in Washington said it was illegal.

I asked about the future of the winery. Michael, who was now standing behind the tasting room bar, seemed to perk up in response to my question. He asked if I would like to taste another wine, and with hardly enough time from me to respond, he poured me a glass of Val Verde Muscat Canelli, unquestionably of Italian lineage, having pleasantly aromatic, semisweet characteristics.

While I was still savoring the aroma of the Muscat, Tommy said, "I'm about to leave the winery operation up to Michael and his sister, Maureen, and what they do with it is up to them. I'm going to work with my olive trees and try to grow a new white grape for us, Blanc Du Bois. I've heard from my friends Raymond Haak at Haak Winery and Jerry Watson in Cat Spring about ways to grow, harvest, and make wine from this hybrid grape. If it will grow in Galveston and Austin countries, it will likely grow here too. I'm optimistic." I asked Michael what he and his sister had in mind for the winery, now that they were in the driver's seat.

Michael said, "Right now we really only have one grape that's grown on the property and that's our Lenoir. We've had success making several wines from grapes that are grown up on the Texas High Plains, like this Muscat Canelli. That's why

my father developed relationships with the growers around Lubbock."

"Right now, I'm in almost daily contact with my sister as we taste and talk about the wines we're making. It's great to have her technical expertise and the commercial experience she's gained in California with her degree in enology from Fresno State. She was just promoted to assistant winemaker at Trione, a winery that has an Italian tradition just like we do here.

"I'm also excited about possibly having Blanc Du Bois growing here and making a white wine. Shoot, Raymond Haak makes it into five or six different styles of wines at his place. It's an extremely flexible grape that's shown the ability to sell well in the mainstream marketplace. It's as good as any vinifera wine that I've tasted."

As I was leaving, we stood together in front of the winery's sign. Tommy, Michael, and I posed for a picture that I was sure everyone who visits Val Verde Winery takes. In the background was the house Frank built for his expanding family nearly a century ago, and to our right was the winery that he made from adobe mud bricks. The sign was a large barrelhead enshrouded by a lone grapevine and etched with the name "Val Verde Winery."

Tommy said, "You know, a bird sitting on this sign must have dropped a grape seed that just took root. For a while, I kept meaning to take it out, but now I want to keep it. That vine's found a way to take root and prosper here, no matter what, just like our family and our winery."

Blood, Sweat, and Tears

7

Bobby Cox pressed up close to the group standing in the vineyard that struggled to hear him over the drone of the ever-present wind of the Texas High Plains as he said, "What makes wine grapes a particularly good crop for Texas is that they take much less irrigation water than mainstay cash crops here like cotton, corn, sorghum, and peanuts. It's particularly important as water here comes from a fixed resource, our subterranean aquifer, the Ogallala. It's not recharged at a high rate like the Hill Country's Edwards Aquifer. Water is going to become a big-time agricultural issue in this area, and wine grapes are going to be an important part of our future in Texas."

Bobby Cox is a larger-than-life character both in stature and reputation among grape growers and winemakers. He's something like a Texas version of Paul Bunyan, and Neal Newsom's large blue grape harvester parked beside him appeared as the mechanical equivalent of Bunyan's large blue ox, Babe. While Bunyan was a legendary lumberman in the American northland, Bobby's a bona fide virtuoso of grape growing here in the Southwest.

Bobby's hands showed the signs of wear and weather, and his furrowed face was etched with the look of lessons learned at the mercy of Mother Nature and hard economic times. At times it is difficult to separate the man from the legend. He's shown an uncanny ability of identifying trends, helping growers select grape varieties that best fit the climate and soil in Texas, and at adapting vineyard techniques that optimize the quantity and quality of their harvests.

That evening when Bobby arrived at a dinner gathering of High Plains growers, he produced his own personal offering of Texas wine history captured in a large, dusty liter-and-a-half bottle of wine.

> "The vineyard he planted in the 1970s is one of the oldest in Texas"

After the dinner blessing, we carnivores lined up to load our plates at the communal feast with steaks piled high—medium-rare to medium, marinated and not. Bobby's blood-rare steak stood alone in its crimson pool, as if the kitchen staff had just rode the critter in, knocked off the horns, and dispatched it moments ago.

Bobby was beaming, bright-eyed, with an ear-to-ear smile. You could see that this was not just any bottle of wine by the manner he and his wife, Jennifer, cradled it as they brought it to the table. The bottle was labeled 1982 Pheasant Ridge Cabernet Sauvignon, but it obviously contained something so much more than wine. What I came to realize was that it had a large dose of Bobby's personal history and spirit: the blood of the grape commingled with large measure of his own blood, sweat, and tears.

Pheasant Ridge Winery, with its estate vineyard in the Lubbock area, was once Bobby's baby. The vineyard he planted in the 1970s is one of the oldest in Texas, with sixty acres of Cabernet Sauvignon, Merlot, Cabernet Franc, Pinot Noir, Chardonnay, Chenin Blanc, and Semillon. He was a believer in the European vinifera grapes from the start, at a time when many people felt that they couldn't be grown here. However, Bobby's blood, sweat, and tears weren't enough. A few years of lean harvests led to the need to borrow money to keep the winery going, but when that ran out, the winery was taken over by the bank and sold in the early 1990s.

Bobby still views his lost winery every day from his kitchen window when he drinks his morning coffee before going out to tend the vineyards of others. Despite this misfortune, he decided to stay in the game as a vineyard consultant to help promote the art and science of Texas viticulture that he loves so much.

The bottle of 1982 Pheasant Ridge Cabernet Sauvignon presented that night was cloaked in a fine covering of red West Texas dust from over twenty-five years of bottle aging, the same red dust that seems to permeate every aspect of life on the High Plains and creates red skies, red rain, red mud, and even, at times, red ice and snow. In a matter of speaking, it reflected the terroir of the same red earth that bred life into this wine a quarter century ago. As we watched Bobby uncork the bottle, there was a gasp from the onlookers when the cork broke. Unfazed by the partial cork in his hand, with deliberate, careful actions he successfully coaxed out the remnant of the cork and gently gave the wine its first breath, like bringing a new life into the world.

The wine's first indication was visual—its abundance of purple color. This was followed with the bouquet of pleasing mature scents: earth, leather, and a strong underpinning of dark berries. Noticeably, it wasn't just any Texas wine being poured, but a fine wine that had withstood the test of time. As I watched the aged liquid in my glass, I could see a reflection of the heart and soul of its maker who, in a similar manner to his wine, is still vibrant.

I stopped to savor the wine and asked Bobby to reveal the secret behind it. He replied, "It's actually quite simple . . . grow good grapes in the right spot, put it in a clean winery and clean barrels." After a moment's hesitation and a deep breath, he added in a somewhat louder, staccato manner, "And, don't mess with it!" This was a Bobby Cox moment manifested, as usual, in a Bobby Cox sound bite.

A voice rose up from the table, saying, "Life just doesn't get much better than this. What makes this industry so great is that you're close to people that love life, camaraderie, their families, and appreciate good food and wine. But, most of all, they know how to work hard." A first toast was raised to the winemaker, then a second to the wine, and the third to the hard-working Texas growers.

After a moment of reflection, Bobby said, "The amazing thing to me is that this wine just keeps getting better with time."

So, we asked, how many bottles were left of his '82 Cabernet? Bobby appeared to be momentarily deaf, showing no immediate reaction. After a few more moments passed and the eating and talking continued, he pulled me close to him and said in a low voice, "It's a state secret."

Bobby was then asked to talk about the vintage and the harvest. Reading from a script of mental reflection, he said, "The vintage of '82 was a hail year, resulting in a smaller than expected harvest. It wasn't necessary to thin that year. The grapes used in the wine were Cabernet Sauvignon with what I'll just say was an unspecified but 'healthy' dollop of Ruby Cabernet. All the vines were self-rooted. And, as I recall, the sugar was a bit low that year, resulting in only about 11.5 percent alcohol in the wine, but the quality of the fruit and acidity were out of sight. We used cultured malolactic fermentation, but the wine was still amazingly crisp."

Because of the extremely small crop in 1982, there wasn't enough wine to sell commercially, so he just bottled it and set it aside. But the wine from the next vintage in 1983 was plentiful, and he entered it in the 1986 San Francisco Fair and Wine Competition, where it was presented a gold medal in a field of almost two thousand wines. His award was one of only fifty gold medals allocated in that year's competition.

Bobby said, "That's a pretty good accolade for a grower and winemaker who started his career making blackberry wine with fruit that he picked on a Santa Fe railroad right-of-way near Burleson. Ya know, I can still remember that my blackberry wine came with the worst case of chigger bites on record."

I asked Bobby what his aspirations were when he started out in the wine business. He said, "Look at the label of that Pheasant Ridge bottle over there." I studied the label, but then had to admit that I was stumped. He gave me a small hint while pointing to the label: "The font."

Then it was immediately clear. Bobby used the same font as the famous Ridge Vineyards in California. He said, "I felt that I could emulate the high quality of the wines from Ridge Vineyards with my own hands right here in Texas. My sights were particularly focused on Ridge Monte Bello Vineyard in the Santa Cruz Mountains, one of the best there is."

Bobby's initial loss and subsequent successes have shown the reality of the situation. The manual for Texas grape growing still has a lot of wet ink on it. People like Bobby and other winegrowers and winemakers around the state are writing it chapter by chapter, a vintage at a time. Unfortunately, the answers they need aren't discovered by simply going to the back of the book. The risks are theirs to take and the mistakes are theirs to make on the new frontier of Texas wine.

It's encouraging that the offspring of the current generation of grape growers have shown interest and appear up to the challenge like their parents, and they are working to learn new lessons. They realize that the lessons gleaned from the previous generations' blood, sweat, and tears benefit them and will eventually define the future of the Texas wine industry.

> ❝ ❝The manual for Texas grape growing still has a lot of wet ink on it❞ ❞

Sun on
the Skins

8

In a matter of just a couple of hours and seven hundred westerly miles, I left behind Houston's vast urban lowland and stepped off my plane in Lubbock onto the high plains of northwest Texas, gaining 3,500 feet in elevation. What took me only a couple of hours took many generations of the tribes that eventually settled this area as they made their way into this region from Asia millennia ago.

Later, Europeans led by Coronado arrived on horseback carrying the red and gold banner of Spain. In their futile attempt to surmount this land, they named this region the "Llano Estacado" (staked, or palisaded, plain). Theories suggest this name came from the cliffs that "stockaded" this flat and formidable region, or possibly from the method the Spaniards may have used to mark their trails on its flat and featureless terrain.

After the Spaniards' retreat, the diffuse native tribes of the Llano Estacado remained. The ingress of more warlike and marauding Comanches added a new and feared label to this region,

Comancheria. Only a century and a half ago, it took a modern military force and the destructive influence of buffalo hunters to overrun the Comanche nation, clearing the way for the wave of Anglo American settlers who found this a still hostile frontier.

This high, flat plain didn't exactly conjure up the image of wine country to me. The scenery was dominated by shades of burnt red below and indigo above. At the conjunction of these two domains, lean and well-drained soil combines with intense high-altitude sun, a little water, and copious amounts of manual labor to define this agricultural region. Surprisingly, cotton and other commodity crops, the local mainstay for generations, now share space with some of the most sought after grapes in Texas.

My first stop was Llano Estacado Winery, one of the first of the modern wineries in Texas. Mark Hyman, its president and CEO, welcomed me. He later described his winery as "the little winery that could." In 1976 it started small and struggled, but by the eighties Llano Estacado Winery was turning heads with national recognition and gold medals won in a major international wine competition in San Francisco. Today, Llano Estacado is realizing its ambitions, surpassing a production of 150,000 cases per year and garnering the distinction of being the largest premium winery in Texas. Its sales currently rank with the in-Texas sales of Kendall Jackson, Sterling, and Mondavi.

Llano's position came about as a result of the winemaking leadership of senior winemaker and vice president Greg Bruni, an immigrant from California. Greg's family founded the famed San Martin Winery, where Greg began working in the cellar, vineyards, and tasting room at the age of twelve. Greg was lured by a new winemaking challenge in Texas.

International awards, accolades, and medals for the wines from Llano Estacado and from other more recently established Texas wineries such as Lone Oak Winery and Duchman Family Winery are now commonplace, but Texas wineries still fight for recognition in the global wine establishment.

Even though Texas is the fifth-largest wine producer, most Texas wines are still consumed within the borders of the state, the nation's fourth largest in terms of wine consumption. Consequently, these wines are not widely shipped to other states and remain out of the spotlight of the national wine media. Why? Texas wineries don't yet have a high enough production to sustain the internal demand, let alone exporting this fine juice to places like New York City and Chicago. However, they do kindly welcome these foreigners to come down to Texas for a sip or two.

It appears that wine aficionados from outside of Texas, and even international enthusiasts, are traveling to this state for a bit of our local agrotourism. At last count, over a million people a year visit Texas wineries. A market research report in 2009 assessed the economic impact of the Texas wine and grape industries at $1.7 billion, a 25 percent increase over 2007, and that was 35 percent over 2005. Surprisingly, while Texas is the fifth-largest wine-producing state, the revenue generated from wine tourism outpaces the next two larger wine-producing states, Oregon and New York, and is nearly on par with the next largest wine state, Washington.

My evening's festivities at Llano Estacado included introductions to the families that own and operate three of the preeminent red-soil vineyards on the High Plains. All were row-crop farmers that discovered they could allocate a portion of their land to growing wine grapes. Neal Newsom started the procession long ago, before grape growing was even thought of as a viable option in Texas.

He said, "It really all began for me when I was in a freshman chemistry class at Texas Tech University in 1973 taught by Professor Roy Mitchell. He compared the climate of West Texas to other wine-growing regions of the world. This got me thinking, and after graduation I discussed grape growing with my father."

As Neal seemed to mentally scan his vineyard, he said, "We now have two vineyards, my mom's and my own, but it all started in 1986 with three acres of Cabernet Sauvignon. Now we've got over ninety acres in vines that include Cabernet Sauvignon, Merlot, Sangiovese, Orange Muscat, Tempranillo, Malbec, Pinot Grigio, and others. But, you know, Russ, if I had to do it over again, I'd plant ninety acres of Tempranillo 'cause it does so well here, and one acre of Cabernet. The one acre of Cabernet would be there just to remind me how hard it's been to grow that darn grape here."

An early wake-up call the following morning with a bright yellow glow on the horizon set the stage for a visit to three major vineyards located between Lubbock and the New Mexico border. Fresh high-plains air in my nostrils and strong hot coffee in my belly primed me for the day's activities. The first stop was at the Newsom family vineyards. Neal admitted that after his first encounter with Professor Roy Mitchell, his association with another Texas Tech professor, Clint "Doc" McPherson, encouraged him to allocate some of the family's land for a vineyard. As we talked, Neal showed off his grape harvester, an odd-looking bulky blue tractor with a high cab and a possumlike underbelly that first shakes the vines and then whisks the berries with a deafening blast of air to overhead bins.

Neal said, "Machine harvesting of grapes gives us significant benefits in terms of quality over the early days when we had to do all this by hand. In

> **"It really all began for me when I was in a freshman chemistry class at Texas Tech University"**

a warm climate like Texas, quicker harvesting allows the fruit to get on its way faster . . . and faster means fresher."

The previous evening I'd tasted Viviano, a premium red blend at the Llano Estacado Winery. It's made from Cabernet Sauvignon and Sangiovese grown by Neal. As I walked the vineyard that morning, I tasted his ripe Cabernet Sauvignon and Sangiovese grapes right off the vine—a venerable Viviano in the raw. The vine-ripened fruit was lush and succulent, with rich berry flavors and a strikingly pleasing acidity. This balance of big fruit flavors and crisp acidity is the hallmark of grapes grown on these high plains. The interplay of altitude and strong sunlight yields daytime highs in the nineties followed by cool arid nights of near sixty degrees and lower as harvest approaches. Neal reinforced this point, saying, "Most people think that heat's a problem for grape growing in Texas, but they just don't understand our climate."

One thought that struck me during this trip was the vast distances in Texas between these quality vineyards and the wineries that want to buy their grapes; some are over six hundred miles away. Haak Vineyards and Winery in Galveston County is one example. I stopped and scratched the math on my pad, then realized it's like harvesting the grapes in Washington State and making the wine in California.

More and more of the growers and winemakers have opted to harvest high-plains grapes and transfer them to a nearby facility where they're crushed. This crushed grape "must" (crushed grapes, skins, and juice) is then stabilized, cooled, and transported by refrigerated trucks to wineries around the state.

Neal provided a sampling of wines made with his Cabernet Sauvignon, Merlot, Sangiovese, Malbec, and Muscat grapes. These wines represented a literal "who's who" of Texas's established wineries, including Llano Estacado, Becker Vineyards, LightCatcher, Texas Hills, San Martiño Winery, Sunset, and Bar Z.

Back on the road again, the next stop was Reddy Vineyards, owned by Vijay and Subada Reddy. They are another story in Texas High Plains determination and diversification. As you might guess from their names, unlike the Newsoms they aren't descendants of the original settlers in this region. The Reddys came here from India for Vijay's advanced degrees in agricultural sciences. After Vijay received his PhD in Colorado, he and Subada settled in Lubbock, where Vijay opened a soils analysis laboratory and started farming. It was his friendship with Neal Newsom and his quest for cutting-edge experimentation that sparked Vijay's interest to grow grapes.

The Reddys were cotton growers and started growing wine grapes in the nineties with five acres of Cabernet Sauvignon rooted in the brilliant red soil. In a few short years his grape plantings exceeded one hundred acres, and he continues to plant and experiment with new varieties of grapes today.

While we watched the harvest, Vijay said, "My scientific background led me to experimentation with many varieties of grapes new to Texas, but I had help from Bobby Cox. Bobby knows the land and has a keen awareness of what growers have done in other winegrowing regions around the world that have similar climate and soils to ours. He encouraged me to try varieties of grapes that some people might not recognize, but have a proven record of making great wines in warmer climates like Spain, Italy, Sardinia, and the south of France. We're now moving from Cabernet to Viognier and from Chardonnay to Vermentino, mostly on the faith that Texas can sustain these warm-climate grapes."

I found Vijay's comments a bit of an understatement. The grape varieties he's planted include Grenache, Mourvèdre, and Cinsault red grapes planted widely in Spain and southern France, but he's also working with Nero d'Avola and Aglianico red grapes grown in southern Italy and Sicily. His white-wine grapes include Viognier and Roussanne from the Rhône valley of France, commonly used in blending but which also make wonderful single varietal wines here.

From there, the list just seems to go on and on. It includes his "big gun" reds: Tempranillo, widely known from Spain's Rioja region, and Malbec, from a similar high-plains region, the Argentine Mendoza. As I walked the vineyard, I was lost in a virtually unending "Mediterranean Sea" of grape varieties.

All this research with new varietals in Texas is a double-edged sword. While most wine drinkers recognize and have tasted Cabernet, Merlot, Pinot Noir, and Chardonnay and maybe Sauvignon Blanc, they may have some trouble deciding on Viognier instead of Chardonnay, Tempranillo in place of Pinot Noir, and Malbec instead of Merlot. With Texas starting to head in a decidedly different direction, wine lovers are going to have to cut loose many of the common wine names from their past experiences and build a new wine lexicon based on these warm-weather grapes. At first, they'll seek out these wines from established wineries like Llano Estacado, Lone Oak, Duchman, Becker, and Inwood Estates. Then, they'll need to look for new up-and-coming vintners at small family-run wineries with interesting names like Bending Branch, Barking Rocks, LightCatcher, and Perissos.

Vijay is even experimenting with a little-known "lost" European grape variety called Tannat, now planted mostly in South America. My first experience with this grape came about a few years ago during a trip to Rio de Janeiro. I was served an impressively inky, mildly tannic, and remarkably

> **"I was lost in a virtually unending 'Mediterranean Sea' of grape varieties"**

food-friendly red wine with dinner, but I didn't recognize the grape. The restaurateur explained that this wine came from the high-altitude region of Uruguay and was made from the Tannat grape.

While originating in the French Pyrenees, Tannat is now considered the national grape of Uruguay. Even in small doses, Tannat can add a bit of color and depth to any red wine as a blending partner. Since then, I've had Tannat wines made from high-plains grapes by winemakers at Brushy Creek, Bending Branch, and Barking Rocks. While Californians brag about their big, brawny Red Zinfandels, Texans may have to look for Tannat-based wines and blends to have a similar experience: a color of purple-black, nearly opaque, rich ripe fruit characteristics and flavor.

The large, ungainly looking mechanical harvester started down a row of Vijay's vines. The scent of harvested grapes trailing the mechanized monster drew me and others down the row of grapevines, leading to an inevitable eating frenzy of the few grapes left on the vines. I later laughed as I looked at a picture of our entourage, each with purple fingers, following the harvester down the row of vines. We were like fish following chum tossed from the back of a fishing boat.

Bingham Vineyards was my next stop, where Cliff and Betty Bingham and their eleven home-schooled children greeted me. Their country-style Texas hospitality included a sampling of local wines, a patio lunch, and an in-home concert by the Bingham family band. Cliff explained that his

expanding grape-growing realm came only after a lot of forethought and even before the first vine was planted. The Binghams have gone from five to over one hundred acres of wine grapes in the span of only seven years, but Cliff approached it with the same business sense and savvy that took the Bingham family farm from growing conventional row crops to organic ones while creatively defining new markets for the products of their harvest.

He said, "In a good year, it's possible to make on a hundred acres of grapes just about as much as on three thousand acres of cotton or a thousand acres of organic cotton, but with a heck of a lot less water. This's something that's gonna be critical for the future of our region."

The day wrapped up with a reception at longtime Texas winemaker Kim McPherson's new winery, McPherson Cellars, located in downtown Lubbock. Kim is a tireless prophet spreading the gospel for growing Mediterranean grapes. He's especially proud of his red wines and blends made from Sangiovese, Syrah, Grenache, and Mourvèdre, his white Viognier and Roussanne wines, and a refreshingly dry rosé wine made from Syrah or Grenache.

The wake-up call the following morning came a little later owing to the previous night's dining indulgence and revelry. The faces of my colleagues appeared a little rosier than the previous morning due to the sun exposure from our previous day's vineyard excursion. We should've expected the intensity of the sun from Bobby Cox's oratory, stationed as he was behind a row of grapevines and motioning to the heavens with his outstretched hands.

He said, "The elevation here is almost a thousand feet higher than it is in the Argentine Mendoza, with many of the same attributes and more. The strong rays of the sun at these elevations result in a noticeable deep coloration in the grape skins. We have to control it by management of the canopy of leaves on the vines." In retrospect, I guess that we should've used more protection from the sun on our skin, as well.

> **"Drink a glass of Texas sunshine"**

Bobby continued: "We find that this high-altitude sunlight also results in higher levels of antioxidants in our wines. I guess that this could stir up a new marketing phrase for us: Drink a glass of Texas sunshine."

I took a last look at the cinnamon soil from the land of Zen-like simplicity that manages to breed complexity in its wines. It's a place where sky and soil conjoin to reflect an indomitable history, a rich agricultural tradition, and a striking bit of Texas wine-growing terroir, all part of a new Texas wine country experience.

A Strong Texas Brand

No sooner did I arrive at the winery than a barrage of words shot in my direction without any encouragement or provocation from my side. "I've been doing this for far too long . . . I get rocks thrown at me. Why? I guess that I just don't play nice in the sandbox. But, hell . . . why play? It's getting harder and harder to create a truly Texas wine. Harder and harder and harder!"

This is how my visit with Kim McPherson started at his new McPherson Cellars winery in a converted Coca-Cola bottling plant in downtown Lubbock. Kim always says his name with a bit of disconnect, so it comes out sounding like "Mac-Pherson." This pronunciation makes me think of a clan of kilted Scotsmen rather than a boots-and-spurs Texan, but Kim is a local, no doubt about it.

In fact, the first time I met Kim was several years ago at the Houston Livestock Show and Rodeo where he was pouring his then CapRock wines at the barbecue cook-off. I was surprised and frankly somewhat impressed by how many syllables he could give to the monosyllabic word *shit* after I asked him to comment about the romantic life of a Texas winemaker.

Looking around me, the McPherson winery appeared an eclectic mix, much like Kim himself. It was a bit of postindustrial Coca-Cola and Zen-like bamboo, with elements of historic Texana beside modern art. The cross-cultural design was well done and nicely integrated with typical winery equipment: a crusher, press, piping, tanks, a bottling line, and case goods ready for shipment. It's located in a town whose claim to fame to most people is not as a wine mecca, but the hometown of Buddy Holly. The winery's as different as Kim is himself distinctive.

Some call Kim a winemaking legend, while others say that he's a maverick, plain and simple. Some have even described him as the tormented artistic soul of Texas winemaking. In any regard, Kim is a straight shooter of the same rootstock as his father, Clinton "Doc" McPherson, who is widely acknowledged as the "father" of the

modern Texas wine industry. Neither seems to shy away from offering the honest truth, even if it's something you're not inclined to want to hear.

Doc grew up on a cotton farm and evolved from Army Air Corps navigator with hundreds of combat flying hours and numerous medals, to PhD college professor and aspiring wine aficionado in a region of the world better known for cotton, corn, and soybeans than for grapes and malolactic fermentation. It was Doc's headstrong attitude and association with Robert Reed, Roy Mitchell, and others that got the whole dang modern Texas wine thing started back in 1970s. Now in his nineties, Doc seems as cantankerous as ever. I recently sat next to him at a wine tasting in Buffalo Gap, and I can say that he's not afraid to say his piece and loudly, particularly if it's about a wine he doesn't find quite right.

Doc showed up along with several of his old-time Texas wine buddies, Bob Reed, Charles McKinney, John Crosby, Frank Carpenter, and others, at what longtime high-plains grower Neal

Newsom advertised as a "Mentors Panel" at his annual High Plains Grape Day in Plains, Texas. To a packed house of winegrowers and winemakers, the moderator started the panel with a short summary of the contributions of each panelist. However, when he introduced Doc, he'd just barely started the introduction with, "Now, here's Doc McPherson. He did all sorts of things early on." Immediately, a voice down the row of panelists blurted out, "Ya know, I can talk for myself!"

When his time to speak did come, Doc, looking slight of build, topped with a dollop of white hair and wearing large spectacles, started his recollection of the beginnings of the modern Texas wine experience. He said, "For those of you that would like to spend the rest of the afternoon here, I can entertain you that long . . . If not, I'll give y'all the short version."

"Bob Reed and I were professors at Texas Tech, and we used to meet over noon lunch. We brought our own lunches because we were poor professors and couldn't afford the food they sold at the union. I said to Bob, 'Let's grow some grapes. We can make jelly and sell it on the roadside during the summer for some extra cash.' We agreed, OK, we'll just do that." Then, Doc stopped for a moment to think, and interjected, "I'll tell you what. If I had all the money that Bob and I made *and lost* with grapes in the early days, both of us would be millionaires.

> **" "Why don't you boys put in a *real* winery" "**

"We finally got five acres of grapes planted in 1969, some for makin' wine. Then, the university president came by and told us that all the assistants and professors had to get themselves a research project. I said *re-search*? So, later I asked him about putting in a small experimental winery in the basement of the chemistry building. I don't remember all the facts and figures—Roy Mitchell might—but I finally got it put in. That's where the modern Texas wine industry all started."

Just about then the panel moderator was prepared to move on to the next speaker, but he found out that Doc wasn't finished with his story, in fact was only getting warmed up. Doc continued: "But one day when Bob and I were talking about what to do with our grapes, a lady came by and asked us, 'Why don't you boys put in a *real* winery?' I said, Ma'am, we're professors, we don't even have enough money to buy groceries, not to mention a winery. She turned to her secretary and said, 'Write these boys a check for $50,000 to get them a winery started.' Today, Bruni is making mighty fine wines over at Llano Estacado, the place I started back in those early days."

Finally, Doc seemed satisfied with his historical account and concluded with, "My five acres of grapes are now fifteen, and I'm still into grape growin' and my sons are makin' the wine now. I would've planted more if it weren't for hails, freezes, birds, and maybe even termites."

Understanding the kinds of problems that Doc described, I figured that I knew what prompted Kim's tirade when I arrived at his winery. What was it that got Kim so riled up?

Well, first off, Kim worked hard to create his own "Mac-Pherson" brand and now has his winery up and running. His biggest concern is all about the growing pains besetting the Texas wine industry of late that have led to a shortage of locally grown grapes and their high prices.

The reasons for this shortage vary depending on whom you talk to. Some simply blame the rapid fourfold increase in the number of wineries since the start of the third millennium. Many of these wineries were propagated by an amendment to the Texas state constitution that now allows local wineries using Texas grapes the exclusive right to make and sell wine anywhere in the state, regardless of the wet or dry status of the area. Yet, others cite the squeeze put on growers by Texas wineries back a decade or two ago when they wanted to keep the price of grapes low and thereby drove many farmers out of the grape-growing business, leading to a grape shortage and high prices.

Still others focus on the past three vintages of grapes decimated by the forces of Mother Nature herself. As it is in the south of France, springtime in this state can be a yin-yang battle between harshly cold continental winds from the north and warm humid sea winds from the south. Spring storms clash over the state and wreak unpredict-

able havoc. I recently experienced the fury of the Texas skies firsthand in Lubbock when an icy cold front hit the state with forty-mile-per-hour winds and a bud-crisping twenty-one degrees; all this only a week after temperatures were averaging in the high seventies. If you think of Texas exclusively as a warm winegrowing region, you best think again.

Damage from hail is a yearly crapshoot in Texas, as it can be at times in central and southern Europe. Hail of sufficient size and duration can locally decimate a vineyard, literally mutilating fruit and new vine growth and, in some cases, killing off the vines.

I've known Kim McPherson for over ten years now, and the one thing that I've learned is that he's not going to hand me a line of bull, in any shape, manner, or fashion. He calls it as he sees it and doesn't care if I agree or disagree, and I respect him for that.

In a similar vein to what Texas ranchers say about their herds of beef stock, what concerned Kim most was keeping his brand pure . . . pure Texas, that is. However, as he said first off during my visit, "It's getting harder, harder, and harder."

There are two things that particularly rankle Kim. One is the price he has to pay for the precious few Texas grapes that he can find. The second and perhaps even more serious issue that he sees is that many local wineries, in an effort to offset the shortage of Texas fruit, are selling short on "Brand Texas" by simply importing cheap out-of-state grapes or juice to make their wines. These "foreign" grapes are cheap by comparison to those available in the state due to near-record-low grape prices in places like California, where there is an overabundance of wine grapes. While these out-of-state grape purchases may be a short-term fix, Kim is afraid that the addiction of Texas wineries to cheap foreign grapes will be a difficult trend to reverse.

As I sat with Kim, he said that his McPherson brand likely constitutes the seventh largest winery in Texas. Based on an average yield of three to four tons an acre, I surmised that he needs the production from about forty or more acres of vines to make his year's allotment of wine. With Doc's fifteen acres of Sagmore Vineyard grapes, I reckon that Kim is still short by twenty-five acres. He has to shop around to fill his winery's needs or strike deals with other winemakers that he trusts and who can share some of their grapes or juice with him. As Texas's native son Dan Rather (well known for his famous "Ratherisms") might put it, "Right now, the market for grapes in Texas is as tight as the rusted lug nuts on a '55 Ford."

Kim said, "Last year, I ran out of wine for my Sangiovese. I could've gone out of state, made wine, and bottled it, but I waited until I could get more Texas juice. That made my distributor furious, but it was worth the wait and I kept my Texas brand intact. If 2009 is a bad as expected, I don't know what I'm going to do."

Kim literally grew up with the wine industry.

He's had his hands in crafting some of the first commercial European vinifera grape wines made in Texas and what are considered today some of the best wines in the industry. He continues to work to make them better in the future, while trying to keep them pure Texas.

Going back to Doc's early days, many didn't believe that the classic grape varietals of Europe could be successfully grown here. Doc and his early wine pioneer buddies advised many of the growers to plant French-American hybrids, such as Baco Noir, Seyval Blanc, and Verdelet, because they felt that these would be a safer bet in the vineyard. After all, the grape grower's old adage was, "You can't grow vinifera east of the Rocky Mountains." They spent several years working with hybrids and came back with words growers wanted to hear: the tonnage looked good. The early Texas experiments in making wines from hybrid grapes showed that while they had potential, the quality of these wines wasn't going to be on par with European vinifera grapes.

Kim's history as a straight shooter came early in his career. After returning to Texas from California, where he learned the craft of winemaking, he was one of the first winemakers to pull the plug on using hybrid grapes on the High Plains in favor of going with classic vinifera wine grapes. He was supported by subsequent experiments in Texas that showed that vinifera grapes like Zinfandel, Palomino, Mission, and Carignan were actually viable on the Texas High Plains. In fact, they found that some vinifera grapes could outproduce the hybrids and had wine characteristics and names customers would recognize.

Kim was also in favor of paying growers well for first-rate vinifera grapes versus the low tonnage prices that the wineries paid for hybrid grapes. While this was good news for growers, the bad news was that they were going to have to pull out their existing vines or graft them over with European vinifera grape varietals.

In 1980, while employed at Llano Estacado, Kim kept working on making wine from Texas vinifera grapes. His work led to some of the first commercially produced vinifera varietal wines in the state: Sauvignon Blanc, Cabernet Sauvignon, and Chenin Blanc. It was a seminal moment for Texas that allowed it to enter the mainstream wine world. Once Kim showed that it could be done on a commercial basis, other wineries started using vinifera grapes in their wine production. It was then only a matter of a few years before his wines at Llano Estacado and others at Pheasant Ridge won gold medals in major international wine competitions.

In addition to focusing on vinifera, Kim has also been on his soapbox yelling at the top of his lungs for the Texas wine industry to steer away from wines made from household names like Cabernet, Chardonnay, Merlot and Pinot Noir. He's an advocate for what he calls "warm weather varietals" commonly found in southern France, Spain, and Italy.

Kim said, "Once, I was on a wine panel with John Bratcher where a Texas winemaker was saying that Texas-made Cabernet was as good as that made in Napa Valley. I thought, Bullshit! Where are they? I know from my California experience that winemaking there was so easy that I just had to slap it in barrels and my job was nearly done. Here in Texas, it's much harder, plain and simple. But it doesn't have to be that hard if we select the right grape varieties."

> **"Here in Texas, it's much harder, plain and simple"**

I asked Kim if things were like that in Oregon and Washington before they got it right.

He replied, "They've had ups and downs, and then they figured out what grew best and what didn't. They picked the winners and ran with them. It wasn't like we have here in Texas with wineries each trying to make and sell sixteen to twenty-four varieties of wines. Whoa there! I'm preaching again, but I think that we should pick five varieties of grapes and go with them . . . find the keepers for Texas. In my opinion, for whatever it's worth, these are going to be the Mediterranean grapes, not Cabernet, Chardonnay, or Pinot!"

We walked a few doors down for lunch at La Diosa Cellars, run by Kim's wife, Sylvia. It's a restaurant and bonded winery, and Kim makes wines for her La Diosa label. Like Kim's winery, Sylvia's place is hard to describe. It's part Bohemian tavern, part Spanish tapas bar and bistro, all under the roof of an art-adorned hacienda. As we discussed the finer points of his favorite olives (Grabers from Ontario, California), I asked Kim how he became the winemaker at Llano Estacado Winery.

He said, "It's actually a funny story. The guy making wine there before me was an Australian, but he was here illegally, you know, here without papers. He basically got a free plane trip home, and that's what gave me my start in Texas after learning how to make wine in California."

Kim also acknowledged that Llano Estacado has had good winemakers since he parted to return to California to make wine with his brother in Temecula. Llano's winemakers included Don Brady, now at Robert Hall Winery in Paso Robles on the California central coast; Mark Penna at Duchman Family Winery in the Texas Hill Country; and Greg Bruni, who came from a family with a long history in the California wine business.

Kim obviously thinks highly of Greg. He said, "Greg's done more than anybody to elevate Llano's winery from 50,000 to 150,000 cases annually and maintain quality in the process. He's the one that I look up to in Texas as a true professional in this industry."

Kim's learned a lot about warm-weather winemaking from his days in Temecula, the coastal winegrowing region between Los Angeles and

San Diego, going inland from the Pacific coast. He said, "It's what everybody called the redheaded stepchild of the California wine industry, but it's a good training ground for making wine in Texas. It's got a similar climate to what we have here and suffers from some of the same ailments we have, including Pierce's disease. But, ya know, they've learned to make good wine there. I brought a lot back with me when I returned to Texas to become the winemaker at CapRock Winery."

I asked why he went to CapRock Winery when he returned, and Kim answered, "It's funny how things work out. The new CapRock CEO back then grew up across the street from me, so I've known him since childhood. After the winery went through a bankruptcy and was reorganized, he called me in California.

"Initially we hired some consultants, real heavy hitters, like Robert Craig who has a big label in Napa Valley and who also put together the Hess Collection there. There was Tony Soter, who started Etude wines in Napa Valley, sold it, and went to Oregon and made a name working with Pinot Noir. Together we looked at new ways of handling warm-climate fruit.

"We knew that in Texas we weren't Napa Valley, and we had to work with what we had. We did innovative things for the first time that helped me appreciate how good the wines could be here. I learned a lot in those days, but things were still difficult financially at CapRock. I started making my own wine while I was there, and I finally realized that I needed to key in on locally grown, warm-climate grapes and my own style of winemaking."

Kim's McPherson Cellars brand focuses on wines made from grapes like Viognier, as it tends to be tropical but not as heavy or as oaked as so many California Viogniers. Because of the grape shortage, Kim had to come up with a creative solution. It was a blended wine made with Texas Chenin Blanc, French Colombard, and Viognier that sold under his second label, Hook, Line and Sinker. Only time will tell what Kim and others will have to do for the long run.

We finished up lunch and exchanged thoughts on how the present situation might improve. He gave me another one of his famous quadra-syllabic exclamations, then said that he frankly didn't think that the weather could get much worse than it was in 2007 through 2009, with all the freezes and hail and rain that eventually caused him to drop the reins on his Texas purebred in 2009. He feels that things naturally have to get better, and it appears so in 2010.

Kim thinks that a more direct approach to bettering the situation will be to get more acres of grapes into production, especially those planted with his favorite warm-weather varietals. He likes the new program sponsored by the Texas Department of Agriculture that provides grants to new start-up vineyards, and he's particularly pleased as it seems that the grants have gone to people with farming and prior winegrowing experience, not professional city folk like me.

Before saying our good-byes, I asked Kim again, Where's this Texas wine thing heading? He stopped a moment with a wrinkled brow and gave out a sigh. Then he said, "Gee, I don't know, Russ. I'm just trying to get enough fruit and make the best wines I can. This year, I had some help from friends like Greg Bruni at Llano Estacado. We see the same picture and we are realists. Sometimes people think that we're just assholes, all bitter and cynical, when we talk about it. That's just not the case. I'm just not telling you that it's going to be all fun, but I am telling you the truth. It's still hard work here, but I have proven that good Texas wines can be made at an affordable price. If I'm willing to do whatever it takes . . . so should others."

> ❝❝I have proven that good Texas wines can be made at an affordable price❞❞

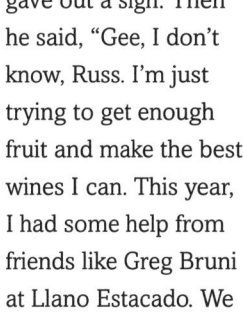

III

Northern Region

The Supreme Expérimentateur

10

"Cross Timbers" was a name given to an area in north-central Texas by early immigrants on their westward journey. The area was dense with oaks and scrub brush, challenging trespassers and posing a barrier to the region's settlement.

I headed out across the vast prairie on Highway 81 past Decatur in the region once dominated by this seemingly impenetrable forest. The land opened around me with only remnant fingers of dense Cross Timbers brush tucked into prairie folds, the last vestige of this barrier once called the "iron forest." Hawks were positioned like sentinels atop the dense vegetation, scanning wide-eyed in search of their prairie buffet. I was on my way to visit with Les Constable—grape grower, winemaker, and owner of Brushy Creek Vineyards in Alvord, Texas.

I found Les sitting on the deck in front of the winery, which had the shape of a small white and green barn; two glasses of wine were already poured. He had the look of a countryman, with his thinning salt-and-pepper hair, faded blue coveralls, and sporting the same green and tan Brushy Creek ball cap that he's worn nearly every time I've seen him for almost five years now. I've come to know and appreciate his look and soft, unhurried conversation.

Les's father was a research biologist, and, for most of his adult life, Les was a nuclear engineer by education and a product of Admiral Rickover's nuclear navy. This background blessed him with an ever-inquisitive mind that he now focused on defining the future manifestations of Texas wine. As we sat and sipped, Les recalled back to 1963 when his connection to wine began.

"While in the navy, I was stationed in Vallejo, California, well before California developed into the wine powerhouse that it is today. My navy associates and I developed quite a taste for fine wines . . . perhaps something you might find unusual when thinking about navy men. We particularly enjoyed it when we went into a port and could locate a fine dining establishment. This environment fueled our passion for the grand wines from Bordeaux, Burgundy, and even Germany, as these countries were, more or less, the 'wine world' of that time."

In the low light and advancing coolness of late afternoon, Les explained further, "There really weren't many wineries in California compared to what they have today. But, whenever I was in my home port there, I was able to explore and find some quality wine producers."

"After leaving the service in 1968, I was in Massachusetts and became good friends with a liquor store owner. Together we tried to find California wines and compare them to our favorites from Europe. We blind-tasted the limited number of California wines that we could locate on the East Coast, but they were pretty bad. I couldn't find the good ones I'd previously had in California."

Not too long after, higher-quality California wines finally became available on the East Coast, and Les continued with his blind tastings. He discovered that these wines were on par with many of the French wines. He actually started doing this before Steven Spurrier's great 1976 "Judgment of Paris" tasting that really caused the world to take notice of California wines. Les's experience made him realize that the wines in Texas had to evolve in a similar manner if they were to be taken seriously in the global wine market.

He said, "At Brushy Creek, I've started to put our wines to the test and pour them side by side with wines from other wine regions. I prefer blind tastings as they remove any bias some might have when they see the word 'Texas' on the label. In such tastings, our wines do very well, and I encourage more Texas wineries to do it rather than fear it."

Les and I then boarded his golf cart to tour his estate vineyard. Along the way I had him stop so that I could get a handful of his vineyard soil. Les mentioned that it's pretty typical stuff for this area of the Cross Timbers region. It was a mix of sandy gravel with high calcium content and nodular clay that yielded some water retention, yet with good drainage. The soil was obviously low in organic matter, which limits vine production, but high in the minerals needed for quality grape production.

Les laughed and said, "As they learned long ago in Europe, it's the type of soil that makes the grapevines think that they're going to die, so they put more energy into grapes than leaves. It's a preservation of the species thing!"

As Les drove farther into the vineyard, he mentioned that, when starting his operation, he had experimented a lot, planting dozens of grape varieties to see which would grow the best. He pointed to the first rows that contained Cabernet Sauvignon, Merlot, and Riesling and quickly mentioned that he's evolved well past these grapes that most people recognize.

"These varieties of grapes do all right and make good wines," he continued, "but it's hard work for me. I've been looking for vines that *like* being in Texas with its heat and sun and that can still handle the freezes that burn us here."

He readily admits to anyone and everyone that he's made lots of mistakes in his vineyard, but he has learned something important from every error. As we got still deeper into the vineyard, Les stopped again and looked out for a few moments. Pointing forward, he said, "Now, these vines are happy campers."

The vines he pointed to were a not-so-common varietal called Rkatsiteli (ar-kat-si-TEL-lee). It originated in Ukraine by the Black Sea over five thousand years ago. From its history, it has the makings of one tough old grape variety and is a survivor in some places where men haven't been so lucky. Les said, "A friend put me in touch with a monk in the Russian Orthodox Church in the Ukraine. We've had an ongoing e-mail exchange, and he's provided me valuable advice on how to grow this grape."

I'll admit that, just about then, I had a weird mélange of thoughts. First, I compared the obvious muscular appearance of these vines to my mental image of a Russian weight lifter with taped wrists, sweaty pits, and all. If that wasn't enough, I had a second image playing in my brain of Les's long-distant Internet relationship with a gray-bearded Russian monk cloistered in his high mountaintop retreat with his PC and mouse in hand. It was like being cast into a surreal movie directed by David Lynch (remember *Twin Peaks, Eraserhead,* or *Dune*?).

Les's voice broke my reverie as he sped up his cart in the ebbing afternoon light. He lamented,

"It's the type of soil that makes the grapevines think that they're going to die"

"After the weather, my real nemeses are coons, birds, and deer. I've most everything else under control, even Pierce's disease. It's the critters that make me want to pull out what's left of my hair."

Continuing our vineyard excursion, Les said, "My favorite wines are Bordeaux-styled red wines, so I planted several Bordeaux varietals—Cabernet Sauvignon, Merlot, Petit Verdot, and Cabernet Franc. From the standpoint of climate I've learned that Alvord is really *not* Bordeaux. Based on my experiments, though, I've figured how to work with the Cabernet Sauvignon grape to produce a high-quality wine, but it takes lots of work both out here and in the winery. Keep in mind that Texas is a big state—about the size of France—and there are some places where these Bordeaux grapes may be easier to grow than right here at my place."

Les is most proud of his experiments with what he, like Kim McPherson, refers to as his "warm-weather varietals," and it's easy to tell that he loves Texas-grown Tempranillo, the national grape of Spain, from its Rioja region. Les said, "This grape does exceptionally well in our summer heat and continues to ripen even when the temperature exceeds a hundred, around the point where the Bordeaux grape varietals literally shut down and stop ripening."

His vineyard experiments that are starting to pay off include growing red-wine grapes like

> **"This grape does exceptionally well in our summer heat"**

Malbec, Syrah, Grenache, Mourvèdre, and Tannat from hotter climates in southern France and Spain. Les said that he and Jim Johnson at Alamosa Wine Cellars were also working with white-wine grapes like Verdejo from Portugal and Albarino from Spain, and Les is even growing a white French/American hybrid grape called Blanc Du Bois that's more common down on the Texas Gulf Coast than in this northern region of Texas.

As he pointed out his plot of vines of Tannat grapes, I mentioned my own experience with an inky-red Uruguayan Tannat wine during a trip to Rio de Janeiro. Les immediately perked up. He said, "Tannat's great stuff. You've gotta try mine." This was followed by a hard left turn and a burst of speed from his golf cart as Les took aim at the back door of the winery and the barrel room (a move reminiscent of Texan A. J. Foyt's early midget-car days. Whoa!).

With glass in hand, Les poured me a taste of his Tannat wine that had the familiar inky red-black color that I'd previously experienced. While he calls it his "work in progress," the tank sample had an exceptionally deep color and a pleasant tannic grip felt as a dryness on the back of my lips similar to that from a cup of strong tea. I was surprised when Les mentioned that these tannins came from the grape itself, mostly the skins and seeds, and that the wine only needed a little time in neutral oak to mellow out the raw fruitiness of the wine.

Noticing my red-stained upper lip, Les said, "This's a red wine that Texas wine drinkers will appreciate. I've made a major play with Tannat, and I'm now working with over ten tons of it from the past harvest. I can't get enough of it. I'm blending it with lots of other grapes like Cabernet and Tempranillo, and my customers love it."

It's also easy to see where Les's current barrel-room experiments have led him. He went from blending his Cabernet Sauvignon with just classic Bordeaux varietals such as Merlot to incorporating the Cabernet with red Mediterranean varietals such as Syrah and Mourvèdre, and now his Tannat.

He added, "My experiments show this is the type of red-blended wine that works well in warm growing regions. It's based on an Australian model where the red wine gets the structure and mouth feel from one grape, and the rich, ripe, fruity character from others."

Last, we tasted barrel samples of the Cabernet and Tempranillo. They had great color that Les attributes to another one of his experiments and to the lessons learned in both the vineyard and winery: more intense field ripening, longer contact time of the juice and skins, and blending. The Cabernet was deep purple in color, with blackberry and cassis just starting to integrate with the oak aging. The Tempranillo, by comparison, had an even riper quality and thicker feel.

"In prior years," Les recalled, "I tasted wines made from these two grapes side by side with customers at Brushy Creek. Most preferred the Tempranillo or its blends; they're always the first to sell out, too. This evidence is useful, as it's dispelled one of the remaining old adages in the Texas wine industry: that customers won't buy wines that have names that are not in the 'big three'—Cabernet, Merlot, and Chardonnay."

Nearing the end of our visit, Les and I stood in the Brushy Creek tasting room and compared notes on Texas's relationship to other superior wine-producing regions. He mentioned that perhaps Texas had a special kinship with Australia, with both regions being rugged places requiring outside-the-box thinking and a willingness to experiment with new, unproven, New World approaches.

I peered out of the Brushy Creek tasting room door into the near pitch black of a clear rural night, but reconsidered my departure when I realized that a visit to Les wouldn't be complete without a brief retrospective glance at his nearly single-handed contribution. It was something that brought winegrowers and winemakers out from the vast hinterlands of Texas and together on the immense yet intimate energy field called the web.

Les said, "Back in 1991, shortly after I made the decision to plant grapes and start a winery, I discovered a few problems . . . like it wasn't legal to operate a winery in dry areas of the state, and most of Texas was, and still is, dry. Actually, it was legal to have a winery here, but the law said that I could give wine away free for tastings but not sell it. It wasn't clear to me how that business model might work."

Well, Les got to work and found other like-minded people like Dr. Bobby Smith, Gabe Parker, and Cord Switzer who'd already been fighting the legal battles for Texas wine. From his knowledge of computers, Les started the "Texas WineGrowers List" (mailing list), now on Yahoo! Groups, before many Texas wineries even had websites and before social networking took on the proportions of Twitter and Facebook. It was initially conceived to get the word out about legislative issues and to round up growers to attend government hearings.

What is now known as the "WineGrowers List," or simply "The List," has, for over ten years, distributed e-mail messages among growers and winemakers throughout this very large state. It's made communication among them across county lines seem like conversations on a small-town party line.

Les said, "Well, I think it worked! The Wine-Growers List helped us get laws passed, change the state constitution, and get research started, all to the benefit of winegrowers and winemakers in Texas, accomplishments no one would've believed possible in ten short years. But even more importantly, many of us use The List to share experiences. It's wonderful to see how this thing's evolved and broken down the barriers of distance and

factions. Growers and winemakers now think of themselves as part of a statewide industry and not just single entities within their county or region."

As darkness descended, I said good-bye and braved the chill of the January night. I headed back down the now-darkened road under the cover of an infinite black sky bejeweled with countless stars and a crystal moon. While captivated by the vast view overhead, I thought again of Les, the Grand Expérimentateur, his inquisitive and ever-searching mind in the vast and still largely unexplored expanse of Texas's wine frontier.

Memories of My Texas Bordeaux

11

I stopped for the night in Denton, Texas, and in the morning I awoke to a clear yellow-orange sky and a rib-sticking Waffle House breakfast. Over the period of a couple days since cold and ice had hit northeast Texas, the weather warmed comfortably. The Saturday sun cast an amber hue on the dry winter countryside, punctuated only by occasional fields of vivid green winter rye. The ground of rich red sandy soil lay beneath in peaceful contrast. As I approached the Oklahoma state line and its defining Red River, bedrock appeared in repeated cuts of erosion, leaving only mineral-rich alluvium where the river, over time, had scoured the northern reaches of Texas.

In a half hour I met Robert Wolf at Lone Oak Vineyard near Valley View, Texas. Robert and Jamie Wolf started this vineyard in the mid-1990s with the provocative intent of capturing a bit of Bordeaux and corralling it in Texas.

As we stood in the vineyard, I kicked at the ocher dirt, admiring its glint in the winter sun. Robert explained, "Lone Oak Vineyard was based on the concept of planting high-density vines, a spacing scheme similar to that used in Bordeaux, France, rather than the lower-density planting that's more common in many California vineyards. The high-density spacing yields a substantial increase in the number of vines on the same amount of land.

"The vineyard's also based on Bordeaux varietals. It consists of mostly Merlot, with some Cabernet Sauvignon, Petit Verdot, and Cabernet Franc. It's a vineyard mix that you might find in France, north of the Dordogne River, somewhere around Saint Émilion. Our goal was to produce either a single varietal Merlot or a blend with Cabernet."

The classic Bordeaux blending of red grape varieties was developed to combine the best qualities of individual grapes, something that tends to vary from spot to spot and year to year, hence the rationale for blending. For example, Cabernet Sauvignon is used for its tannic structure, sometimes called "backbone," Merlot for roundness and silky mouth feel, Cabernet Franc for color and herbal complexity, Malbec for body, and Petit Verdot for aroma and color.

While we kicked about in the vineyard, ducks on the adjacent pond took flight. We stopped briefly to follow them, and then Robert continued describing his experience. "As with many things necessary in starting a vineyard, they sometimes get done 'back-asswards.' In this case, we anticipated using well water for the vineyard, but the well was too salty and a deeper well was cost prohibitive. So, we decided, as a secondary plan, to develop these ponds to retain rainwater for irrigation. So far, the ponds have worked well, but this exercise taught us that water should've been our first consideration, not left as an afterthought."

Robert also focused on elements of terroir beyond the land itself, and he hit on what he felt was the real key to the vineyard's success: its proximity to Lake Ray Roberts, which was apparent as I approached the vineyard site by car that morning. The vineyard was surrounded on three sides by the lake, which seemed to come to within less than a mile of the vineyard.

He said, "The closeness of the lake and the prevailing summer wind results in a cooling effect for the vineyard, creating a mesoclimate here. We oriented the vineyard to take advantage of the lake-effect breeze. We see later bud break in the spring. Additionally, our grapes ripen two to four weeks sooner than those in other locales to the west of us that do not have this lake effect."

This seemed counterintuitive to me: cooler in summer, but earlier ripening. Then, he described how the lake effect reduced the summer daytime temperatures, which cut back the tendency for the Bordeaux varietals in his vineyard to stop ripening during periods of intense summertime heat. Robert pointed to the Merlot vines and said, "They're the real workhorses in this vineyard, just like you'd find in Saint Émilion, and they consistently put out high-quality fruit.

"We've had good success with Merlot and, to a somewhat lesser extent, Cabernet at this location, but the Petit Verdot is particularly impressive, and it adds a lot of color and character to the red wines made from our grapes."

Before my departure, Robert took me inside a small office building, and we tasted wine drawn from three small oak barrels labeled Cabernet, Merlot, and Petit Verdot. He said, "The real wine-making goes on at Gene Estes's Lone Oak Winery in Burleson. I just like to play here, as it helps me understand what the grapes in the vineyard are doing."

As we tasted from the barrels, we blended aliquots of purple Merlot and Cabernet and eventually dosed it with the inky, near-black Petit Verdot. We created a single bottle of red wine to my liking to be tasted later at a quiet time when I could reflect on my personal Texas Bordeaux moment. Departing, I headed northward for an overnight stop before tomorrow's return trip through Burleson, Texas, to see the goings-on at Lone Oak Winery.

After a leisurely drive north, I stopped for lunch in McKinney and visited the Landon Winery, producer of several excellent red wines. It's located on the town square, which resembles a mini-version of one I'd previously visited in Sonoma, California. Later, I stopped in Denison for dinner with friend and writing colleague Henry Chappell. It was getting late as we arrived at his house on Lake Texoma where the last rays of winter sun filtered through the trees and sparkled on the water. We sat at his kitchen bar that night, talking late into the evening while sharing a bottle of a decade-old Texas Cabernet that I had packed for this moment. The bottle's label read "Blue Mountain Cabernet Sauvignon, Davis Mountains Appellation." It was a worthy bottle, the last of its kind.

Blue Mountain was a West Texas vineyard known for its hearty Cabernet Sauvignon that was probably the best Texas had to offer in its day. Regretfully, the vineyard was unexpectedly lost to Pierce's disease long ago, before the countermeasures commonly applied today. It was especially worthy for sharing with a friend while swapping memories of wine experiences, history, kids, corporate life, dogs, hunting, travels, writing, and, of course, back to wine. As I poured the last taste of this extraordinary wine, I realized that it too would disappear into that special place in my mind where fond and distinctive memories reside.

> " "I realized that it too would disappear into that special place in my mind where fond and distinctive memories reside" "

Before leaving, Henry and I shared the breakfast he prepared, consisting of a tall pile of sausage patties, eggs roughly scrambled, and biscuits large and irregular. It was all brought together with thick milk-white gravy and chased down with Henry's strong caffeinated brew. When we'd finished, Henry said, "Follow me: I think that I have something you'll want to see."

We walked across the street from his house and through a patch of short brush into the vestiges of a small family graveyard nearly obscured by time and vegetation. It was a simple plot, a scatter of raw-cut headstones with weathered names—the only memorial left for the Grubb family that settled these wooded hills over a hundred years ago. There were many Texas settlers like the Grubbs, people of modest means left unnamed in history but for a worn and weathered headstone. They came to Texas from places back east . . . West Virginia, Tennessee, and Kentucky and from across the broad tier of southern states. This was a special place for Henry, a place to commune with the souls of Texans past, about their coming to a much younger and more hostile Texas than we now experience. It was a place of somber significance, where memories also linger.

In the 1800s, Texas was a frontier, and many chose to suffer the difficulties of this rural land in exchange for a new way of life. From these meager beginnings, the Texas agricultural tradition was born and continues to evolve today. Surely Henry had shared something with me that weekend that was much more than shelter and friendship.

After departing, I progressed down the highway on that Sunday morning recalling my earlier readings of Henry Renfro, a migrant to Texas from his native Tennessee. In 1853, Renfro befriended Dr. Rufus Burleson, president of Baylor University and an influential Baptist minister. Renfro prospered as a farmer and rancher and, with Burleson's guidance, also gained prominence as a North Texas Baptist minister. Renfro acquired land in central and northern Johnson County and sold some of his holdings to Mellen Dodge for establishment of a town site.

The Texas town-now-city in my sites was Burleson, named for Renfro's mentor and friend. Dodge divided the town of Burleson into blocks and lots, selling land to dozens of the area's pioneering merchants and settlers. His efforts established a growing North Texas community known for quarries of limestone, sand, and gravel, and an agriculture based on cattle, cotton, and now grapes and wine.

After my early Sunday start from Lake Texoma, I arrived along with the warm noon sun overlooking Lone Oak Winery. Owner Gene Estes and I sat and talked about his entry into the world of Texas wine that found a new purpose for the local limey, sandy, and gravelly soil.

Gene explained, "I've had an interest in making wine since college, where I studied and degreed in microbiology. While still back East, I started making fruit wines from blackberries, plums, and, Lord knows, even bananas. With the help of local winemakers, I expanded my talents by making wine from Muscadine grapes and furthered my studies by correspondence."

In the mid-1990s after a thirty-year career in pharmaceuticals, Gene took an assignment in Alsace, France. For the next two years, he met local grape growers and visited Alsatian wineries. By his own admission, he knew at that point that when he got back to Texas he needed to try his hand at what he called "real winemaking."

He knew that starting a winery was a big investment and that many past Texas wineries were undermined by an absence of sound business strategy. From time spent in Alsace, he learned that many French wineries were smaller, family-run enterprises that had operated successfully for generations.

Gene said, "I noticed that the Alsatian wineries had a very simple business plan. It was based on selling every bottle of their wine directly from their tasting room. From this, I decided not to have unrealistic plans about getting my wines into Walmart or Costco or exporting wine to California or New York City. My plan was to focus on making good wine and selling it from my own winery tasting room. I also realized that the main element of our success would be to draw people to our winery."

In 1998, Gene partnered to start his first vineyard. It was only one acre of land, and he planted lots of what he referred to as his "cold-climate grapes" from his experience in Alsace as well as hybrid grape varietals. In his straight-talking manner, he confessed that his cold-climate grapes simply "bit the bullet" here in Texas. Gene replaced some with Syrah, which continues to be a good producer for him. In 2001, Gene sold some of his grapes to Robert and Jamie Wolf at Lone Oak Vineyard. He also helped them prune their vineyard, and soon he and his wife, Judy, became good friends with the Wolfs.

"Back then, Robert was starting his Rudy's Barbecue franchise and literally had too much on his plate," Gene said with a short chuckle. "I was especially impressed with Robert's Lone Oak Merlot and his Bordeaux vineyard concept up in Valley View. So, I purchased Robert's winery assets and moved them to Burleson after I bought this property on the fringe of town. In keeping with my business plan, I thought that this would be a great, high-visibility location. Since then, it's a story of just trying to keep pace with growth."

Gene and I walked his vineyard while he elaborated about new experiments with what he calls his "warm-weather grapes," which include Syrah and Ruby Cabernet. He uses these grapes along with those from Robert's Bordeaux vineyard. Gene's white grapes include Malvasia Bianca and Blanc Du Bois, a hybrid grape with a Muscat lineage. Gene also purchases Tempranillo and Merlot from Texas growers in other locations around the state, and especially likes what he gets from the Texas High Plains appellation near Lubbock.

He said, "I am particularly impressed with grapes from the expanding number of major Texas High Plains growers like Newsom, Wilmeth, Bingham, Reddy, and Timmons. They just know how to grow things up there, do an excellent job, and do it in a big way, too."

We segued into Gene's barrel room and tasted some of the handiwork of his winemaker, Jim Evans, including the soon-to-be-bottled Lone Oak Tempranillo made from Newsom Vineyard's rich, red, high-plains fruit. In obvious excitement, Gene climbed the barrel racks with his wine thief in hand, searching for our taste. Though still not a finished wine, the Tempranillo had appealing color, and a smoky aroma punctuated with traditional American oak and a scent of rich berry. This tasting was clear evidence to me that this wine was destined for high marks. (It later won gold medals at the *Dallas Morning News* and San Francisco International Wine Competitions.)

The more we tasted, the more Gene made his way rack to rack through the barrel room. He thieved a barrel sample of Merlot from Jet Wilmeth's high-plains Diamante Doble Vineyard in Tokio, Texas. As he held up the wine-filled thief, Gene said, "Look! This's inky dark stuff, isn't it?"

Before leaving, we talked about his term as president of the Texas Wine and Grape Growers Association (TWGGA). Gene said, "Most importantly, I've tried to help growers and winemakers in Texas focus on quality. We can't afford to let the smaller wineries fall behind. We need to give everyone the opportunity to improve, but then it's up to them. We're processing a lot of new information in Texas, and new experiences abound. Growers and winemakers alike need to share these experiences and, most of all, be willing to learn important new lessons."

> " "A smoky aroma punctuated with traditional American oak and a scent of rich berry " "

Gene likes the efforts being made here to emulate warmer-weather wine regions like those in Spain, southern France, Italy, and Australia, and the pursuit of red wines made from what are to many consumers unfamiliar names. He's particularly keen on Tempranillo, but he emphasized that his own experiences with Merlot and Cabernet have taught him that Bordeaux varietals can also work well at particular vineyard sites and should not be abandoned.

After our farewells, with each passing mile southward the winter air became a little sultrier as I approached my next stop.

Later, over a few evenings, I savored my recently blended red wine as I studied its shiny, label-less bottle. It yielded an incredibly pleasing and palatable experience; this smidgen of North Texas Bordeaux had improved as the aromas and flavors now melded together. Alas, it would have undoubtedly benefited from further aging, but one bottle can only go so far. It too, like the once great wines from Texas's Blue Mountain Vineyard that I've shared with friends in faraway places, is gone. Now, these wines exist only in the vaults of my memory, but I still savor them every chance I get.

Younger, Dumber, Older, Smarter

12

It was a warm, muggy morning, and the drive from Granbury on the Brazos River to Springtown, west of Fort Worth, was pleasant enough. I was to meet Dr. Robert Smith, whom most everyone calls "Dr. Bobby." Back about twenty-five years ago, his Smith Estate Winery (known then as La Buena Vida Winery) was one of the first new wineries of the modern era of the Texas wine industry.

To get to Dr. Bobby's place, I snaked along country roads and skirted the small rural community of Springtown. When I arrived, the winery door was unlocked, and no one responded to my hellos yelled through the open door. I tried a call to Dr. Bobby's cell phone, but got his voice mail. So I sat in the shade of an arbor eating plums from a nearby tree and viewing the lush green vineyard. After a few minutes I got a phone call from Bobby saying he'd be right down.

While enjoying the sweet warm plums, I heard a noise coming from behind the barn that sounded like the whirl of a large fan overlaid onto the low rumble of a cement mixer. I looked around and spied a petite-looking orange-red tractor with its driver enclosed in a dusty white cab.

It stopped, and out popped Bobby Smith in baggy tan work pants and a plaid shirt. His physique betrayed his age, but his eyes were bright with the look of a much younger man still engaged in his passion. He said, "Howdy, Russ! Come on into the winery where it's cool. I've been out spraying the grapes before the clusters get too tight."

I'd barely gotten through the door when he pulled a bottle of wine from a rack and set it on tasting room bar, then walked over to a cooler and retrieved a package of firm white cheese. A pungent and acerbic aroma permeated the room as soon as he opened the package. That done, Dr. Bobby and I started talking.

He said, "Ya know . . . what I've enjoyed most of all through my years in the wine business is seeing Texas go from nothing at all, in terms of the wine world, to what it is today." I asked him where he thought the Texas industry actually was today.

He replied, "I know it's still got things to work on like quality and distribution, but it's the way the laws have changed since I started this winery. Gosh, we've come a long way. In the beginning, we were all new to it, and, looking back, what amazes me most is that we really *didn't know what we didn't know*. What we had going for us was that we were young, excited, and passionate about wine.

"When I bought this place, I was really pretty young and dumb; I didn't know I couldn't make wine out here in Springtown. The area was dry with respect to production and sales of alcoholic beverages. So, very early I knew that I had to come up with a plan so I could legally make wine here."

He slowly scratched his head and took a deep breath of cool winery air, then said, "Help yourself to some of this cheese. It's my mother's recipe that includes a good helpin' of garlic." He opened the bottle of his La Buena Vida, Smith Estate 2005 Tempranillo and poured a taste in a slow, deliberate but shaky manner, one hand steadying the other. It was easy to see that these were the hands of a man who didn't mind a hard day's work.

Bobby said that he had quickly realized there were two possibilities: get this area voted wet for alcohol or change the laws in Austin. Well, Bobby knew that this area had been dry since the turn of the twentieth century, and the plethora of Methodist and Baptist churches in Springtown convinced him that voting wet just wasn't going to happen in his lifetime. He surmised that changing the law was the only answer.

Years ago, Leon Adams (who's considered by wine enthusiasts to be the seminal American wine historian) paid Dr. Bobby a visit and helped him understand the problems new wineries faced in many states dealing with wine laws.

Bobby said, "Leon told me something that I consider, to this day, to be the most important advice I've ever received. He said that if I could convince the legislature to change the laws in some way, there are four things that a legislator will never vote against and I *only* had to include one of them: God, country, family, and farming. Since family farming was such a strong tradition in Texas, he thought I should be able to get something into legislation on farming that would help me out of my wine-making dilemma."

Bobby linked up with another early pioneer of the modern wine movement, Ed Auler at Fall Creek, to deal with the wet/dry issue and wine laws in the state. Professor George Ray McEachern at Texas A&M University, originally a pecan specialist, got involved because he was starting to help grape growers with their early tribulations with Texas viticulture. He couldn't participate in the legal dealings because of his job with a state-supported college, but George Ray could testify in front of legislative committees on grape growing and rural farming issues, if needed.

"What we did," said Bobby, "was we pleaded to the Texas legislature that the finest land for growing grapes in Texas was predominantly in dry counties, and the grape industry had tremendous potential for the benefit of rural Texas farms and family farmers."

I asked him what it was like back then and what was driving this newly founded movement to grow grapes in Texas. He related that in the seventies, a new wine awareness had struck the nation and was then spearheaded by the winemakers and grape growers in California. This was a time when Ernest and Julio Gallo and a young Robert Mondavi were traveling from coast to coast. It was something like the traveling revival meetings that spread the gospel across the South, but this time it was aimed at opening people's minds to wine.

He said, "Leon finally convinced me that, hell, I could do it. Shoot, I didn't know anything about how the legislature worked, but I spent a total of five months in Austin going to meetings and learning the ropes. Leon's advice was that if I could get things to where I could just make the wine here in Springtown, I could eventually figure out things on the marketing and sales side. So, we decided to put nothing in the bill about selling wine. Our bill had the word "Farm" in its title (one of the words Leon recommended), and it was totally about allowing the making of wine in the dry rural areas of Texas and not much else."

Bobby paused. His recollections were sharp and personal, as though the events of this story had taken place just this morning on his way to the winery. I touched my glass to his, then raised it

> ❝❝Shoot, I didn't know anything about how the legislature worked❞❞

to direct a lingering glance at the purple-red fluid before touching it to my lips. He did the same.

After a swallow, he said, "Gosh, I love this Tempranillo. A guy from the Rioja region of Spain helped me make it. His name is Antonio Palacios of Viña Herminia, where he makes traditional wines and presides over their cooperative winery."

Bobby first met Antonio in California at a wine-making conference, but when Bobby made this wine, Antonio was in Spain. They did the whole thing in Spanish and via e-mail. Bobby sent him questions, and Antonio sent Bobby instructions.

He said, "I remember that Antonio was emphatic about using American oak to get the true essence of the Spanish Rioja style. I recall specifically what Antonio told me. It was, 'Don't be *deceived* by French or Hungarian oak. American oak *is* the thing that gives Tempranillo its character.' It's the power of gripping tannins that's associated with the best tradition of Spanish Rioja wines." Bobby must have followed Antonio's advice, since his Tempranillo had all the key components: essence of ripe red berries and a respectable tannic structure.

After our respite, Bobby said, "Our wine bill was introduced in March or April 1977, and in June it was passed as the Texas Farm Winery Act of 1977, and then-governor Dolph Briscoe signed it." Bobby straightened up and walked from behind the bar to the back wall of the tasting room to point to an aged photograph. "This was taken at the signing in Austin. Here's Representa-

tive McFarlin who sponsored our bill, Ed Auler, Jim Cooper, and here's a good-looking young guy named Bobby Smith."

In the photo, Dr. Bobby looked young and lean, with a head of dark, bushy hair. He recalled that a reporter asked Governor Briscoe what the bill was going to do for Texans. According to Bobby, the governor said, "It's going to help the farmers of Texas," and that's all he knew. Leon Adams's advice appeared to have paid off.

He continued: "My plan was to make a few improvements to the winery and then make some wine the following year, but then I realized I still had a problem. How in the hell was I going to sell my wine? Springtown is dry and I won't be able to sell it here. While I was thinking about that, I got a call from the district supervisor for the Texas Alcoholic Beverage Commission (TABC), who back then was Virgil Stevens. He called me and said, 'Doctor, you've got this bill passed. We're gonna have a meeting in Austin and try to figure out how to get things to where you can sell the wine.' He figured that since I was behind the bill, I could tell them how I was gonna to do it."

Bobby told Virgil that he'd be glad to come down, and by that afternoon Bobby was in Austin. The drive gave him time to think, and he hatched a brilliant idea; the sale wouldn't actually occur until the point when the wine was delivered to a wet area in Texas.

Bobby took another few sips of his deep red wine and said, "Next, I talked to Joe Darnell, a

TABC lawyer, and asked him, 'What if I bought a piece of property in a wet area and set me up a little winery there.' This way I could make wine in Springtown, then sell it to my other winery located in the wet precinct. I asked if that would pass muster, and, without hesitation, Joe said that it would be OK as long as I stayed away from churches or schools."

Bobby then got ready to buy some land over in Lakeside, on the edge of Fort Worth, where sales of alcoholic beverages were legal. He went back to Joe and told him about it. Bobby went through it from start to finish, and again Joe said that it would work.

However, several years later the state highway department called on Dr. Bobby,

> ❝❝I got somethin' else that I want you to taste. Follow me!❞❞

saying they were going run a six-lane highway right through his Lakeside winery . . . or at least that's what Bobby admitted to hearing. They were offering him nearly nothing for the property and even threatened condemnation if he didn't sell. The highway department was playing hardball, and it had nothing to do with his winery's legal wrangling. Realizing that he would be fighting a losing battle, he told them that he would sell but needed some time to figure out where to go.

Struck by a flash of inspiration, Bobby said "I got somethin' else that I want you to taste. Follow me!" We exited the cool of the tasting room

and walked around to the side of the large metal building ablaze with the heat from the afternoon sun. Bobby held the door open for me to enter, after which we climbed over equipment scattered around the large, dank, and dusty room to where oak barrels were stacked two high, all in a row.

As he pointed to the barrels before me, he announced, "This is all my port. Some of it goes back all the way to the eighties. Everybody that comes here wants to buy this stuff."

Looking at the collage of business cards stuck on the side of the barrels, I believed him. There was even a card from his air-conditioning man. Evidently, he had tasted it during the last repair job on the old AC unit and fell in love with the sweet juice.

As Bobby ambled up a metal ladder laid against a barrel, he said, "Steady the ladder with one hand and raise our glasses up here with the other." After he siphoned some samples of his port-style wine, we swirled and savored it while seated on stools across from each other in the warm, shadowy room. He said, "I made this port from Cabernet and a little Chambourcin back in the fall of '87." After my first taste, I said, "Man, this stuff is really smooth and tawny."

"I've a story to tell you about this wine," Bobby said. "In 1979, a guy came by after hearing that I made a port. He asked me if I was interested in using a new strain of yeast that he said would stay active up to really high levels of alcohol, making fortification of my port with brandy unnecessary. It resulted in a smooth, drinkable wine without having to age out the sharp taste of the brandy. This sounded interesting to me, so I said that I'd try it.

"Over the many years that I've had this wine, it's gone tawny with a bronze color and this nutty aroma that I just love. But, you know what? It was smooth from the moment that it came out of the fermenter. In '85 I made the first all-fermented, non-brandy-fortified port wine in Texas. I never wanted credit or recognition for being the first. I've helped others make port this way, and several others have gotten a lot of notoriety for it. But, ya know what? I really don't care, especially when I'm sippin' this stuff."

With the taste of this wine fresh in my mind, I told Bobby that I could envision a time when a much younger Bobby Smith made this wine. To this he quipped, "The younger and dumber Bobby Smith!" As we continued to slowly savor his port-style Texas wine, Bobby continued with his saga.

"Before my run-in with the highway department, P. W. McCallum, with the convention bureau in Fort Worth, wanted to do a travel deal for convention planners and taste some Texas wine. The problem I realized was that there wasn't much Texas wine, and most of it back then was crap, including some of my wines. However, we worked out a deal where I would select and serve the wines at this event. After that, P. W. asked me if I would move my Lakeside winery to Grapevine.

But I didn't have the money to move right then." Later, after his deal with the highway department was struck, Bobby called P. W.

He said, "I called his office at seven in the morning and he told me to be there for a meeting with the mayor an hour later. Well, the mayor was there and we mapped out a strategy. Then they showed me a few places, but I didn't care for any of them."

He then noticed an old vacant church next door to one of the properties. Bobby invited Camille McBee to come look at it with him. After they went through the old church, Bobby called the owner, talked price, and told him that he would take it subject to two things: proper zoning and changing the property from dry to wet for sale of alcohol (a problem that just seemed to follow the young Dr. Bobby no matter what).

He said, "The property was zoned residential, and there was a nearby church congregation, so P. W. suggested that we get the full support of the neighborhood behind the project. We held a neighborhood social on a Sunday afternoon, and I went over. Camille did the socializing, and, if you knew her, she was a classy lady and that was one thing that she was really good at."

Well, the neighborhood social went well and Bobby's spirits were high, but when they tried to get the consent of the planning and zoning commission, they were voted down five to two. After the meeting adjourned, Camille returned to her car wiping the tears from her eyes.

Bobby said, "Ya know, a few minutes later, the

mayor walked by her car and patted her on the shoulder and told her in his characteristic broad slow drawl, 'Little lady, don't ya cry. You'll get your winery.' Then, as he passed me, he said in a muted tone, 'or I'll get me a new commission.' You know what? He did, and we eventually got that new winery in Grapevine.

"Last year I brought in a bunch of my friends, about fifteen, for a tasting of my ports to commemorate my thirty years of making wine. I included what I felt were some of my best vintages. It was before Camille McBee passed. She was a grand lady and, I'm pleased to say, a good old friend of mine. She picked out which food went with which port. It was a grand affair, and it made me feel like I was able to share a portion of my winemaking career with her and those that attended."

In tribute to both Camille and Bobby's winemaking career, we tipped our glasses and downed the last of the port wine. It produced a sweet, mellow, and warm feeling down deep in my soul while I envisioned the two Bobby Smiths: the younger and dumber man that helped to spearhead the Texas wine movement, and the older and smarter man that now felt blessed by the experience.

> ❝It produced a sweet, mellow, and warm feeling down deep in my soul❞

Tastes of Time

13

"**I**'ve been around the Texas wine industry a long, long time. I've been in many places and worn many hats over the years." This is how Dr. Roy Mitchell described himself to me during a midsummer class on wine quality at Grayson County College in Denison, Texas.

Perhaps the most interesting hat in his collection is the one that he wore that day in front of the class billed as "a wine quality boot camp." I thought that this boot camp thing was going to be more figurative than literal. However, as Camp Commander Roy Mitchell marched in to start the class, he wore a helmet from his early college days as a member of the Aggie Corps of Cadets. Roy said, "The last time I wore this here helmet was in 1957 at Texas A&M University.

"I get to wear this helmet 'cause I'm Camp Commander. They tell me that this designation entitles me to drink just as much wine as the rest of you, and I get just about the same other privileges, too. Basically, we're gonna have a few winemaking experts here this week along with one old codger, me, who's got lots of experience. So you better ask me lots of questions before I get a headin' for home."

I concluded that Roy, as the self-proclaimed old codger, had been witness to and participated in more of the Texas wine experience than anybody still active in it. Prior to this meeting, I'd met Roy only once, at a Texas wine industry meeting in Austin a few years ago where I tasted his sherry. Roy said, "It's something I call 'La Bodega de Mitchell, Crema Del Sol.' I think it's pretty damn good, if I say so myself."

Roy's winemaking career goes back to the genesis of the modern wine movement in Texas. In 1973, Roy was a professor in the Chemistry Department at Texas Tech University. As unlikely of a place as it was, this is where he first made wine from Texas grapes grown on an arbor on the patio of another Texas Tech professor, horticulturalist Robert Reed. Roy also made wine from grapes grown at Sagmore Vineyard. Sagmore was owned by another Tech professor, Clint "Doc" McPherson.

These were Roy's first experiences with winemaking. They built his career while jump-starting the modern Texas wine industry. Doc, Bob, and Roy became like the proverbial "Three Musketeers." Their adventures and misadventures stem from their proclivity for grape growing and winemaking in a land decimated by Prohibition and post-Prohibition wrangling.

In a conversation, I asked Roy which one of them was Athos, the musketeer who retired to his estate, which one was Porthos, who married the widow of a rich lawyer, and finally which one was Aramis, who entered the priesthood. In response, I just got a gravelly laugh, after which Roy said, "You might know that we eventually had a falling out of sorts. We ended up going our separate ways, I reckon just like those other good ol' boys seemed to've done."

The wines that Roy made in his Texas Tech basement laboratory were experimental wines. Back then, it wasn't a given that wine grapes could be grown successfully, not to mention commercially, here in Texas. For that matter, no one knew whether Texas-grown grapes could be made into decent wines either. According to Roy, their research, plain and simple, was to prove that palatable wines could be made from local grapes, and he demonstrated how to do it.

While at Texas Tech, Roy met and became closest of friends with another professor in the Chemistry Department, who, Roy admits, was into wine consumption in a bigger way than he was at the time. Being originally from Texas A&M, Roy and his friend, who had roots extending from the University of Texas, had a standing bet of a bottle of Harveys Bristol Cream Sherry on the annual UT–A&M football game. That's when Roy starting drinking and learning to appreciate the finer qualities of sherry.

He said, "After that, I started saving leftover white wines in a five-gallon jug. I had three rules that I followed for what went into the jug: Rule #1: It had to be a white wine. Rule #2: It had to be grown in Texas. Rule #3: It had to be from vinifera grapes, the classic grapes of Europe. My sherry-making operation started small with some of my first experimental Texas Tech wines from the seventies, and as I continued, I expanded it several times since."

"Doc, Bob, and I were the three Texas Tech professors who started the first modern-day Texas winery, called Llano Estacado, but I'm not one of the names that gets mentioned very often." The reason for Roy's anonymity stems from the selling of his Llano Estacado stock early in the venture when funding for the winery started to roll in from other shareholders. The main reason for the sale was that Charles McKinney was starting to look at growing grapes in a big way for a project on University of Texas lands and needed help with the winemaking. Once he asked Roy to do the winemaking for the UT project, Roy had to make sure he was clear of any conflict of interests that his ownership in Llano Estacado might present.

Roy's stock transaction is something that he looks back on with a certain amount of tongue-in-cheek pride. He said, "Incidentally, I made a small profit selling that stock. It's probably some of the first profits made from a Texas wine venture back in those days. Things were pretty dicey, ya know." Actually, the profit from Roy's shares in Llano Estacado was likely the *only* profit made from a Texas wine venture during those early years.

Roy was also around at the inception of the wine industry's first trade and technical organization that promoted grape growing and education. With a chuckle, Roy said, "I was a charter member of TGGA, the Texas Grape Growers Association started up by George Ray McEachern and a bunch

> **"Their research, plain and simple, was to prove that palatable wines could be made from local grapes"**

of the early grape growers and winemakers. You notice that the word 'wine' wasn't in it at that point. I'm not a lawyer, but I wrote the bylaws and I made sure that I only mentioned grapes and grape products in these bylaws and nothing that had anything to do with an alcoholic beverage. I knew enough about the situation in Texas specifically not to use the word 'wine.'"

Despite the deficiencies in Roy's legal background, he was astute, if nothing else. Compared to today, back then Texas was not quite what you would call cosmopolitan. Several old-timers of Roy's vintage told me that even though National Prohibition ended in 1933, most of Texas really didn't emerge from it until well into the seventies, or in some parts, even later. Until just recently, some said, "Hell! There are parts of Texas that are *still* in Prohibition," referring to the totally "dry" areas of the state.

In this same light, Roy's early compatriot, Doc McPherson, acknowledged that back in the early going, people in many parts of Texas, particularly in and around Lubbock, still saw alcohol in any form of beverage as the "devil's drink." When Llano Estacado was being formed, Doc tried to convince farmers to convert a portion of their acreage in row crops to growing wine grapes. In several instances, farmers got a personal visit from their preacher once the word got out that they were going to grow grapes for the new winery in Lubbock.

When the pastor stopped by, he usually conveyed to the farmer in a subtle yet clearly understandable and God-fearing way that the farmer could go ahead and grow wine grapes if he wanted. However, if he did, he and his family wouldn't be welcome any longer in the church's congregation.

It was Roy's awareness of these situations in Texas that allowed the fledgling wine industry and its new organization to get its foothold. It also allowed them to do this without getting growers and winemakers into trouble with their teetotaling opponents around the state.

Eventually, when the time was right, TGGA evolved into TWGGA (Texas Wine and Grape Growers Association) and the taboo on the use of the word "wine" finally came to an end. From there, Roy was able to focus on developing TWGGA's educational programs, which included sessions at many regional meetings and state conferences.

Roy said, "Unfortunately my employer, Texas Tech University, really didn't back me in all this work. They never really saw it as part of my job description. All they wanted me do was to publish more research, but I felt that I needed to do more practical things that would benefit our new struggling wine industry."

Since these early days, Texas Tech University has found a renewed interest in Texas grape growing and winemaking and is pursuing it in a big way. It now offers a new viticulture degree, with classes in winemaking and wine tourism included. With growth, the plans are to expand the curriculum further to include business planning for wineries, marketing wine, and vineyard management.

During the period that Roy worked for the University of Texas project with Charles McKinney, UT was in the lead-up to a large vineyard and winery operation on its vast university landholdings. Charles was involved in evaluating grape-growing possibilities at several central and west Texas vineyard sites, while Roy, as winemaker, led the winemaking trials using the grapes from the university's experimental vineyards. The results of this work eventually led to the establishment of Cordier Estates, better known now as Ste. Genevieve Winery and Mesa Vineyards near Fort Stockton, Texas. They're the largest combined vineyard and winery operation in the state.

From his days at Texas Tech through his period at Llano Estacado and making experimental wines for the UT mega-project, Roy continued to grow his collection of white wines for his sherry-making operation. Roy also met and was good friends with Mark Penna and Don Brady, who were then two young upstart winemakers at Llano Estacado. Eventually Don and Mark moved on, going from Llano Estacado to work in the big Ste. Genevieve winery.

According to Roy, "Mark and Don had a couple barrels of old white wine that they saved up and took with them down to Ste. Gen. These were the only two barrels in the whole winery, something that made them pretty conspicuous. One day the federal inspectors were performing an audit at Ste. Gen and they found those two barrels of wine and asked what was in them as they weren't on the books."

Don decided that they'd better get these barrels of wine out of the winery . . . and fast. So, he got hold of a guy with a truck that was making a delivery at the winery that day and paid him to quickly load the two barrels onto his truck and deliver them to his house.

When I talked about Don's story with Roy, he said, "Yep, that's just where I found them, in Don Brady's garage. I bought those two barrels of wine from Don and added them to my sherry-making collection. I bet that some of that wine had its origins in the fledgling days of the Llano Estacado winery, not to mention maybe a smidgen or two that may have wandered in from Ste. Gen."

Roy acknowledged that his job while working on the UT winery project was challenging. Although it took him out of the classroom for several years, he got to work full-time in Midland, where Charles set him up with a good lab and winemaking facility.

Roy said, "Eventually, things were set for the Ste. Gen winery project, and then the UT funding dried up. So, in 1988, I went to Teysha Cellars, now known as CapRock Winery, in Lubbock. It was a big new commercial winery, and I actually gave up my university tenure to take the winemaster's position at Teysha."

Roy's time as Teysha Cellars winemaster didn't last long. Teysha, like many start-up Texas wineries in the eighties, suffered financially, filed for bankruptcy, and was later resurrected as CapRock Winery. The problem with Teysha Cellars, and what was seemingly repeated later with CapRock, was that they planned too far ahead, speculating on rapid growth that never materialized. The failure of Teysha Cellars was a first for a publically owned winery in Texas. At the time, it was simply too big for its young britches.

In the fall of 1989, Roy retreated to the Chemistry Department at Texas Tech as a part-time faculty member and then moved to a full-time position in the Horticulture Department in 1990. This is where Roy stayed with his growing collection of white wine until his retirement a few years later. Those who know Roy often comment about the personal energy that he dedicates to education and his passion for winemaking. It wasn't a surprise to anyone who knew him when he announced that he just couldn't stay retired.

Roy said, "In the nineties, I started consulting for several wineries and was eventually hired to manage Pheasant Ridge Winery in Lubbock; it previously won some of the first out-of-state medals for Texas wines. It was in the post–Bobby Cox era after the bankruptcy. Around the same time, I purchased more oak barrels and started my pet project. I picked up surplus white wine that was lying about Pheasant Ridge gathering dust, and I finally got my sherry operation up to a commercial scale, another first for Texas."

From Pheasant Ridge he moved the sherry to Bobby Smith's La Buena Vida Winery in Spring-town for a spell, and later on moved it again to Gabe Parker's Homestead Winery. Roy said, "It was like a rambling road show looking for a home. Finally, once at Homestead Winery, my sherry operation got up to twenty-two barrels of wine."

Roy's love of teaching persists into his "retirement." He helped Grayson County College develop their original curriculum, and he's taught one or two enology/chemistry courses every semester over the years. Roy's kept this finger in winemaking through his association with Gabe Parker at Homestead Winery.

When he could just be sitting back sipping and chilling, Roy continues to vent some strong ideas about problems that need solving, such as the need to develop more effective educational programs in Texas. He feels that education is key to the development of an industry that's growing grapes in diverse growing conditions over such a vast region as Texas. It's like trying to train grape growers and winemakers to practice over an expanse as large and diverse as the whole country of France. Texas is like its own country, and growers and winemakers need to have an assorted set of skills to grow and process wines around this state.

Roy said, "I don't have the energy or stamina I used to have, but I still enjoy making wine. At Homestead, I can help out with Gabe's winemaking and do what I need to do with my sherry makin', while doing some teaching and lab work at Grayson. I'm not really looking for many new projects, but my old friend and cohort Charles McKinney (who we let escape from here to the Carolinas) and I need to write a book of our stories. We ain't getting any younger, ya know."

In the middle of the 2010 crush, Roy turned a young seventy-four. He appears to be in pretty fair health and is active beyond a doubt. He now relies on his six-year-old pacemaker to keep him going: traveling, teaching, and making wine. At this level of activity, Roy is a bit snappy and approaches bragging when he says, "I wore out my last pacemaker much faster than anybody expected. Who knows how long this one's gonna last before it'll need a tune-up or a trade-in just so it can keep up with me."

Finally, Roy explained a very interesting and historical aspect of his Texas sherry-making operation, his solera. Solera is a winemaking technique whereby every year the wine from the present vintage is combined with wines from previous vintages before bottling. Then, some of the mixed wine is saved for the coming year where it is again blended with the new wine. There is always an amount of wine in the barrel that dates back to the original wine used when the solera was started. In Roy's case it dates back to the genesis of the modern Texas wine industry. Roy is particularly proud of his sherry both for its taste and historical value.

He said, "I've entered it into many competitions year after year. Since the blend of wine in the solera continues on year after year, and now dates back a ways, I think that I could advertise it as winning more awards than any other wine in Texas history. There are parts of it that date back nearly forty years that came from the first modern wines made in Texas from my early days at Texas Tech."

In essence, Roy's sherry is a living entity that grows in flavor and complexity with every year. Even more importantly, the solera encapsulates many fragments of Texas wine and wine history along the way. It's a legacy of the notable places Roy's traveled to and touched, including the hallmark days of Texas Tech, Llano Estacado, Pheasant Ridge, Ste. Genevieve, Bobby Smith's La Buena Vida Winery, and Homestead Winery. If Roy had more time to think about it, I bet that he'd come up with a few more historical footnotes about what's in his solera.

As I later savored Roy's sherry at Gabe Parker's Homestead Winery tasting room, I finally realized the depth and complexity contained in this deep aromatic fluid. It traces its maker through place and time. Its dark-golden color, warm vapors, and sweet lingering flavor contains some of the most important molecules in the history of Texas wine. In this creation, Roy has prepared a lasting tribute to the Texas wine experience in a wine that holds venerable tastes of time.

> "I finally realized the depth and complexity contained in this deep aromatic fluid"

Coming to America

14

Scenic hills with tall pine trees fringed my East Texas path to produce a cloistered environment with an emerald cast. As I drove, I thought about how modern man conjoins with nature on a grand scale in Texas: acres under barn, vast countryside dedicated to row crops, white wooden fences extending to the horizon guarding the domain of domesticated animals. With the tenacity and cleverness of early farmers, augmented with the tools and treatments of modern-day agricultural technology, Texans are developing a fresh, new definition for the word *terroir*.

My path circumnavigated the sprawling East Texas city of Tyler, following four-lane thorough-fares into the piney woods. Once at Tyler's southern reach, I entered what I soon realized was the "Province of Kiepersol," the domain of Pierre de Wet and his daughters. A man of immense vision and strength, Pierre, with his daughters Marnelle and Velmay following closely in his footsteps, has crafted a new life and realm.

I navigated the Kiepersol Estate, a maze of manor homes on streets named for the classic grapes of Europe. My drive terminated at a nearly clandestine B&B and restaurant. Inside the comfortable surroundings were images of Pierre's South African family and their wild homeland amalgamated with their present American endeavors.

Marnelle Durrett, Pierre's married daughter and craftsperson of this domain, stopped by to greet me. She's the estate manager and head winemaker at Kiepersol Estate Vineyards, overseeing the production of the family's five wine labels: Kiepersol Estates, KE Cellars, KE Bushman, 4 You, and Barrel 33. She's assisted by Velmay, the domain's chief financial officer.

Marnelle and I drove to the nearby Kiepersol Estate winery overlooking its adjacent vineyards and meandered through vineyard blocks seemingly plucked from the estates of Bordeaux, the Rhône valley, Italy, and Spain. My preconceived notion of East Texas as the ragged edge of the realm of Texas grape growing was shattered by what I saw.

When I started my travels in search of Texas terroir (the sense of place for Texas viticulture), many said with conviction that European grape varieties couldn't, and simply wouldn't, grow here. They cited East Texas as being just too damn hot and humid, as well as too "hot" in terms of

Pierce's disease. Yet here were vines of Cabernet, Merlot, Syrah, Chardonnay, and Muscat alive and well in the Texas sunshine—all a lush green, gestating this year's abundant crop of grapes.

Entering the winery, I was dwarfed by a large room with shiny stainless steel tanks defining its perimeter. Across the room, I saw a tall man in a white shirt and jeans, topped with a cowboy hat. His jeans had the fade of outdoors, and his boots had the scruff of a man who walks the land, not an office. I recognized immediately that this was Pierre de Wet.

> **"The most powerful statement about terroir I've heard since starting my search"**

He leaned against the wall just outside the small winery office/laboratory as we entered. He was preoccupied with a cigarette in one hand and his cell phone in the other. After we assembled in the office and exchanged greetings, it was obvious that he already knew what had become "my quest."

After our introduction, Pierre said, "Sense of place, terroir, for me it's very different than the old conception that you read about in all your wine books. With modern-day technology, man can change the terroir. I'm a good enough farmer to change it to get what I want."

His voice carried the interesting intonation of his South African homeland, but his message was pure unadulterated American freedom. It also carried what was perhaps the most powerful statement about terroir I've heard since starting my search. Facing me was precisely the confluence of man and nature about which I've penned ten thousand words, and yet he described it in only a dozen.

Pierre continued: "Our palate at Kiepersol defines our terroir. We use nutrients, micronutrients, pruning, vine spacing, and even new wind machines to get the precise qualities in our grapes for the wines we taste."

Marnelle seamlessly continued Pierre's thoughts, saying, "When we started Kiepersol Estate Vineyards, Daddy and I looked to California, Washington, Australia, and other growing areas for ideas. Our approach utilized the wine philosophies of wine gurus like Robert Parker and sometimes even anti-Parker philosophies. My father has an interesting combination of skills: an international palate and knowledge on how to farm just about anything."

I could already feel the headstrong, can-do determination that Pierre manifests. Furthermore, I sensed that Marnelle and Pierre shared a strong bond that starts with family but extends outward into their wine endeavor. They think as extensions of each other, so much so that in their verbal volley they complete each other's thoughts with nary a gap for breath. Consequently, when asking either a single question, I received replies incorporating multiple perspectives that started with a serve into the dirt of the vineyard, continued with a back-

hand to the winemaking operation, and finished with a hard forehand smash covering the quality of the finished wines. Whew!

Pierre stood up, walked over to the doorway, and lit another cigarette. I asked Pierre how he and his young daughters got started in Texas and how he chose this state. Before responding, his cell phone rang. I immediately recognized the ring tone as the theme from the old Marlboro Man TV commercials from years ago. I thought, how appropriate.

Finishing his cigarette, Pierre fanned the air as he closed his phone. He walked back, sat on a table near the door, and said, "Twenty-five years ago we came here. We left South Africa by choice, for personal and private reasons. I wanted to be part of the rose-growing industry in this area and start a simple life. When we came here, my goal was simple. We were going to start anew in America, live a debt-free life, and stay away from promises that we can't keep."

I asked him why the family became involved in vineyard operations and winemaking in Tyler, Texas, not exactly recognized as prime real estate for grape growing like Napa or Sonoma. Marnelle replied, "The grape-growing idea came from Daddy in 1996 when I said that I wanted to be a farmer. After all, both my sister and I were involved in agricultural activities since high school, and I finally concluded that I wanted to be a farmer."

Pierre, as I expected, finished Marnelle's thought, and said, "You know, when my kids were growing up, I must've done something right. Usually, farmers complain so much that their kids just want to leave the farm as soon as they can. When Marnelle came to me, she said that people in the area used to grow peaches many years ago. I thought to myself, she wants to grow peaches, so I said 'That's awesome!' However, I suggested that if she wanted to proceed into agriculture, do something that's not as perishable as peaches . . . try grapes."

The wisdom in Pierre's recommendation came from his global knowledge of agriculture. He knew that grapes are grown in North Africa, in South Africa, and from France to Washington State to Australia. He figured they should be able to grow good-quality grapes right here, good enough for making wine. And, if the wine didn't sell right away, it wouldn't perish. They would still have another eight years or more to sell the wine once it was in the bottle.

For the past three decades of the modern Texas grape-growing experience, there is probably only one thing that nearly every Texas viticulteur could agree on: classic varieties of wine grapes like Cabernet Sauvignon, Merlot, and Chardonnay just wouldn't grow east of a line defined by Interstate 35 extending from San Antonio to the Dallas–Fort Worth Metroplex because of Pierce's disease.

Nevertheless, Marnelle and Pierre started their winegrowing venture by journeying to several Texas colleges and universities that offered classes and degree programs in grape growing and wine-

making. Pierre judged the agricultural expertise of these institutions to be inferior to his own, which came from over thirty years of hard knocks, farming everything from mangoes in South Africa to apples in Washington State. So, they decided to plant a one-acre test plot with several varieties of the European grapes to see the results firsthand.

Pierre said, "The one thing that I've learned from my years in farming is that every place has its agricultural challenges. It's usually a matter of just figuring out how to provide healthy nourishment for plants to overcome these challenges."

At roughly the same time, over ten years ago, Pierre and his girls decided to open a restaurant on their Kiepersol Estate. With what he calls his growing "sense of patriotism to Texas wines," Pierre decided that the restaurant would serve only Texas wines.

He followed his statement with a grimace, saying that back then he tasted over a hundred wines from Texas and it was hard to find even a few that he really felt comfortable serving in his new restaurant. While disheartened at the time, he acknowledged that there has been substantial progress made since then. Their restaurant now carries over a hundred wines from all around Texas that he is proud to serve.

In a rare gap in the discussion, I finally got to ask the questions that had nearly burned a hole in my brain since I arrived at Kiepersol Estate: What about Pierce's disease? When did you realize PD was a problem?

In response, Pierre said, "When it comes to this disease, we are simply growing outside the box. PD scares everybody in Texas, but I ask, what do they do about it?"

Marnelle added, "Every one of our vines tested positive for the bacteria that causes Pierce's disease, but now most don't die. From the start, we knew that PD could be a problem, but in 1997 Daddy simply approached it very matter-of-factly, as a farmer would, saying let's just figure out what'll grow here."

Pierre said, "Frankly, I was more worried about fungus. That's what drove out the rose business from Tyler. I figured that we would try some Cabernet, Merlot, and Chardonnay, but I also did my research and found other grapes varieties that had thicker skins that would be more resistant to fungal problems."

Marnelle followed with her volley and said, "Actually, things started off very well in the experimental vineyard, and, in short order, we proceeded with planting fourteen acres."

While Marnelle was in California interning at Trefethen Vineyards in Napa Valley, Pierre ordered the vine stock for their initial fourteen-acre vineyard, but didn't have enough money for trellising. So, in early 1998, after the vines arrived, he walked the rows and stuck in flags where they were to be planted. Then, he temporarily closed his fourteen-person business office and told his employees to put on their jeans and boots and show up at the vineyard the next morning to plant grapevines.

Pierre said, "By Easter weekend, we were surprised. The vines looked like they'd found paradise. But now, we really needed the trellising and I still didn't have much money. So, I brought in a post-hole digger and got some used wire that we cut apart and re-spliced. I bought a load of used posts from a vineyard in California and trucked them to Texas. It didn't look very good when we put it all together, but it got us started. The vines grew to the top of the trellis the first year, and we didn't lose a plant."

In May of the following year, the vines started blooming and then started to die. Pierre realized that he really didn't understand Pierce's disease, but that he had to do something. From past experience, he started using zinc treatments.

Pierre described why he used this approach. When he was a farmer in South Africa, if a plant got damaged, he treated it with zinc. Still later, when growing citrus in Florida, after a hurricane he used an MZF spray that contained magnesium, zinc, and iron to help plants recover from sea salt blown into the orchards by the storm.

He admits now that what he did first to fend off the vineyard disease was another one of his "poor-boy" tactics. Pierre mixed his own zinc concoction and scattered it around each vine. Unfortunately, it didn't help. After some analysis of the vines, he realized that the vines weren't taking up the zinc. So, he broke down and bought a commercial zinc formulation and applied it throughout the vineyard.

With a stern look, Pierre said, "By the following year, many vines had succumbed to PD. So, we cut them off near the ground. But, the next spring, they were growing up again. After one more year, we still lost some vines, but it really wasn't that bad. It was like the unhealthy vines died, but then the healthier ones took up the zinc and things improved."

Marnelle said, "We were really excited, but at first nobody in Texas seemed to want to confirm our results or do any research to find out why the zinc worked. Some people said they were afraid that the levels of zinc would be so high that it might be toxic. However, when we analyzed the zinc in the grapes we found only normal levels. For some reason, the leaves are the sink for the zinc and this gives the vines added protection from PD."

Marnelle and I left the gathering and went up to the winery tasting room, where we had a retrospective tasting of her Kiepersol Estates Cabernet Sauvignon. The first pour was from the 2003 vintage, and it showed a fabulous purple color, an underpinning of dark fruit character, and the development of secondary aromas of leather and cigar box.

Marnelle, commenting on the wine's age worthiness, said, "I can't believe it. This was one of my early vintages as a winemaker, and everything I did seemed to work better than I expected."

She appeared generally disappointed in the 2004 and 2005 vintages of Cabernet, chalking up these vintages to experience, a period where she was still developing her winemaking craft. Both wines were more austere than the 2003. She attributed this to the overuse of neutral oak in the winery, and also indicated that these wines were made before the feeding regime they use in the vineyard today was fully implemented.

The 2006 Cabernet, while well made and improved over 2004 and 2005, was not as intense and complex as the 2003 wine. She acknowledged that in 2006 she went back to her winemaking comfort zone that resulted in a wine with an easy drinking, lighter style, but less age worthiness.

As we tasted her 2007 Cabernet, I commented that this wine had darker fruit attributes, a notable complexity of aromas and tastes with a distinct smoky character. The bottom line was that it was a better wine than any of her previous vintages.

Marnelle was also pleased and said, "This is the vintage where I decided that I was going to push things a bit. I didn't just want to make good wines; I wanted to step up to making world-class wines."

To finish the tasting, Marnelle and I trekked down into the barrel room for a sample of her 2008 Cabernet Sauvignon still in barrel. From one taste, it was obvious that she had reached the level of a confident winemaker, something that only comes with courage and even a bit of cellar room bravado to coax every last bit of fruit and character the grapes have to give.

I told her that I had the feeling that many Texas winemakers haven't had the courage to reach their full potential yet. Perhaps it's because of the shortage of grapes in Texas for the past several years. I surmised that winemakers are generally afraid of screwing up the precious few Texas grapes they've had in these short vintages. They often found it safer to tack a sure course rather than explore the extremes of their grapes and their winemaking abilities.

Marnelle said, "You should've seen the skins when I was finished with this 2008 Cabernet. They were nearly white. I got all that the grapes had to give, and I gladly took it."

After the tasting, Marnelle drove me back to the Kiepersol B&B and provided me a bottle of Cabernet Sauvignon from her new 4 You brand to sample later that evening.

> **❝❝I got all that the grapes had to give, and I gladly took it❞❞**

As we drove, she pointed down the hill into the vineyard's low spot to one of two wind machines her father installed. It was whirling and oscillating back and forth across the vineyard. She said that it was originally Pierre's idea to provide air movement in the vineyard in the spring for frost protection. However, they were using it more in the summertime to move the air around the vineyard to reduce fungus and mildew problems, especially after an afternoon rain like they'd had that day.

I could see only an occasional limp and yellowing vine; row after row after row of vines were green and vigorous and well into their ripening phase. Being close to the first of August, some of

the white grapes would be harvested in only a few weeks, while some of the red varieties would hold on for possibly another month.

Back at the B&B, Pierre joined me at the corner of the long wooden bar under subdued lighting with an array of fans revolving overhead. He was in what I realized was his classic pose, leaning against something, looking downward or talking on his cell phone, while smoking a cigarette or, in this case, drinking a soft drink. I asked Pierre about the vastness of his East Texas domain.

Pierre told me that it's something not measured by thousands of acres but in the diversity of his interests and ventures. He provided a litany that started with their sixty-acre Kiepersol Estate vineyard and winery, followed with the development of nearby estate homes, an RV park, the neatly cloistered B&B with its gourmet restaurant, a Hereford and Angus cattle-breeding operation, KE Bushman's winery and meeting center, KE Cellars winery, and even a recording studio.

As I perused the restaurant's dinner menu, Pierre checked his cell phone, lit another cigarette, then said, "Do you like a good New York strip steak? If you do, try this one. It's from our own Hereford cattle and we use only the top prime plus, USDA quality grade. It's as heavily marbled as you'll find."

I settled in with the bottle of KE Cellars 4 You

Cabernet Sauvignon and the New York strip, all from within this, Pierre's East Texas domain. That evening I was a locavore getting a true taste of Texas terroir, both in the glass and on the plate.

I finally decided to ask Pierre about his Marlboro Man ringtone; but Pierre said something that I really didn't expect.

He said, "It's also the theme from the movie *The Magnificent Seven*. To me it's a classic American tale, the story of people victorious, overcoming fear and unfavorable odds. It's a story that has a deep and very personal meaning to me in our own coming-to-America story."

Then Pierre asked me if I'd heard his phone's ringtone when Marnelle calls him. Even before my response, he called her and asked her to call him back. In a moment, Pierre's phone rang alive with the voice of Neil Diamond singing "Coming to America," the song that speaks of the vast history of immigration to the United States and the opportunities realized by the hard-working hands of new Americans.

It's All Legal Now

15

hile geographically proximate to the Dallas–Fort Worth Metroplex, northern and northeastern Texas just doesn't seem to garner near the interest that the Hill Country gets as a tourist destination or what the High Plains region near Lubbock gets as a premium grape-growing region.

I was alerted to a change in this situation by author Henry Chappell, who recently wrote about the Texas wine industry: "Much of the recent growth occurs in North Texas, where producers are learning to match grapes and growing methods with challenging weather and varied soils." Additionally, just a few years ago marked the addition of the state's newly recognized American Viticultural Area (AVA); over three thousand acres of North Texas along the Red River bordering Oklahoma is now termed the Texoma AVA.

I left Houston in the morning on the interstate, traveling north facing a wall of tall, bristly green conifers of the piney woods. North of Dallas, I traded the tall trees and interstate for two-lane country roads, a bit of suburban sprawl, and, finally, rural villages. A left turn in the hamlet of Ivanhoe had me rambling along something just a tad wider than a backwoods trail. The red dirt and caliche crunched as I drove, then flared up behind me in a cataclysmic cloud of liberated dust.

At last, in front of me, at the intersection of an even smaller dusty road, I found my final vector on a well-weathered sign that read: *Homestead Winery–Ivanhoe, Texas.* Tucked between groves of trees was a nameless metal building. As I opened the door, a voice addressed me from the subdued light within.

> **"Back in these woods, I half expected to find a still and some bootleg whiskey rig rather than a winery"**

"Russ, welcome. Let's chat a bit, and then I'll give you the cook's tour." The voice rambled on, "It's sure been hot up here." As my eyes adjusted to the limited light, I saw the mustachioed and smooth-topped features of winery owner Gabe Parker.

I responded, "How long you been up here in the backwoods?" Gabe answered with a laugh, "You mean the boondocks, don't ya? We're on a dirt road off a dirt road—can't get much more backwoodsy than that."

As we walked through the winery to the tasting room, I said, "Back in these woods, I half expected to find a still and some bootleg whiskey rig rather than a winery."

Gabe said, "You betcha. This's heavy bootleggin' territory. I reckon that I'm the first North Texas Parker to make a legal alcoholic beverage. Years ago, my uncle, 'Dog' Parker, was notorious in these parts. He had a still and apparently knew how to use it."

Once in the tasting room, Gabe sat down in an old rocking chair next to the bar. I positioned myself on a folding chair in front of him with a window AC unit whirling at my backside. The room wasn't fancy, with a decor based on well-worn barn wood and looking something like a small-town country store.

Gabe said, "I've made wine for some time now. I started growing grapes in 1983 here in Ivanhoe on my family land. In '89 I started the winery, but since this area's dry, I opened tasting rooms in Denison and Grapevine, Texas. Those areas were wet for the sale of alcohol, but here, it's all legal now."

Gabe and his wife, Barbara, recently refurbished Gabe's ancestral home as a new tasting room and guesthouse just around the corner in what he jokingly referred to as "downtown" Ivanhoe. The Parker House carries its centennial plaque proudly, and Gabe agreed to put me up there for the night.

However, he gave me what he called his "standard disclaimer" just in case any "ghosts of Parkers past" decided to pay me a visit.

Gabe comes from a long line of Parkers that were Philadelphia Quakers who later moved on to Indiana. He said, "My granddad was too young to serve in the Civil War, but likely wouldn't have anyway, as they were what you'd call conscientious objectors. However, he had cousins that enlisted to fight in the conflict that resulted in the whole Parker clan being expelled from the Quaker community. After that, Granddad Parker was a carpetbagger of sorts, coming down to Texas to teach school and later moved the family to Ivanhoe. He bought a sixty-acre parcel for farming wheat and corn, and built the Parker House in 1891. Then, my dad came along in 1902."

"Farmin's in my blood. I'd always thought of row crops and cattle raisin' in hundred- to thousand-acre increments. When I started to grow grapes, planting my first five acres back in '83 damn near killed me. I didn't realize how hard it was going to be, but I made it a point to get out to California to see how it was done out there, which helped a lot."

As we talked, Gabe seemed conversant in the system that governs wineries in Texas, which includes a legal labyrinth of local and state laws and federal regulations. He threw out a three-tiered alphabet soup of state and federal regulating agencies that track taxes and distribution of alcoholic beverages.

A lot of Gabe's experience came from working on lobbying efforts to evolve the legal system in Texas that now governs wineries. The trouble is that most of the laws that regulate alcoholic beverages in Texas were written long before much thought was given to the modern Texas wine industry. For wineries, it's a matter of playing legal catch-up in the hardball game of Texas politics. As many have told me, politics in Texas is governed by one rule: if someone else stands to gain, you likely stand to lose. This is the situation that's kept a Hatfield and McCoy feudlike situation going between the wineries and the distributors of alcoholic beverages in Texas.

Gabe's involvement in Texas wine legislation started in the nineties well after the initial success with the Texas Farm Winery Act in the late 1970s. Gabe calls the period from the eighties through the late nineties the "dead zone" for both the Texas wine industry and winery legislation, with no significant accomplishments.

Gabe attributed these doldrums to two things. First, there were so many huge crash-and-burn stories, with as many wineries going out of business as there were new wineries starting up. Second, there was a lot of self-serving special-interest maneuvering by the wineries going around the Texas capitol that didn't help the industry as a whole.

Gabe and I took a short break to stand, stretch, and visit his estate vineyard that was hiding out back of the winery. The vines were laden with clusters of grapes still green, with some just starting to show the blush of ripening. Gabe said that most of his Cabernet Sauvignon wouldn't harvest until mid-September; however, the Syrah that seemed to better handle the heat might be ready in as little as a few weeks. Gabe, recalling his previous years' experience, acknowledged the ever-present threat of late freezes in Texas.

He said, "I don't start pruning until after the twentieth of March. I prune the vines that bud last, first. Then, I prune the vines that bud first, last."

His regime sounded like viticultural double-talk to me until I thought about it. Simply put, late pruning delays bud break. The nugget of wisdom in Gabe's short Texas grape sermon was to wait as long as possible to prune, especially for the early-budding varieties.

As we returned to his tasting room, Gabe said, "Ya know, Russ, for Texas to be a long-term player in the wine business, I don't think we can use California as a model: big wineries mass producin' wine for ten dollars a bottle. Here, it's going to be something more like you find in Europe where smaller local wineries are integrated into the local customs, lore, and cuisine. It's already starting to happen in East Texas at Kiepersol Estate near Tyler and at Los Pinos Ranch Vineyards around Pittsburg, Texas. Other examples are Lone Oak Winery over in Burleson, Brennan Vineyards in Comanche, and Haak Vineyards in Galveston County. These folks are all successful 'cause they're the local winery for the local people."

Gabe knows what it takes for his Homestead winery to "sell" itself. It has to market wines that go with the type of foods people eat right here in northeastern Texas. In Gabe's neighborhood, the barbecue's always pork, not beef, and it's slathered with a sweet sauce made with brown sugar and molasses. There's an emphasis on simple chicken dishes, but, as a rule, they're pretty spicy. Gabe knows what kind of wines pair well with this local cuisine. They're sweet.

Previously, people told me that Gabe was the creator of what most now refer to as simply "Texas Sweet Red." He gave me a quick nod and followed with a story.

Gabe said, "I left my day job back in 1992, and the family wanted to leave Dallas to move back here to the old Parker farm. We were looking around for a church to join up with. I was raised in a fundamentalist Church of Christ, but I knew that I wasn't going to be welcomed back there. After all, in their eyes I was makin' the 'devil's brew.' So, some of the locals suggested that we check out the local Presbyterian church."

By then, he had his winery going, and Dr. Roy Mitchell, one of the original Texas Tech professors that started making Texas wine in the seventies, was consulting with him on winemaking. They had what they thought was a darn good dry red wine, something mostly from Cabernet Sauvignon. Gabe always considered it his "good stuff."

Gabe continued, "At the Presbyterian church, they customarily have a Seder dinner at Easter time where they serve wine. One of the parishioners told me that since I had a winery, maybe I could help out and bring my wine. During the planning stages of the dinner, the matriarch of the church, Nikki Williams, got in touch with me and said, 'Oh, I hear you're going to bring the wine. That's real nice, but Gabe, one thing, please don't bring that sour stuff.' I guessed that she was referring to my dry wines."

What Gabe did next was take some of his good stuff, put it in a five-gallon jug, and sweeten it up to about 6 percent residual sugar. Gabe and Roy agreed that it was really pretty flat, so they juiced it up a bit on the acid side and got something that they thought was mighty tasty: sweet, crisp, and refreshing, especially when served cool.

Gabe said, "I went on over to the dinner toting this five-gallon jug with a flexible hose hangin' out of it. It really didn't look appealing served that way, but it worked. I also took several bottles of my dry red wine. At the end of the dinner, nearly all of the sweet red wine was gone, but most of my dry red was unopened. At the dinner, everybody was asking me when I was gonna bottle the sweet red wine so they could buy it."

From there Gabe made up a hundred cases and called it Homestead Winery, Rose of Ivanhoe. Frankly, Gabe pondered if he could sell that much. To his surprise, the first batch of Rose of Ivanhoe sold out in a month, and right now this wine accounts for about fifty percent of sales. Similarly, Texas sweet red is the lifeblood for many rural country wineries all around the state. While many wine snobs think of sweet red wine as just an introductory or transitional product, Gabe sees sweet red as something more fundamental for many local wine drinkers.

He said, "I've stopped apologizing for it. It's a hell of a lot more enjoyable with a well-slathered slab of pork ribs in the middle of a Texas summer than a glass of hot Merlot." Later in the day our discussion turned to Gabe's experience with the continuing saga of the wine laws in Texas.

According to Gabe, the pinnacle of Texas wine legislation occurred in 2003 with an amendment to the state constitution. This legislation had several facets, but in one way it was a game changer for wine in Texas. It essentially gave Texas wineries a bridge over the troubled waters of the existing patchwork of dry, wet, and damp areas for sales of alcoholic beverages set up by local option elections since the end of Prohibition.

Many parts of rural Texas are still dry today. Since grape growing and winemaking are more or less agricultural endeavors, it's a fact of life that most of the new wineries end up in dry, rural areas that prove to be a considerable barrier to the development of the Texas wine industry.

Former Speaker of the Texas House Billy Clayton was the lobbyist for the Texas wine industry during the early nineties. Gabe said, "During the nineties, they'd not gotten much of anything passed in Austin. In '99 we tried, but nothing got passed. In 2001, we got a piece of legislation passed that enhanced a few things for wineries, but there was a small glitch."

After that session, there was a meeting with then Texas agriculture commissioner Susan Combs and her staff to discuss this issue. Afterward, her chief of staff called on wine lobbyist Billy Clayton.

According to Gabe, "Susan's chief of staff told Billy that they wanted to talk to the wine-lobbying group. At the time it included Bobby Smith from La Buena Vida and Les Constable from Brushy Creek Vineyard. The gist of the meeting was one thing. We love you boys, but don't get any more damned unconstitutional laws passed! We were lucky that nobody challenged the legislation. We needed to fix it and do things right, going forward."

Gabe painted a vivid mental picture for me. He described walking back to Billy's office from the meeting. Billy was feeling the hands of time, and he walked slowly. They were all wondering what to do. When they got back to Billy's office, they continued to bat around several options. Then, Billy brightened up a bit and said that he had a constitutional amendment idea that would allow wineries to sell wines by the glass. But then Billy's eyes opened up wider as he said, "Why play around with just wine by the glass? Why not get the whole dang thing?"

Gabe said, "The long and short of it was that separate house and senate bills for the amendment to the state constitution were passed. However, things were not finalized yet. What happened then was classic Billy Clayton."

The house and senate bills that went to the conference committee in Austin were two very different bills. Work to try to get them into agreement and signed by the governor hadn't yet gotten anywhere.

Gabe said, "Billy went to Speaker Craddick of the Texas House and said that the people of rural Texas needed this legislation. I've helped you out in the past, so I want you to let me pick the legislators on the conference committee who'll settle this bill. In the Texas Senate, Billy went to Frank Madla and essentially did the same thing. Of the ten votes needed on the conference committee, Billy positioned the conference committee to have nine 'friendlies.' Then, he called a meeting."

According to Gabe, Billy, with help from the wine-lobbying group, then proceeded to rewrite the bill. It was different from either existing version of the bill. Then, Billy got his draft bill hand-carried over to the legislative liaison committee and got it approved, but apparently he didn't actually give them time to study it.

Gabe said, "The next step was to get the 'friendlies' on the conference committee to sign off on it. His instructions to the courier were, 'If anybody changes a single word, you call me. If you mess up, it'll be the last job you'll ever have in Austin.' Billy had the nine friendly votes taken first and finally the very unimportant and likely negative vote last. As was typical of Texas winery legislation, it was finally ratified on the last day of the session. Then, the voters of Texas confirmed it in the following general election. This bill was Billy's last hurrah and a good one. He later died in 2007 after a lengthy illness."

The way Gabe described things, the success in 2003 developed a new framework for Texas winery laws. It essentially created a special place for wineries, taking them out of the local-option, wet-dry jumble. It did this by allowing wineries to make and sell wine in dry areas in Texas so long as they sold wine that was at least 75 percent fermented juice from Texas grapes. It also gave the state government, not local-option elections, the power to control future decisions on Texas wineries; so it's all legal now, and constitutional, too!

Gabe said, "Since the constitutional amendment became law in this state, a quick set of changes to the winery laws in Texas was enacted. They included legislation to allocate excise tax money for vineyard and wine marketing and research [funds reallocated in 2011's legislative session to the general funds to help balance the budget], allowing shipment of Texas wines within the state, and the ability for wineries to participate in and sell wine at festivals and farmers' markets on par with other farm products. Texas wineries also got the right to make brandy and sell it to other wineries for making fortified wines."

As I stood to leave, Gabe just sat there rocking with a big smile on his face. Then he said, "Ya know somethin', Russ? Back thirty years ago, we had some of the most oppressive wine laws of any state in the Union. Today, Texas has some of the most supportive wine laws of any state. That's not bad in my book. No sir, not bad at all! And it's all legal."

> **❝ ❝ So it's all legal now, and constitutional, too! ❞ ❞**

The Munson Spirit and Legacy

16

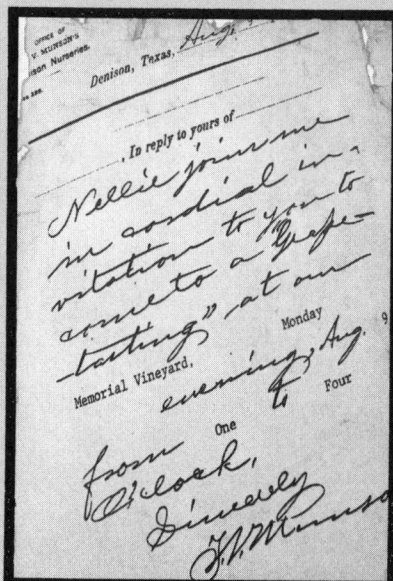

"**I**'d read and knew something about what T. V. Munson did here in Texas. He extensively traveled the state on horseback, hunting wild grape varieties and breeding them. I also knew the role he'd played in saving the French vineyards from phylloxera with Texas rootstock in the late 1800s, something other states like to take credit for."

As Ed Auler from Fall Creek Vineyards recounted the legacy of Thomas Volney "T. V." Munson, I felt a momentary rush of excitement. He mentioned that after Fall Creek became a winery, he had to load up his wines and deliver them to retailers. On one of his stops, he talked with the elderly wife of one of his retailers.

Ed said, "While I was delivering wine, Mrs. Krause told me that her father used to talk about a day when he was out riding and a guy came up mounted on an old horse and leading horses with tote sacks full of grapevine cuttings. She said that the man mentioned that he saw some vines he liked nearby. In exchange for gathering up samples, he said he'd like to leave some. Mrs. Krause said that a grapevine from those cuttings was still growing on her property and was about the size of a tree." Ed continued, "I thought, that's pretty wild. Just ten miles away as the crow flies. That guy was probably Munson; he gathered some vines, but left something in return."

Several months later, I had the chance to visit the home of T. V. Munson, who was known as the "Grape Man of Texas," in Denison, Texas. It was a meetup with Dr. Roy Renfro, who perhaps more than any other living soul had many opportunities to commune with the spirit of Munson. I asked Roy how this came to be.

He said, "It must have been in 1973 or early '74. I'd just arrived on the Grayson County College campus, and I was ready to go to work as their horticulture instructor. About a month after I'd started, a meeting was held in the president's boardroom, and I got an invitation to attend, but I didn't really know why."

The W. B. Munson Foundation (formed by the descendants of T. V. Munson's older brother W. B. Munson) wanted to honor their famous ancestor's brother and requested a meeting. At that time, T. V. Munson's story really hadn't been told. His vineyard had long been untended and eventually plowed under. It was getting to the point where many of the grape varieties hybridized and identified by Munson were going extinct. They would totally disappear unless someone did something. In the meeting, they discussed setting up a memorial vineyard and needed someone to find the Munson grape varieties and bring them back to Denison where they'd begun their existence at the hand of their originator.

Roy said, "Well, the task fell on me. I didn't realize then how deeply it would take me into the life and spirit of T. V. Munson. I've looked so deeply into his life, technical accomplishments, writings, business dealings, and beliefs that, at times, I almost feel like I've been transformed into that man."

Immediately, Roy got to work trying to find the

Munson varietals. He wrote letters to universities and organizations around the world. It was an eye-opening experience, as Roy found out that in addition to being shipped to France, Munson's vines had been dispatched to nearly all the European countries and to distant places like South Africa and Japan. As Roy's work continued, the vast scale of the agricultural disaster wreaked by phylloxera on European viticulture in the late nineteenth century became apparent. He realized that the European vineyards that remained in the post-phylloxera era were only a small fraction of those from before and that all benefited from Munson's work.

He said, "Within the first year, my team located about forty Munson grape varieties and made arrangements to get cuttings from these existing vines. The following year we collected them and built a small greenhouse where they could root. The inherent vitality of the Munson grapes surprised us. Even with little tending, they grew vigorously; they literally grew out the roof of the greenhouse. Obviously, we needed a bigger place."

The next spring and all that year, Roy looked for a vineyard site. Eventually, the retired Perrin Air Force Base, situated about a mile from Grayson's main campus, became available and was acquired by the college. Part of it was used as the site for the T. V. Munson Memorial Vineyard.

" "Hanging under the canopy of green leaves were the many hues of Munson grapes " "

Over two decades later, on a hot summer morning, I had my first look at the Munson vineyard. It lay before me on the downward, easterly facing slope from the building that's now the T. V. Munson Viticulture Enology Center. As I peered through a chain-link fence at a gangly array of trellised vines, the herbal smell of the vineyard's freshly mowed grassy border permeated the thick humid air.

I opened the gate and began meandering through the diagonal rows of vines backlit by the low morning sun. Hanging under the canopy of green leaves were the many hues of Munson grapes: lusciously ripe reds and purples, pastel pinks, vibrant yellows and gold, and the glowing lime green of still unripened grapes. The diversity of the Munson grapes is a tribute to the immensity of Munson's work, his passion for his studies, experiments, and business in what he called "his grape paradise in Texas."

I found the Munson grapes not only of varied color and hue, but also in various states of maturity. Approaching August, some of the grapes were raisinated, while some were just approaching their prime. Still others were barely through berry set, not likely to be ready for harvest until late fall or early winter. While Munson was a consummate scientist and grape breeder, he was also a practical businessman. He realized that if grapes were to be a successful business option for Texas farmers of his day, they had to be a full-season crop.

The urge to taste the grapes, a venerable taste of history and the Munson legacy, was uncontrollable. I felt like a child in a candy shop. The grapes had a multiplicity of flavors, some with characteristic grapy and foxy notes oft associated with native American grapes. Others had a full set of enjoyable red and dark fruit qualities, surprisingly close to the classic vinifera grapes of Europe, but yet different. Some of Munson's grapes were passive and mellow, while others were tart to startlingly acidic, each with its distinctive character created and nurtured by the hand of Munson over a century ago. By the time I departed, my encounter with the Munson grapes left my lips tingling and my tongue verging on numbness.

Later that day, I continued to move southward en route to Tyler, Texas, following roads that snaked among rolling hills, tall green pines, rambling farms, and languishing lakes. For about a year, I had corresponded with R. L. Winters, a master horticulturalist and owner of Fairhaven Vineyards in Hawkins, Texas. His vineyard and winery was just a short stretch of road north of Tyler, so I decided, on a lark, to visit, and I'm glad I did.

There I learned that R. L., like Roy, was focused on French-American and American hybrid grapes, and especially the grape varieties developed by Munson here in Texas. Imagine how shocked I was to find that he not only studied and grew some of the Munson varietals, but that his passion was making wine from them!

R. L. believes strongly that the Munson varietals possess qualities that make them uniquely adapted for success in Texas. They were bred from the same genetic material found in the native grapes Munson gathered from creek beds along the Red River, the white limey knolls of central Texas, and railroad easements in Denison near his home that he called Vinita. These are hardy grapes able to withstand heat and drought, many of the common grape fungi, rot, and mildews, phylloxera, and Texas's own scourge, Pierce's disease. I learned that last year R. L. had his first major success when he made a small but commercial release of wine from Munson's Lomanto grape grown in his vineyard.

Sweet Jesus, could this be? Munson often referred to himself as "the Originator" of his hybrids, and now, only hours after I'd come up with the half-brained idea of a Munson tasting, could R. L. be "the Facilitator"? I got an eerie feeling, the same feeling I had that day at Fall Creek Vineyards when Ed Auler described hearing the Munson story from Mrs. Krause. I began to think that Munson's spirit was at large, still roaming his Texas grape paradise, and that I was on his trail or perhaps . . . he was on mine.

As soon as I returned home, I phoned Roy and told him about my visit with R. L. and that I thought it might be possible to have a tasting of wines made from Munson grapes. Roy suggested that, if this were true, he would set up the tasting at Vinita, the Munson family mansion, a site that Roy worked for many years to restore to its late-nineteenth-century glory.

About two months later, I met Roy at the gate to Vinita, and we walked into the house where we awaited a small gathering for this special tasting. As I walked into the parlor and perused the living room with its period furnishings, I thought, What better venue to enjoy these wines than at Munson's home; it would be a fitting tribute. If Munson's spirit still made its way around Texas, perhaps it would grace us today with its presence.

Along with Roy and me, our tasting assemblage included R. L., Gabe Parker, Rick Mears, and Bob White. They represented several northeast Texas winery operations: respectively, Fairhaven Vineyards, Homestead Winery, Grayson Hills Winery, and Texoma Winery.

Later, R. L. opened his box of wines and laid out four bottles, but only one had a recognizable commercial label, which read "TVM Lomanto 2009." The other three, as R. L. explained, were just works in progress, not yet commercial, and sported only duct-tape labels with handwritten names: Wine King, Nitodal, and Extra. As he arranged the bottles and started popping corks, R. L. mentioned that there were other Munson wines back in his winery that bore still more unfamiliar names given them by Munson: Ben Hur, Brilliant, and Delicatessen.

Roy asked R. L. where he got the vine stock for all of his Munson varietal wines. R. L. replied, "In

some cases, I've had to search out the vine stock. I've gone to old, nearly defunct vineyards in places like 'Nowhere, Tennessee.' In one case, the whole vineyard was dead except for two vines sticking up, and, as I expected, they were the Munsons."

To prepare for this tasting, I traced the ancestry of these grape varieties through Munson's own words in his book *Foundations of American Grape Culture,* published in 1909. He documented the lineage for all the grape hybrids in his collection, each in painstaking detail, and included their characteristics and even their commercial merits; some include his recommendation for making wine.

In the case of Lomanto, it was like a potpourri of American and European grape varieties. Munson traced it back to its distant great-grandparents, Delaware and Lindey, in 1883, grandparents that were a cross between a native Champini grape and Brilliant in 1893, and ending up with a cross made by the hand of Munson between Salado and a Portuguese vinifera grape called Malaga in 1902.

As R. L. finished pouring the Lomanto, he splashed a bit of the wine on the table. He said, "You'd never guess that I just got my first-level sommelier certificate and now here I'm pouring wine like a Methodist. Can I swear y'all to secrecy?"

When I swirled the Lomanto wine in the glass, the dark purple-blue liquid gave testimony to what some might refer to as good "teeth staining" purple wine, along with red-fruit aromas but darker fruit flavors with nuances of leather and cocoa. Roy mentioned the smoky characteristics, while Gabe, Bob, and Rick were into the deep weeds commenting on the wine's hints of plum, not the fruit but the skin.

As we tasted the wines, Gabe said, "I think to understand these wines, and what Munson probably tried to accomplish, we should think about what kind of food he might've eaten back then.

"Munson's period was before refrigeration was common in north Texas. From what my kin have told me, a good piece of beef, like a slab of prime rib, might have aged for a few weeks to a month before it was cooked and served. What I really mean is that the prime rib likely got tied to a rope and hung down a well to keep it somewhat cool, but not cool enough to completely stop spoilage. So, its flavor, let's say, would've been quite powerful."

"They reminded me more of the rustic wines of Europe"

Based on Gabe's viewpoint, Munson's prime rib dinner likely needed an intensely flavorful wine, which perhaps explained the full-bodied character of the Lomanto. In fact, back in those days, some made wine that had a healthy bit of sweetness to help it marry with the savory and deep-aged flavors of the beef. Port wines were also very common, and practical, too. However, there are no records to show which style Munson preferred.

There was another interesting observation made by several at the tasting. Contrary to what we expected, there wasn't a hint of off-putting characteristics to the Lomanto. Old-timers familiar with wines derived from hardy native American *Vitus labrusca* cultivars like Concord, Niagara, and Catawba called the unpleasant qualities "foxy." These are the musty-mellow, animal-like scents that betray most wines derived from native American vine stock.

By comparison, the Munson wines were best described as unique. They reminded me more of the rustic wines of Europe, like Spanish Mencia and Nero d'Avola from Sicily, but still with a twist. They had berry descriptors that were what I described as "lesser" berries like mulberry, boysenberry, and loganberry.

R. L. made another comment, but this time from his winegrower perspective. He said, "Lomanto has good-sized grape berries and is very much like Cabernet Sauvignon on the vine. It makes beautifully shaped, actually very sexy-looking clusters, and it can also easily produce seven tons an acre." Gabe reacted with an exclamation: "Whoa! For northeast Texas that would be phenomenal, even if it was just used for blending."

R. L. continued: "These Munson grapes are absolutely bulletproof, too. They love our hot climate, even the limey soils, and show no symptoms of Pierce's disease. Even better, the wines that come from these grapes are true Texas wines; they're a living tribute to Munson and our Texas wine heritage that we can still enjoy today. They're our Texas heritage grapes!"

This statement seemed to stoke a fire inside R. L. As we neared the end of the tasting, he announced that he wanted to take us in a different direction. He asked Roy if he'd ever envisioned Munson as a thinker, an inventor, a man of religion, and perhaps as the only true Renaissance man to step foot in Texas. While making grand oratorical gestures with his hands, R. L. likened Munson to Thomas Jefferson, Henry David Thoreau, and even Leonardo da Vinci. He then asked Roy to sum up his thoughts garnered while writing his book on T. V. Munson, *The Grape Man of Texas*.

According to Roy, Munson was a man of nature, a scientist, and yet very entrepreneurial, something that speaks to the breadth of his abilities. He was a man who understood history and the value of innovation. He was also a religious man, but not really interested in what organized religions offered. In fact, he appeared to have detested them, preferring private and direct communion with his God.

Munson was especially interested in the bonds between God and man, believing that there was a God over nature and all mankind, but perhaps not one that sat on high with a long gray beard. It's something that comes from the words in the dedication poem that he wrote for his *Foundations* book

" "They're our Texas heritage grapes! " "

and in the self-eulogy that he wrote for presentation at his funeral service. Then, as if touched by the spirit of Munson, R. L. asked for Roy's copy of Munson's *Foundations* and rapidly leafed through the pages until he found a particular passage that obviously had been tugging at him for some time.

R. L. said, "In Munson's own words, above all else, there's one thing that I've noted. Munson discussed topics on grapes and horticulture in a strictly scientific and technical manner. He'd be talking about things like grape varieties, their properties, and technical specifications to be sought out in grape hybridization like here on page 129. Then all of a sudden, he'd veer off down a philosophical path and discuss the qualifications for 'The Originator.' This is the term Munson used for himself and others engaged in what Munson appears to have considered the deeply religious experience of breeding plants, something akin to God-like creation.

"Munson stated that 'The Originator' must be enthusiastic, with an ambition to 'add something to the general fund of human development,' and have 'an intense love of close communion with nature,' causing him to 'admire the infinite correlated life movements.'" R. L. stopped abruptly and said, "Are y'all following me?"

Then R. L. turned to a verbatim quotation of Munson for guidance to "Originators." R. L.'s voice started softly, but built up steadily to a crescendo, and eventually joined by the waving motion of his outstretched arms, it was though Munson himself was giving his oratory before the assembled gathering.

His instructions were "to study the loves and hates prevailing in all organic life and growth, discovering the great fundamental truth in ethics, as well as in the development of organic beings, that *love breeds life and hate breeds death.* Such a spirit of investigation leads the student of biology . . . to the contemplation of the all-binding energies and impulses belonging to and circulating through, by mutual reciprocation, influencing and controlling all objects, thus creating the best concept of the *self-governed Infinite.*"

Not a word was spoken as R. L. returned his arms to the table and took a long, deep breath. Then he said, "Wow, that's really heavy stuff, isn't it! That's something you don't expect in a grape-growing textbook. Shoot, it's even hard to believe that it's something that I just quoted at a wine tasting, either! I'm not even sure I know what it all means. All those words about love and hate and the 'self-governed Infinite' require deep thought and hours of discussion, after a glass of wine or two or three—shoot, maybe more!"

Silence returned to the room for a minute, maybe longer, or it could've been only a few seconds. I was consumed in reflection over the vastness of Munson's thoughts, the power of his words, and the presence of his spirit around me.

IV

Central Region

A Personal Place in History

d Auler and I stood in the shade of an old live oak tree on the flat western bank of Lake Buchanan. The Colorado River once ran like a wild horse through westerly canyons before the dam was built and this lake was formed. Back then at this spot, the river slowed and deposited its load of sand and minerals where Ed's Fall Creek Vineyards now resides.

Ed said, "Russ, here's the old oak tree I wanted you to see. It's called the Proctor Tree. George Ray McEachern, who helped us start our vineyard, also helped size up this tree. According to George, it's the second largest live oak left in Texas. It's over a thousand years old and played an important role in history. The last two Indian treaties in Texas were signed under this tree."

All I could say at the time as I craned my neck to take it all in was a drawn out, "It's in-cred-i-ble." The shade of the tree and the cool breeze coming off the lake provided respite from the summer heat.

From our vantage point, we scanned the four hundred acres of valley land of which Ed's vineyard occupies only a small parcel. After I photographed Ed beneath the stately tree, we drove back to the winery where we settled ourselves. Ed's wife and collaborator, Susan, interrupted us to say hello, then disappeared into the kitchen. He then started to talk about what he calls "their early days."

He said, "My great-grandfather, like many of my other relatives, was a cattle rancher. I also grew up with cattle ranching and didn't give much thought about using this land for anything else. But, in 1973, things started to change after Susan learned a little bit about wine. Back then, I knew absolutely nothing about wine and, frankly, I had little interest in it.

"Shortly after that, Susan talked about us taking a trip to Europe to learn more about wine. At the time, I was ranching a pure Aberdeen Angus herd and wanted to look at the French breeds, so I figured that we could go to France and I could look at cattle while Susan pursued her new interest in wine. Well, the long and short of it was that we spent three days on French cattle ranches and three weeks at some marvelous French châteaux, and during the tour we both fell in love with wine."

Their time in France was enlightening because Ed and Susan found similarities between the land there and the land they had back in Texas. There were some common features, with lots of limestone, sandy soils, and an arid climate.

Ed said, "And to think, the French were growing grapes and making wine over there for darn near a thousand years; that's as long as our old oak tree's been here. It really got me thinking, especially after the bottom fell out of the Texas cattle market."

Ed decided that the cattle were staying, but that he had to do something else, too. After considering peaches, pecans, apples, and even olives, Ed got in touch with the county agricultural extension agent. The agent told Ed that a fellow was putting in a winery down in Fredericksburg called the Haversack Winery. As it turned out, that venture was more talk and wishful thinking than an actual winery. Ed moved our conversation into the winery dining room, where he had three bottles of Fall Creek wine awaiting us. We sat at a large dark wooden table while Susan served lunch.

Many think of the Auler family as the "Mondavis of Texas," prime players in the state's wine development. While Ed focused on making the wine, Susan explored its relationship to the culinary scene. She's worked tirelessly to bring together the fine cuisine and wines of Texas. Susan created the Texas Hill Country Wine and Food Festival in Austin in 1986, an activity that helped establish the Texas Hill Country as a recognized American Viticultural Area, something secured by Ed in 1990, and more recently founded the Texas Fall Fest in Marble Falls.

As we sampled the Fall Creek Sauvignon Blanc, Ed likened the style to what Robert Mondavi referred to as his Fumé Blanc. It had fresh fruit flavors augmented with light oak aging to give the wine a toasty quality. Ed said, "That's the way we've done it since 1983; it's a classic style."

Back then, he started making wine with the grapes from the University of Texas experimental vineyards before the university got the Ste. Genevieve winery venture up and running. When their Chenin Blanc grapes arrived at Fall Creek, Ed admitted he really didn't know what he was going to do with them.

He said that in those early days of his wine production, he was "just darned pleased" because the Texas Chenin Blanc actually tasted like the ones from his trip to France. He tasted batches of his fermenting juice while its sugar content was decreasing and stopped the fermentation at two percent; he really liked it. He then clarified it and added a touch of oak, and it was done.

In 1983, *Wine and Spirits Buying Guide* liked this wine too and rated it the top Chenin Blanc in the United States; he hasn't changed the style since. Ed knows the value of consistency. It's helped build a consumer market for his wine that's kept it on store shelves for over twenty years. We finished our lunch, and Ed continued with the story of his startup winery.

He said, "The story of the Haversack winery

> ❝ He then clarified it and added a touch of oak, and it was done ❞

made me think that maybe we needed to do the real deal right here on our property. The county agent sent us to see George Ray McEachern at Texas A&M University for more information on viticulture. George Ray was a horticulturalist specializing in growing pecan trees in Texas, but he started to support vineyards due to the increasing interest here in growing wine grapes. We formed an instant friendship, and he eventually told us that if we wanted to put in a test plot, he would help us out. So, I thought, what the heck, let's give it a try."

From Ed's account, George Ray didn't pull any punches and warned of the many hazards of growing grapes in Texas, among which were Pierce's disease, nematodes, cotton root rot, and phylloxera, not to mention all the potential fungal and insect problems above ground. He also told the Aulers that they could use PD-resistant grapes (native American and French-American hybrid grapes), but suggested that Ed put in some of the common European varieties to see how they might perform in a future commercial vineyard.

According to George Ray's triangulation at the time, PD was mainly a problem east of Interstate 35, which runs from San Antonio to Dallas, suggesting that Ed's vineyard should be in the clear. I've heard from several parties that over the years George Ray took a lot of grief, particularly from growers like Ed who lost vineyards based on his early predictions of PD susceptibility.

In 1975, Ed and Susan planted their first quarter-acre plot of grapevines on the shore of Lake Buchanan, and since then they've had little time to look back. Ed recalled that the vines grew with vigor; they were "like an erupting volcano" of canes, leaves, and grapes, which surprised even George Ray.

In 1977, the Aulers had their first small crop, and the grape chemistry looked pretty good. By that time, Ed and Susan got the bug for making wine and not just for growing grapes. However, the university support was spread thin, with numerous vineyards and winery ventures all starting up at the same time. There wasn't a coordinated effort from Texas A&M, University of Texas, and Texas Tech like we have now to technically support the state's vineyard and winery operations.

Ed remembered looking for winemaking support and found a little home winemaking shop in Austin called DeFalco's. Ed recollected that a nice couple owned the shop, and he just asked them to help him make some wine. They took the grapes and used a basket press and helped him make his first batch of wine in five-gallon containers.

During all this, Ed started meeting people like Doc McPherson and Roy Mitchell, the former college professors who started Llano Estacado Winery, and Charles McKinney and his folks at the University of Texas experimental vineyards. With things looking mighty fine in their own experimen-

tal vineyard, Ed and Susan decided to expand the Fall Creek vineyard to seven acres.

While talking, an overpowering zeal percolated through Ed's normally soft-spoken words. It must've been a frenetic time in the Texas wine industry back then, full of unbridled optimism. I noticed that we were so engaged in his story that we hadn't tried the third wine on the table. It was Ed's Fall Creek Meritus, his top-of-the-line red wine. It's based on a Bordeaux-style blend consisting mostly of Texas Cabernet Sauvignon and Merlot usually grown by Alphonse Dotson at Certenberg Vineyards, one of Ed's primary grape growers.

Ed said, "With our Meritus, I take a different route from my other wines. I basically let the chips fall where they may. It's a deep red wine and has great body and intensity. The blend of grapes may vary from year to year. In fact, I don't even make it every year, but if I do, it's going to be something special." After only a few slow sniffs and sips of Ed's Meritus, he jogged me back to his unfolding story.

He said, "You can keep sippin' and I'll do the talkin'. Ya know, the big issue I had after starting the vineyard was that making wine at this location, in a dry precinct of an otherwise wet county, wasn't exactly legal. The law had to change."

One thing that's amazed me as I've talked with Ed Auler and others who played seminal roles in the start-up of the modern Texas wine industry in the seventies is how they started things off without actually realizing the legal "lay of the land" in terms of alcoholic beverage production and sales. It was like pushing a cart down a steep hill and jumping in without even knowing if the damn thing could be steered.

Ed finally admitted that, even for a lawyer like himself, the wine laws in Texas back then were written for an industry that didn't exist. He either had to try to get the laws changed or move his operation to a nearby wet precinct. This was the point when he met up with Dr. Bobby Smith, who had a similar issue at La Buena Vida Winery in Springtown up in north-central Texas.

Ed and Bobby helped draft a bill that they took to Billy Clayton, who, at that time, was speaker of the Texas House of Representatives. Ed half expected to get run out of Billy's office, or maybe clean out of Austin.

Well, the long and short of it was that the law was passed. It was called the Texas Farm Winery Act, and it got the laws changed to allow wine to be made in dry areas. However, wineries in dry areas had to find a location in a wet area to sell their product.

Despite this first legal step, there was still some basic confusion in the embryonic winery laws. For example, did a winery tasting room have the legal right to sell or distribute wine itself, or did the wine have to be handled through wholesalers and retailers? Neither Bobby nor Ed were selling very much wine at the time, but they could see the day coming when they would need the laws cleared up on distribution, particularly with respect to sales

from their winery tasting rooms.

Shortly after the first law passed, Gretchen Glasscock started Blue Mountain Vineyards in West Texas near Fort Davis. She was convinced that she could get the laws changed to allow unlimited winery tasting room sales, but the beverage distributors were opposed to it and didn't want *any* winery tasting room sales. It looked like they were about to have one hell of a riot on their hands over this issue.

Ed said, "There was a last-minute compromise of sorts on the last night of the legislative session that I'll never forget. Senator Bill Moore got the representatives of the beverage distributors and a few of the winery people in his office. He asked for Bobby Smith and me to be there as part of the winery delegation, probably since we'd worked on the previous bill."

Ed grew more animated and his face gained a flush as he worked up to describing the events of this meeting. "Bill Moore looked at the beverage distributors while pointing to us wine folk and said, 'These are my friends.' Then, with a similar sternness, he looked to our group, pointed his finger in the direction of the distributors, and said to us, 'These are my friends.' Bill followed with, 'I guess before y'all plan on leaving here tonight, ya need to come to a resolution on this here bill.' After a pause, he continued, 'But I suggest that y'all do it before midnight when we close up shop here, and it's already after ten o'clock.'"

Ed and Bobby were able to help get some provisions into the bill that weren't perfect, but that would make it legal for wineries to sell wine from a winery tasting room (in a wet area) with, as he recalled, a limit of twenty-five thousand gallons of wine per annum.

Ed said, "I looked at Bobby and asked, 'how much wine is that?' Bobby responded, 'If my math is right, it's about ten-thousand-plus cases.' Shoot, that's more than either of us were makin' at the time, and it seemed like an unlimited amount to me."

Well, the revised bill was written up and submitted to the legislature that evening and was approved before midnight and the end of that year's legislative session.

Taking a deep breath followed by a long sigh, Ed said, "Ya want to go up on the property? We can see the springs and the waterfall that give our winery its name."

As we drove in his truck, gaining elevation over Lake Buchanan, past the wild brush growing next to the dusty caliche road, I could see the winery at the lake's edge. Ed said, "Look at it over there. As I said, the lake was originally our best friend, with its cooling breezes in the vineyard. However, later it turned out to be our worst enemy."

I knew what he meant. I'd spoken to many vineyard owners in Texas who had issues with Pierce's disease. Riparian and lakeside environments harbor a terror to Texas winegrowers called the glassy-winged sharpshooter, *Homalodisca vitripennis.* It's a massive leafhopper insect that looks more like a cross between a Bradley M2 fighting vehicle and an F-117 stealth fighter than a creation of nature, and it can fly higher and farther than any other type of leafhopper. It carries and injects the vines with bacteria, *Xylella fastidiosa,* that cause PD. Once this happens, the vines lose the ability to move water and nutrients up from their roots. In most cases, death of the vines comes suddenly and extensively. Ed deflected my next question about the extent of his vineyard's PD problem, choosing to focus on another problem that he admitted was like running into a brick wall.

> **" "We can see the springs and the waterfall that give our winery its name " "**

He said, "The first devastating thing to happen in Fall Creek's vineyard was the freeze of 1990. It got down to minus twelve degrees here. That year, we had to buy grapes from other growers (many out of state) to make our wines, and then we had to replant everything. It was like starting from scratch."

It wasn't until 1998 that Fall Creek started to see PD damage, and it rapidly worsened. Ed decided that he wasn't going to win the battle with PD in the short run. Furthermore, his experience with the killing freeze got him working with other vineyards so that he could continue making Fall Creek's wines. This situation helped diversify his grape supply before PD hit, with grapes purchased from other vineyards in Texas or from sources outside the state. That's why today you see wines from Fall Creek Vineyards with either the American or Texas appellation on the label, depending on the source of the grapes.

Ed said, "I actually sleep better and my banker sleeps better now that we aren't just dependent on this one vineyard site at Fall Creek. It's just like having a diversified investment portfolio. The concept with Texas grapes is the same, and it hedges my bets against the big three of vineyard disasters: PD, freezes, and hail."

Ed mentioned that he's not given up on his Fall Creek estate vineyard. He's using new vineyard perimeter techniques and a new spray program developed in California to target the sharpshooters that reside in and around Fall Creek's lakeside location. He said, "If I stick at it long enough and if I live long enough, I'll find a workable solution."

At this point we topped a hill and I could feel the vibrations of the crashing waterfall nearby. We walked along a short, narrow trail to the rocky bluff overlooking it. Nowhere on the ranch was the clash of geology so apparent. Looking down I saw the valley land awash with limestone, sandstone, and granite silt brought from far upriver. High on the hill where we stood were stone outcroppings of what Ed called hard lime and friable lime (referring to limestone) lying among weathered pink crystalline granite and honeycomb quartz.

Looking out from the bluff, Ed told me stories of geology, his waterfall, and the ancient people who settled here. With fervor he recounted his start-up story and legal wrangles with the Texas wine laws. Ed, a man who clearly knows and appreciates the history of his surroundings, humbly acknowledges his own personal contributions to the genesis of the modern Texas wine industry. While trekking the Fall Creek backcountry, Ed stopped and reflected on one aspect of his narration. He said, "Haven't seen George Ray lately, but I'd like to."

"I know that you haven't always seen eye to eye," I said.

He shrugged, then continued, "I don't want people to forget the contribution that he made to the overall success of the Texas wine industry. He was there when the industry was young and had no one else to turn to. Susan and I certainly thank him for his support. Another fellow that's almost been forgotten is Ron Perry. He did his thesis at Texas A&M back in the eighties. His work was the first attempt to put some sound economics to the business of Texas wine. I hope people still read it.

"Gosh, we've all had our personal place in history. But, Russ, none of us could have done it alone."

From Mediterranean Shores

18

Long before I had the opportunity to experience the winemaking legacy of Provence, France, I spent many late evenings reading about its history, terroir, and wines. My interest was piqued because Texas growers were planting Mourvèdre, a grape synonymous with this French region's leading appellation of Bandol. Mourvèdre vines were being planted in many hot, dry Texas locales: the High Plains, the Hill Country, and even far west Texas.

I decided on this trip after a conversation with Texas Hill Country grower and consultant winemaker Don Pullum, when he said, "I'm amazed at the similarity of the terroir of Bandol to what we have right here in Texas." This I had to see for myself.

My mission was to absorb what I could of the Provence wine culture, and experience firsthand its resemblance to the Texas terroir. My first stop in France was in the diminutive yet very relevant appellation of Bandol on the Mediterranean shore between Marseilles and Toulon. I was surprised to learn that Provence has many environmental similarities to what we have right here in Texas. There are dry sandy hills with limestone outcroppings, crape myrtles, sycamores, and even prickly pear cactus, all resembling the scenery back home.

While Bandol is one of the oldest winegrowing regions in France, it was almost relegated to a historical footnote in the late nineteenth century following the great phylloxera devastation of the vineyards in France. After a long recovery, this region received its official *appellation d'origine contrôlée* (AOC) designation in the 1940s, mainly through the efforts of Lucien Peyraud and several other local *viticulteurs*. This classification came with strict requirements to base wine production on the region's historic and classic grape varietal, Mourvèdre.

I'll confess to an ulterior motive for this trip. In addition to experiencing the French wine history and culture, I wanted the French to experience the fruit of our Texas exploits. Call me crazy, but in my suitcase was a bottle of Texas wine from my friend Don. It was one of his best to date, a special cuvée

he called "L'Évier" (French for the "kitchen sink") that was a blend of too many red Mediterranean grape varietals to count (which led to the wine's name), but dominated by Mourvèdre.

I approached Bandol during an afternoon rainstorm. My first French driving lesson was on slippery highways with speeding traffic and mountain curves. In a wet blur, I saw a road sign that indicated the road to Bandol and made a hard right turn up a small winding hillside road in the direction of Hostellerie Berard in La Cadière d'Azur near Le Castellet.

Frazzled from the drive, I parked and checked into the hotel, went up to my room in the former eleventh-century convent, and threw open the shutters. There to behold was a scene worth going halfway around the world for: a breathtaking afternoon view of a rainbow arcing down from the sky into a Bandol vineyard in the valley below.

The following day I walked through the vineyards planted in yellow-orange sandy soils intermixed with white stones. The main ingredients of this winegrowing region usually cited are its aridity (on average only twenty inches of rain a year) and its sandy, limey, mineral-rich soils. I recalled Don explaining to me that these conditions are a microcosm of Texas terroir.

He said, "There's a growing bit of evidence suggesting wine grapes like Mourvèdre grown in the intense sun in Bandol, Spain, or Texas on such mineral-laden, sandy soils produce intense and highly aromatic wines. I like to make small batches of wines driven by my local terroir. My wines are red blends made with Mourvèdre and other Mediterranean varietals where the floral and spicy components are overlaid on rich red to dark fruit based on what the particular vintage gives me."

Departing Bandol, I drove north up the Rhône River and spent a day in Avignon with a stop at Châteauneuf du Pape and then drove on into the Gigondas hills farther up the road to spend the night. What I didn't tell Don was that I'd already sought an audience with one of the leading estate winemakers in this region, Yves Gras, the owner and fourth-generation winemaker at Domaine Santa Duc. I arrived to find a simple stone-faced building with a twenty-two-hectare vineyard of old vines consisting of Grenache, Syrah, and Mourvèdre located under the Dentelles de Montmirail, a high ridge of limestone outcroppings.

I found Gras and his friends from Germany inside the winery with a few opened bottles of Santa Duc's recent cuvées. They graciously invited me to join them. We talked a bit, tasted some wine, and then I presented him with the bottle of Don's L'Évier. The name drew immediate laughter. After tasting a selection of recent vintages from Domaine Santa Duc, Gras opened the L'Évier and began swirling, sniffing, sipping, and smiling, but did not say a word. He poured some for his guests.

The men seated around the table began their own swirling, sniffing, and sipping. Then, one of them caught the eye of Gras, and smiles broke out from the group. After further discussion I realized that they were astonished that a wine with such flavor and aroma came from Texas vines that were only on their fourth year, merely *enfants* on the French viticultural scale.

> **"The men seated around the table began their own swirling, sniffing, and sipping"**

When I returned to Houston, I called Don to let him know what I did with the bottle of L'Évier that he'd given me some time back. Don responded, "Oh, my God! If I'd known that you'd taste my L'Évier in the company of Domaine Santa Duc wines, much less personally with Yves Gras, I probably wouldn't have given that bottle of wine to you! Many of Domaine Santa Duc's wines are rated in the 90s by the *Wine Spectator*."

Nonetheless, Don appeared very pleased with the outcome, and I felt like I'd proven something, too. Texas wines *could* be poured and enjoyed at the same European table with those from a first-rate French wine producer and fare admirably.

Now, six years later, I had an opportunity to repeat my French/Texas wine tasting in Houston with Gabriel Mata, the son-in-law of a French colleague of mine, Jean-Paul Giraud, who recently retired to his cottage in Bandol (and in the shadow of Le Castellet). Gabriel said that he and his business partner were importing the rich red wines from Bandol, and he was asked by his father-in-law to arrange a tasting of his wines for me.

After a prelude of several whites, rosés, and a Côtes de Provence, Gabriel poured the grand wines of the evening: 2004 Domaine Sorin, still a youthful prodigy, and 1996 and 1998 Domaine La Suffrène, both strong and mature. They all sported the Bandol AOC appellation, ensuring that they were Mourvèdre-laden, with a supporting cast of other red Rhône varietals.

As we tasted, Mata commented on the capability of Mourvèdre-dominated wines to age gracefully. He went on to say, "These wines take their lead from the women of Bandol," which he followed with a loving glance to his wife across the room.

Mata was right. The wines of Bandol with their "patron" Mourvèdre grape did show a vast potential for aging, and these 1996 and 1998 vintages were showing nicely. Both were still fresh, crisp, and dominated by rich fruit flavor, though they were starting to show deeper and more genteel nuances of age.

After a light bite, I opened a bottle of wine that

I'd brought and asked my hosts to accept it as a present from a different locale, but made from grapes with kindred DNA and terroir to the Bandol wines. It was another Don Pullum wine: 2006 Sandstone Cellars III, a red blend from Mason County, Texas, having much the same varietal composition of the wines of Bandol.

Mata said its color, fruit intensity, and aroma were comparable to those found in the youthful Domaine Sorin. We both wished for a way to time-travel forward a decade or two to experience these wines again; but alas, we'll just have to do it the old-fashioned way—cellar the wine and wait.

Gabriel gave me an additional bottle of his Bandol wine to taste at my leisure. I later decided to share his wine with Don and his Sandstone Cellars collaborators, Manny Silerio and Scott Haupert. In honor of this occasion, "Chef" Don Pullum planned an intimate gourmet dinner experience to accompany a side-by-side tasting of Mason County and Bandol wines.

My wife and I headed west on Route 290 from Fredericksburg where the limestone roadcuts at the eroded edge of the Edwards Plateau disappeared. The countryside morphed into outcroppings of even more ancient, burnt-orange sandstone with a magnificent view of the Llano Basin. The convergence of water and wind on rock in Mason County appeared before us, a visible slice of geological time that produced Don's very particular Mason County Texas terroir.

When we arrived at Sandstone Cellars, we found Chef Don and his sous-chefs Manny and

Scott in good spirits from their afternoon of culinary endeavors (and wine). The dinner venue was a house adjoining the winery that once belonged to Lucia Holmes in the late 1880s. As we relaxed in anticipation of the evening's dinner delights, we perused Lucia's memoirs in which she described Mason County's colorful history and the setting for the so-called Hoodoo Wars. These skirmishes were replete with cattle rustling, shootings, hangings, outlaws, Confederates, Unionists, marauding bands of local Indians, and sharpshooting Texas Rangers, all trying to kill one another for various reasons. History has it that the whole episode finally came to an end only when there weren't enough enemies left standing to sustain the fighting any longer.

As we talked about the historical setting, we sat down for the first dinner course, featuring two of Don's creations: a spicy mulligatawny soup and Sandstone Cellars' first wine, a 2004 Syrah. The spicy richness of the soup paired one-for-one with the wine's natural fruit richness and the hint of pepper spice on the finish. Near the end of this course, Don raised his glass to the gustatory pleasure of his guests and gave a toast: "Now this is what mulligatawny's all about!"

Next out of the kitchen was broiled quail with a selection of raspberry and cilantro sauces, served with Sandstone Cellars II, a red blend of eight different Mediterranean grapes all from Mason County. I immediately commented on the style of wine, reminiscent of his memorable L'Évier from years before. Don responded with a big smile showing his pleasure at the tribute and indicated

that, in fact, his goal had been to recapture the spirit of his L'Évier.

Don said, "I really shouldn't have given you that bottle of my L'Évier, but it must have been a wonderful day at Domaine Santa Duc. I would've loved to be a bug on the wall while you tasted it."

The final course was Don's three-hour, red-wine braised lamb shank, a hearty blend of ingredients, including ginger, banana, and soy sauce. It was accompanied by collard greens with smoky bacon for a Texas Hill Country meets low country fusion. We toasted Don's global palate, but Don downplayed his culinary concoction as nothing more than a world-beat version of the renowned Luby's restaurant Lu Ann platter.

The use of the word "fusion" to describe both the food preparation and the Sandstone Cellars method of winemaking seemed appropriate. Here the winemaking approach is similar to what many high-profile chefs are doing—a fusion of flavor elements that cut across different cultures and cuisines. The wines of Sandstone Cellars are a fusion of flavors from three, four, five, or more grape varietals grown in Texas that have a lineage going back to countries all around the Mediterranean. Don said, "In Texas, we find spicy and savory on the same plate; for example, Southwestern and Asian cuisines. Our friend Chef Terry Thompson-Anderson (author of *Texas on the Plate*) always talks about how European, African, Hispanic, Asian, and Native American cultures and cuisines have integrated here in Texas: from gumbo to chili and stir-fry to deep-fried. The savory and spicy qualities of my wines work exceptionally well in this type of setting."

Paired with the lamb dish were several Sandstone Cellars red blends (III, V, and a VI barrel sample). We also used the occasion to revisit the 1998 Domaine La Suffrène Bandol wine gifted from Gabriel Mata at my Houston tasting.

The 1998 Domaine La Suffrène Bandol, the true grand dame of the event, showed elements that make Mourvèdre-based wines so attractive to lovers of bottle-aged wines. This wine still had considerable clout encased in its dark purple-black color and rich fruit flavor. The unusual aspect of this wine was that its intensity was tempered with a refined elegance. (If present, Gabriel no doubt would have made another comparison between the wines of Bandol and its women.) Before leaving, I asked Don a question that had been tugging on me since I first took his wine to Europe. How had he settled on the sandy soils of Mason County for his vineyard?

"Brother Fabian, a Carmelite hermit who founded the Mount Carmel Hermitage in Christoval, Texas, called it my spiritual journey," Don told me. "In December 1997, I stumbled upon the hermitage while searching for a vineyard site in Texas. I learned that the hermitage was the result of Brother Fabian's own spiritual journey."

Pausing to savor a sip of wine, Don eased back in his chair and continued swirling the wine in his glass. "While in Rome, Brother Fabian was groomed for a position at the Vatican, but discovered that prayer, silence, solitude, contemplation, penance, and labor were more important to his devotion than climbing the religious hierarchy. Realizing this, he traveled far and wide and finally staked a tent on rugged land in Schleicher County. It was probably a site more suited for scorpions than salvation, but, after erecting his tent, he began to pray. He eventually built a small chapel there, and, in time, other Carmelite monks joined him in his retreat."

❝ ❝ My vineyard site in Mason County simply appeared on my path ❞ ❞

Don's gaze dropped low and he continued: "I sat in Brother Fabian's cold chapel on a December morning with monks chanting in hypnotic Gregorian monotone. I listened to Father Fabian tell me his story. It was a story that offered me solace. I'd only a vague understanding of why I was relinquishing the challenge and rewards of the corporate world for a more bucolic livelihood working in a vineyard. As I said good-bye to Brother Fabian, he told me that he'd have the brothers pray for me."

"Well, almost immediately after that unexpected visit," Don said, his eyes sparkling with tears, "my vineyard site in Mason County simply appeared on my path. Two months later, I was plotting the vineyard layout and scratching about in the Hickory Sands of Mason County."

19

Passports to the Wine Experience

Hobbling with his cane, Franklin Houser entered the barrel room of his Dry Comal Creek winery with me in tow. The door squeaked shut behind us, blocking out the hot, humid clime of the Texas summer. We were talking about the year's massive crop of Black Spanish grapes that he expected from his winery's estate vineyard and from other vineyard sites around the state that supply his grapes.

In fact, Franklin and his former Washington State winemaker, Joe Donnow, already had some grapes harvested, crushed, and soaking in cold, sweaty, stainless-steel tanks in front of me. Franklin yelled out, "Give 'im a taste of that cold soak you got going, Donnow." Then, in a much softer voice intended for my ears only, Franklin said, "I just like sayin' that. It almost makes me feel like I'm on *Hawaii Five-O*."

As Donnow extended a glass, I saw that this was going to be a mouthful of thick, dark, raw grapiness. It wasn't yet refined or elegant, but held great potential for this banner Texas harvest year of 2010, what some have called the "Vintage of the Century for Texas."

Franklin said, "I went to a TWGGA meeting once. I told them, 'Let's face it. Texas is going to have a hard time producing enough of the European grape varieties—you know, Cab, Merlot and Chard—to handle all of our needs. We have to unlock the potential of the Black Spanish grape. Shoot, it can be grown nearly everywhere in the state and with a lot less effort and money.' Well, you'd thought that I'd killed the Pope, or something. But later on, the president of TWGGA stopped by the winery for a visit, and privately he mentioned that he remembered what I said and acknowledged that I was very likely right."

Many people still don't know about the Texas grape phenomenon known as Black Spanish or by the various other names the grape's been given throughout history in the United States, and in parts of France and Spain: Le Noir, Lenoir, Jacques, or Jacquez, to mention a few.

By the mid-1800s, as phylloxera devastated the French vineyards, the vines (known in France as Jacques) were sent from Texas to France since they were highly disease resistant. This created a great demand for Black Spanish grapes stateside to the point where few were available for use in the states or shipment to France. Back then, and still to this day, many don't realize that the Lenoir and the Black Spanish vines cultivated in Texas are the same as Jacques in France and Jacquez in Spain and Portugal.

Franklin mentioned that he was having some visitors in for a tasting at the winery that day: the McNews, Tom and Anne Marie. I admitted that I didn't know much about them, but I'd heard they were the couple that, to date, had visited more Texas wineries than just about any other living souls. Tom, an army major, was soon to deploy to Iraq.

Franklin said, "Tom and his wife, Anne Marie, have hit more than a hundred wineries across the state, which is nearly half of the total number of

Texas wineries that are presently licensed."

I decided to stick around for the day. Their visit might allow me to find out more about them and the insights they've acquired from their own Texas wine experience. In the meantime, Franklin and I talked further about his estate vineyard now made up exclusively of Black Spanish grapes. It wasn't exactly what Franklin originally planned for.

He said, "Way back when I started planning this vineyard, I was told by experts like George Ray McEachern that because I was west of Interstate 35 and north of San Antonio, I should be able to grow the European varieties of grapes. Well, as it turned out, these so-called experts didn't know what they were talking about. I planted Cabernet, Chardonnay, and the like, and they all up and died. While the experts were still trying to figure out what happened, I pulled out the first vineyard and replanted again with the same types of grapes." By this time, the verdict on the cause of death of his first vineyard was back. The jury of Texas grapevine experts declared that the problem was, in fact, Pierce's disease.

In those days, the understanding was that PD occurred only east of Interstate 35 and south of San Antonio, but since those days the PD line has progressed westward and northward across the state. The vineyards testing positive for PD now take in most of the state. Some sites, like the Blue Mountain Vineyard in the dry desert region near Fort Davis, unexpectedly succumbed to PD. Other locations, such as the vineyards on the High Plains region near Lubbock and some in East Texas, while showing positive for PD infection, mysteriously remain healthy and produce wonderful wines. However, the front line in the battle with PD back then was in the Texas Hill Country vineyards like Franklin's. There were skirmishes and personal one-on-one battles with PD being fought all across the state, not unlike the Indian fights over a century ago, but with the outcome still very much in question.

So, after losing his second vineyard battle with PD, Franklin decided to replant exclusively with PD-resistant Black Spanish grapes. The only question was: Could it be made into a palatable modern-style red table wine? Up to that point, Black Spanish grapes were mostly relegated to producing sweet dessert and port-style wines. That was Franklin's dilemma.

Shortly after we moved our discussion to the tasting room, Tom and his party came through the door. Tom, sporting a Hawaiian shirt, cargo shorts, and a stylish fedora, said, "Sorry about being so late, guys. We got a late start out of Fort Hood. I had some soldierin' stuff that held up our departure."

I could see that Major Tom and Anne Marie, along with Tom's brother Tim, were well focused on their mission: to take in and enjoy as many Texas wineries as they could before Tom's deployment. They apparently had their mission plans and necessary logistical and family support for a successful outcome.

Franklin responded in a manner typical of his sardonic self: "Are y'all here for some wine tasting or what? Let's get the show started."

As Franklin and his daughter Sabrina got the tasting lined up, Tom gave me a short background that sounded more like a briefing. He and Anne Marie lived on the base at Fort Hood. Anne Marie was from Chicago, while Tom and his brother grew up in West Texas and the Panhandle area.

> **"Are y'all here for some wine tasting or what? Let's get the show started"**

Then Tim added, "Just for the record, Tom knows that I'm a beer man. So, to get me here, he told me that we were going to stop at a new Shiner brewery." I guess being a military man, Tom knows the finer points of how to get people to do things, even if it's not something they've done before, or had in mind to do in the first place. I asked Tom and Anne Marie if they were wine people from way back or if their foray into Texas wines and winery was something new.

Anne Marie said that before she married Tom, she and her sister would go to wine tastings in Chicago, some that they found a bit daunting, with over 150 wines tasted in one evening. The two of them also did a little wine touring and tasting in Napa Valley. In her early drinking days, Anne Marie admitted that she was more of a Captain Morgan drinker than a wine drinker. Later she started to favor white wines. By the time she made it to Sonoma, California, she admitted, she had evolved into mostly a red-wine drinker, but didn't consider herself a wine expert in any manner of speaking.

Following Anne Marie, Tom said, "Before we were married, I was at Fort Leavenworth, Kansas, while she was in Chicago. We met on eHarmony.com, and once we linked up online, we talked by phone for months. In fact, we talked nearly every night and had lots of long phone calls. Finally, we decided to meet on neutral ground at the Anheuser-Busch brewery in St. Louis."

Franklin was ready to roll through the tasting of seventeen Dry Comal Creek wines. However, just as we were about to start, a lady entered the tasting room and introduced herself as Elizabeth Hadley from the Texas Department of Agriculture (TDA).

It was no mystery why Elizabeth happened to stop in for this tasting. Part of her responsibility with TDA was the Texas winery "passport program." It's what helped get Tom and Anne Marie started on their somewhat grandiose mission to visit all of the wineries in Texas.

Only a big bodacious state like Texas that started life as a Spanish frontier territory and morphed into its own independent republic would have the audacity to print up its own passport—especially one for people to use when they visit the growing list of Texas wineries . . . and receive rewards for doing it. Based on Tom's current recon, by the end of today's visit they would have reached a milestone somewhere around 106 to 108 Texas wineries.

When Tom and Anne Marie received their first passport, they really didn't know what it was. They just took it around to the wineries they visited, got it stamped, and Tom sent in the results to TDA. When they started to get rewards, he said to Anne Marie, "Hey, this is cool." Later, when the rewards started to get even better, like big wine glasses and stuff, they both agreed that it was *way* cool. That's when they really got into the passport program and looked forward to what the next reward level might bring.

Sabrina started the festivities with pours of a white wine. Franklin's unpredictable commentary indicated that it was made from French Colombard. After that we moved through tastings of Dry Comal Creek's wines, some with quirky names that just seemed to fit Franklin's own jovial and curmudgeonish style.

The wines included a white blend with a grape that Franklin thought might be Muscat and the juice from another grape that was of even less certain lineage, so he named the wine Mongrel Bastardo. The bottle sported the words, "Great Mongrel Bastards in History," complete with a list of those that made Franklin's top-ten list.

Then, Sabrina came in with a round of a blended red wine that Franklin announced was called

Footpress. Once he made sure we had tasted it, he revealed that he had given the wine its name for one reason only. That's exactly how the juice for the wine was made—trodden by the gentle yet gamely feet of the winery's female visitors. It's become so popular that pressing day is now an annual festival at Dry Comal Creek.

Tom talked about wines and his Texas wine experiences with a carefree ease. Even though he confessed to being a wine novice, he had no trouble piping up with his own wine descriptions and favorite food pairings. As Franklin poured, Tom tasted. Interestingly, he described his wine experiences in terms not found in any wine books that I've read, but in terms familiar to him.

Tom said, "We walked through Neal Newsom's vineyard up in Plains, Texas, where I was struck by the differences in the grapevines and the way the grape clusters grew. Merlot grapes grew in small, tight clusters, something that Neal and I agreed looked like a hand grenade of grapes. I seem to recall that those were Neal's words, but maybe they were mine."

Anne Marie also sounded like she was a bit further along than a mere wine novice when she said, "I was surprised by how different types of grapes tasted. I particularly fell in love with the pungent flavor and aroma of Orange Muscat grapes as I picked them off the vine. That was incredible. I would never have guessed that would be the way grapes could taste."

As we sipped Franklin's White Black Spanish

wine, a blend of Black Spanish and the juice from white grapes to make a semisweet rosé, I asked Tom what wines he and Anne Marie liked. His response was that they now tended toward dry red wines. Tom mentioned that they have more red blends in their cellar than anything, raising two fingers from each hand to put air quotes around the word "cellar." He declared a preference for blended red wines rather than straight varietals like Cabernet, as they were a bit more interesting.

Tom was actually turning into what he might have previously called a "wine geek." What he was saying about blended red wines being "a bit more interesting" might be captured in winespeak as "complexity." As I learned early in my own wine-tasting career, if you plunge right in like Tom, where excitement leads vocabulary will eventually follow.

Both Tom and Anne Marie also admitted that they now focus on seeking out new white wines because they realized that there are times when red wine just isn't right. Anne Marie said that they are buying Viognier, which she finds a bigger white wine, perhaps intended for people that are normally red-wine drinkers. She's also developed a fondness for another special Texas grape: Blanc Du Bois, either dry or only slightly sweet.

Franklin was anxious to pour the wine for which he is best known around the state of Texas: his Dry Comal Creek red table wine made with Black Spanish. Franklin and Sabrina had this part of the tasting well choreographed. Right on cue, as we sampled the wine in our glass, Sabrina plopped down a bottle of Franklin's 2002 Black Spanish wine weighted down with the various gold and silver medals it had won in a host of wine competitions.

Franklin said, "We made the Black Spanish into a reserve wine, submitted it to some leading wine competitions, and lo and behold, it won lots of damn medals. People love it, and they find that it's completely different from what they've experienced with other red wines like Cabernet and Merlot."

I said, "You know, Franklin, this wine *is* really different from Cabernet or Merlot. It's got this deep red-garnet color and initial aromas of black cherry that's common enough, but what makes it unique is the distinct taste of mulberry, something not observed in European wines."

We completed the tasting with Franklin's offerings of port and his special rancio-style (oxidized) red wine, which had the distinction of being barrel-aged for 1,096 days outside in the Texas weather: a wine style common in Banyuls on the French Mediterranean coast.

I was still trying to dig deeper into Tom's and Anne Marie's personal wine experiences. As I continued to ask them questions between sips of wine, it was becoming apparent that Tom got great pleasure from their explorations into Texas wine country. He indicated that it's been a way to share a portion of his Texas "Republic" with his new bride.

Following this tasting, I've stayed in contact with Anne Marie and Tom to try to gain better insight into how everyday people interpret the Texas wine experience. From their base of operations near Killeen in central Texas, Tom and Anne Marie found so many wineries close by that they started taking short weekend trips to visit them. They've found it fun and really not very expensive to travel by car in the countryside, with an occasional overnight lodging.

One recurring aspect of their wine experience that Anne Marie mentioned is how much she likes and appreciates the firsthand information they've gleaned from winemakers, growers, and other hands-on people that are usually present at wineries and vineyards. She's found that this makes the Texas wine experience so much more up close and personal than her visits to the large commercial wineries in California.

I asked her what Texas wineries were on their personal top-ten list. She had no trouble focusing in on her top six, which included Red Caboose, Brennan Vineyards, Perissos Vineyards, Texas Legato, Bar Z, and Solaro Estates. From there, her list of favorites shot around the state like a ricocheting bullet in hard-rock country. McPherson Cellars, Messina Hof, Sandstone Cellars, and Wales Manor

rounded out her top ten. When I asked about things that they did not particularly like, Anne Marie forwarded a message from Tom, who at that point had already made it to Kuwait and was awaiting his final deployment in Iraq.

Tom said, "There are still some Texas wineries that haven't learned what it takes to do it right. In contrast, the wineries on Anne Marie's list were the wineries where we felt the most welcome and engaged in a learning experience about wines. We didn't like some of the wineries in the 'tourist' trap locations that seemed much more interested in selling us wine than making us fans of their wines and for the industry as a whole."

Texas wineries need to come to attention and listen up. Anne Marie plans to continue her Texas winery trek in Tom's absence. When Tom returns stateside, they'll be back to a fighting-strength brigade, ready to make the final thousand-mile assault covering wineries on opposite ends of the state, from El Paso to Beaumont. Wineries across the state had better be ready for them and the many new Texas wine aficionados that will follow in their footsteps. They are already learning what they like and are critically evaluating their own Texas wine experience.

> "Texas wineries need to come to attention and listen up"

Not My Granddaddy's Cowboy Country

20

Anxiety ran high as I drove north from Fredericksburg, Texas, with my near-term mission set: hunt and eat rattlesnakes and pair them with a rattlesnake-friendly wine. I was headed to Sweetwater, Texas, home of the world's largest rattlesnake roundup.

Why a roundup? Well, rattlesnakes are venomous critters, and they're packed with a healthy dose of attitude and a particular fondness for the Texas outback. Over fifty years ago, this situation encouraged the area's ranchers to join forces with their local Jaycees to get rid of as many as they could while raising some money for charity at the same time. Now, I wanted to add a new wrinkle: enjoying these rattlin' reprobates along with a fine Texas wine.

I started out north of Fredericksburg on the limestone caprock (a harder or more resistant rock overlying a less resistant rock type) of the Edwards Plateau. Looking ahead, I saw the plateau disappear, revealing still older red sand beds of the

Pennsylvanian epoch farther to the north. In these parts, the road is like a time machine that yields an account of geological history of more than three hundred million years.

For the past tens of thousands of years, a mere snapshot of the state's history, this area was home and hunting grounds to the Native American tribes of north-central Texas. In the eighteenth and nineteenth centuries, these peoples fought back hard against the Spanish conquest, Mexican settlement, and then the onslaught of Anglo American settlers. History shows that as the native fights became less hopeful, they became more brutal.

My path took me past the ruins of the old Mission Santa Cruz de San Sabá near Menard, Texas, established in the mid-eighteenth century. With the building of this mission and its adjoining presidio, it seems as if the good padres could've stayed longer and perhaps tried to plant a vineyard in the limey soils near Menard to produce their sacramental wine.

The goal of this mission was to extend the Spanish reach north into central Texas through religious conversion of the area's Lipan Apache. One day in March 1758, the Apaches inexplicably vanished from the mission. Accounts state that shortly thereafter, over two thousand mounted Comanche armed with bows and lances overran the mission and killed nearly all of its Spanish inhabitants, save a padre and two of his parishioners to tell their horrific story.

To exact revenge, the Spanish government in San Antonio dispatched one of the largest contingents of soldiers ever assembled in Texas, only to be decimated by the established force of Comanche warriors. The Spanish left the remnants of the San Sabá Mission, never again to regain a penetration into north-central Texas. Now, all that remains are the vestiges of the mission's presidio resting peacefully in the county park.

In the early 1990s, over two hundred years after the demise of the nearby mission, Menard was the location of another, but different type of Texas incursion. This time it came from California and involved the establishment of a large, two-hundred-acre Texas vineyard. Dale Hampton, a man with Texas roots and considered by many the father of California's Central Coast wine-growing region, started the vineyard as an investment.

Hampton selected Texas based on his winemaking experience gleaned from thousands of California vineyard acres and recommendations from his vineyard manager. His new venture in Menard was the first large Texas vineyard established with out-of-state, private investment money. While large investments are deemed critical for the long-term success of the state's wine industry, this vineyard failed dismally; some called Hampton's venture snakebit from the start. Many Texas winegrowers say that the failure of the Menard vineyard was caused mainly by one thing: an attitude of "what works in California will work in Texas," local input be damned.

Charles McKinney, longtime Texas viticultural

consultant, said, "The negatives with Hampton's Menard vineyard were almost too numerous to mention. River water was originally going to be used for irrigation, but as anyone who experiences Texas summers in this area knows, surface water becomes a mighty scarce commodity come around August.

"An overhead sprinkler system was selected for irrigation, but it increased local humidity around the vines and that brought a raft of fungal diseases. Additionally, this irrigation system couldn't be used for delivery of nutrients needed to fight chlorosis of the vines in the limey Menard County soils. Limestone-laden soils are just something that Californian growers generally don't know too much about."

The Menard vineyard was also cursed by a mistake that's probably the most common one made in Texas . . . location. The vineyard was placed near where the vineyard manager wanted his daughter to go to school. To make things worse, the vineyard was situated in a low spot that acted as a sink for cold air from the surrounding hills, making it susceptible to freeze damage.

In its short history of less than a decade, the vineyard contributed some award-winning wines. However, after seven years, as one person described it to me, "It was simply nothing but a bunch of sticks in the ground," and eventually was abandoned. Today, people can see more of Mission San Sabá than the Menard Valley Vineyard.

While this unfortunate vineyard saga likely caused other large vineyard investors to reconsider funding similar ventures in this state, the lessons learned from the Menard Valley Vineyard brought about a seminal moment for winegrowing in Texas. It proved to all that Texas was not a carbon copy of another wine region and couldn't be handled the same way with the anticipation of success. Texas winegrowers had to start anew to craft their own path forward to long-term sustainability and profitability using different tactics, different grapes, and different procedures.

Dale Hampton realizes it now, too. On a phone call from California, he said, "I just wasn't close enough to monitor and react quickly enough to the situation in my Texas vineyard. If I had to do it again, based on this experience and those of other growers that are now established in the area, things would be done completely different, with a much better chance of success."

A spring storm was brewing and brought a ten-degree drop in temperature, along with a gusting wind that made banks of tall wind turbines come to life with the low-frequency "whoosh" of their blades. An ominous dusty red glow arose from the western horizon, with a blackening sky overhead giving the countryside an eerie, otherworldly appearance. The scenery was made even more surreal by the harsh tight brush of horny mesquite and prickly pear cactus that covered nearly every square inch of ground. I thought this must surely be the bizarre, foreign world where rattlesnakes rule supreme. What had I gotten myself into this time?

The following morning just after ten o'clock, I donned my snake chaps, tested my snake hooks and tongs (I selected the longest ones possible), and caravanned with other hunters to a nearby ranch. However, the reception from the snakes was a bit cool. We were told that the cold, wet winter in Texas was keeping them deep in their burrows, with hardly a forked tongue, fang, or rattle being extended to scare off this year's hunters. I found this situation particularly interesting, as my winegrowing friends in these parts were singing songs of joy as the prolonged cold, wet El Niño winter made things look good for their grapevines.

> ❝ ❝ My mind played with the thought of 'man bites snake' ❞ ❞

After about three hours of prodding into just about every crack, fissure, or hole in the red rock and clay, our group came back with seven snakes. I hefted a four-foot squirming hunk of muscle and venom on my tongs that left me satisfied with this experience of the "hunt." While I headed back to the rattlesnake coliseum for my personal wine and food pairing, my mind played with the thought of "man bites snake."

At the coliseum, I unloaded my stash of Texas wines and my long-stemmed glassware. Then, I bought a plate of "chicken fried" (breaded and deep fried) rattlesnake. I proceeded to chew, savor, swirl, sniff, and taste as the arena announcer gave his play-by-play. He said, "I gotta admit, this is the first time in the fifty-two-year history of our rattlesnake roundup that we've had a wine taster here. And, he's tasting *Texas* wines and matching them up with some of our rattlin' rascals!"

The tasting went well and seemed to follow a simple wine-pairing rule: match white and light foods with white wine. The rattlesnake meat was light, white, sweet, and tasty, which along with the simple deep-fried preparation paired well with my dry white wine: Viognier from the Duchman Family Winery. Viognier is a signature white wine in Texas in spite of its challenging spelling and pronunciation. Locals try it, generally enjoy it, and quickly pick up on the pronunciation: "Vee-on-yay."

After departing Sweetwater, I headed east from the old red sand beds back into the younger gray-limey blocks of Cretaceous stone. These materials were pulverized long ago into fine alluvial soils by the raw power of the Brazos River. These processes occurred over an unfathomable time and now offer fine frontier winegrowing terroir on the broad Brazos River valley.

By the mid-nineteenth century, this region

was the epicenter of the war between new Anglo American settlers and its native populations. They battled for ownership of the land, a combat of survival. As I drove on, I recalled stories of the hard life on the north-central plains of Texas back then, a landscape still harsh today.

My next destination was the city of Comanche, named for the proud and fierce people that brought trepidation and death to settlers here. In the 1850s, bands of marauding natives were common, seeking to gather horses by whatever means possible and, in warrior tradition, add scalps to their collection.

Back then it would have been hard to picture this region as a future wine country on any scale, even though, at the same time, there was a boom in California for growing grapes. According to an 1859 census, California was producing half a million gallons of wine by then, but Californians never had to contend with the ferocity of the Comanche nation like the Baggett family did here in Texas in 1850.

The fate of John Baggett's family typified many unfortunate frontier experiences in the 1800s. The story goes that John's wife, Bettie, tried to gather her seven children into their small split-log house as a party of Comanche natives rounded up the family horses in the pasture. Fear turned to horror when she spied the bloody red-haired scalp of her foreman on the belt of a raiding party member. Too far away to return quickly, two of her children

were captured by natives and summarily lanced with arrows in every conceivable way while their mother could only stand witness. Son Joel was scalped while still alive, and daughter Betty was left to run bleeding until she fell dead. With Bettie and the remaining children secure in the house, the natives, fearing discovery, remounted and rode off with their cache of horses and scalps.

As I arrived on the square in Comanche, Texas, I spotted a preserved historic log house from the period of the Baggett family's tragic experience. Viewing the house up close, I could sense the extreme sadness of the horrific events of the past. It's no wonder this region of Texas had to wait until civility would rule and still longer through the secession of states, National Prohibition, and for the advent of modern viticultural technology before a wine culture could develop.

I later sat in the Brennan Vineyards tasting room in Comanche converted by Dr. Pat and Trellise Brennan from the old McCreary family house that was built in 1879, only a generation after the Baggett family but in a decidedly more settled time. It was hard to put aside my thoughts of this region's events in frontier times and concentrate on discerning the nuances of the wines. I realized that I was having a metaphysical moment: a confluence of personal experiences consisting of a sense of place, a place in time, and my taste of wine.

A lady walked into the tasting room and was

welcomed by Trellise with a friendly refrain, "Would you like to taste some wine?" The response was immediate: "Actually, I'm a beer drinker but want to buy a bottle of wine for a friend hosting a party. Do you have a Chardonnay?"

Trellise paused and then explained that Brennan Vineyards, like a growing number of Texas wineries, didn't make Chardonnay because it's a difficult grape to grow in Texas. However, Trellise offered, "How about our Viognier—it's our signature wine." The look from the lady on the other side of the tasting room bar was one of puzzlement. She said, "What, no Chardonnay? Is this a winery or what?"

Sensing an impasse, I pitched in with a comment of my own and said that, "Viognier is to Texas what Chardonnay is to California. When you taste the wine, it'll be dry like a Chardonnay, but with the taste of a crisp white peach." After a taste, she accepted the wine with a smile and a nod of her head. Then she asked, "What do you have that's like a Merlot?"

By this time, I'd moved on to the red wines: the Brennan Vineyards Cabernet Sauvignon, Syrah, and their Austin Street Red, made from a blend of red grapes. Before Trellise could say that they didn't have a Merlot either, and sensing a tasting room kill shot in the offing, I suggested to the guest that she try the three Brennan Vineyards red wines and decide which she liked best.

So, which did she like best? Her preference was the Syrah, the softest of the three reds and most like Merlot to her taste buds. This Texas beer drinker ended up taking home not one bottle of wine as intended, but three. This is precisely how I find the Texas wine experience is gaining converts: one Texas beer drinker at a time. Not bad, not bad at all.

Before she left, I asked her what she was doing in Comanche besides tasting wine. She said, "I was looking at bulls, Brangus to be specific."

Well, I'm no expert on bull (a point that some may argue), but this sounded like a wine marketing opportunity for Comanche's only winery that no Texan should pass up. Imagine getting a hefty discount on a case of red wine with the purchase of a bull. I left my bit of marketing genius for the Brennans to assess. After all, there *is* a common wine rule that says "red wine goes well with beef."

I returned that evening to Brennan Vineyards for their monthly music event. It was a night of country and western honky-tonkin' in the winery's Austin House event building. In lieu of the traditional Texas beer and barbecue, the Brennans offered a selection of red and white wines and a grand selection of gourmet foods, not exactly a repast I'd expect to find in my granddaddy's cowboy country.

Now we can all talk a little bull, enjoy some boot scootin' to fiery country and western music, while enjoying a glass or two of "Texas Chardonnay."

Mañana Has Finally Arrived

21

It was one of those sunny, dew-laden Houston mornings when the doorbell rang at nine thirty. Walking over to the door, I caught a glimpse of a broad-shouldered man of substantial proportions peering back at me through the door's leaded glass. He was sporting a mile-wide smile just visible under an impressively large cowboy hat. In the short span of a few seconds, my mind flashed back in time to a previous close encounter with this image.

It was in a small conference room at Wildseed Farms in central Texas, a magnificent emporium of wildflower seeds, flowers, and associated bric-a-brac, located on a stretch of highway now called the Fredericksburg 290 Wine Road. My mental cinema played an image of this same man with the big hat and his noteworthy ear-to-ear grin. I remembered thinking that perhaps the diminutive dimensions of the room were playing tricks on me, magnifying the size of both the man and his hat.

In his characteristically slow and deliberate

manner, he navigated the narrow space around the people seated at the table and made his way to the only open seat down from where I sat. As he passed me, he leaned over and planted a kiss on my check, after which he continued on and took his seat.

As the silence in the room reached a deafening pitch, I managed to blurt into the awkward abyss something like, "What's that for, Alphonse?"

In a slow, low, and nearly lyrical voice, Alphonse Dotson responded, "I just wanted you to know, that I love ya, man."

With a second ring of the doorbell, I snapped back to Alphonse's questioning gaze staring at me through the door. I opened the door, and he entered with his wife, Martha, looking much the smaller following in his wake.

Alphonse isn't a young man—I guess probably five or six years my senior—but impressive. In his prime, his stats were impressive, too: six foot four and 240 pounds, All-American defensive tackle, Grambling University, 1964, first from a small college to make an All-American football team. Now, only tinges of silver in his dark black hair hint at his age; it's something that he proudly refers to as his "Oakland Raider hair."

We sat leisurely in the living room and chatted about friends, family, and common acquaintances as I poured their new wine proffered from a tall slender black and silver bottle that they had brought with them. It was the first wine under their new Wines of Dotson-Cervantes label, with the fascinating name of Gotas de Oro. Alphonse

acknowledged that the name was a "Martha contribution" that translates from her native Spanish to "Drops of Gold."

The silky yellow liquid had a pure tropical expression: sweet, ripe pineapple, and overtones of apricots and nectarines. The perfumed wafts of jasmine and musk from the glass helped me identify the wine's central Muscat grape.

Unless you're interested in Texas wines or good with football history, you might not know who Alphonse and Martha are. However, as a couple they are helping to redefine rural Texas as wine country.

My acquaintance with Alphonse goes back only a decade, to my early days as a member of the Texas Wine and Grape Growers Association where he served as president. I've seen Alphonse command a room of dissenting winemakers and growers with the mastery he once had over opposing linemen and quarterbacks; however, he used only slow, softly spoken words. In contrast, Martha, his petite counterpart and at times his alter ego, is normally a bit more excitable. That morning, they both radiated their anticipation of the possibilities of their new wine release, and Martha's excitement was palpable.

She said, "This wine was the result of a full year's work. It took a lot of personal involvement; actually, more than I know Alphonse expected."

Alphonse and Martha talked for years about starting a winery and making their own wines. However, Alphonse confessed that they kept saying "mañana, mañana, mañana" for far too long. They finally decided to go forward with the project, albeit in a different way than others had before them.

Their decision was prompted by the harsh slap of Mother Nature's hand—a series of late spring freezes, episodes of damaging hail, and ill-timed rain that affected Alphonse and many Texas winegrowers in recent years. That's what made it necessary for them to seek a creative solution to the problem that many in the Texas wine industry refer to as "château cash flow."

Acknowledging the problems caused by the past season's weather, Martha and Alphonse mentioned that they were still nursing their vineyard back to health. Several years ago, they reached a high of over a hundred tons of grapes harvested from their twenty-plus acres, but last year they reached both a harvest and emotional low with a crop of less than ten tons. With a smile, Alphonse said, "Our vineyard's made good progress this year, with a grape harvest in the vicinity of thirty tons. With that, the future looks bright."

Their first wine was a blend of grapes, some from their Hill Country vineyard. However, because of the shortage of Texas grapes from the previous year's harvest, they had to mix some non-Texas grapes into the blend. As a result, the first release of Gotas de Oro didn't bear the Texas appellation. It carries an American appellation that acknowledges that some of the fruit came from outside the state. Alphonse said, "While we couldn't reach our goal of Texas appellation in our inaugural vintage, our vision is to use as many Texas grapes in the mix as each season will allow."

I asked Alphonse what got him to consider growing grapes. After all, how does one go from being an All-American defensive tackle and having a professional football career with the Oakland Raiders to something that's basically farming . . . grape farming. This is only one of many questions one might ask about this man, whom I've come to know as more complex than any wine that I've ever experienced.

> **" " Their decision was prompted by the harsh slap of Mother Nature's hand " "**

Alphonse said, "Look here: as for grapes, definitely the thought was planted in my mind by my grandfather Alphonse Certenberg back when I was ten years old. He took me home with him to Houston and helped raise me. He had two acres of land with a big carport on it where he kept his fishing boats; I can still see it, nearly fifty foot wide. There was an arbor of grapevines that covered the carport, and one of my jobs was tending those vines. I'd remember that grapevine arbor several times a month for years. Years became decades before I realized that it had a grip on me. It was nearly forty years before I told anybody about that grape arbor and that I wanted to try to grow grapes."

With this thought of growing grapes still rooted

in the back of his mind, Alphonse retired from professional football and settled in Acapulco, Mexico. That was where he developed a hankering for a Mexican girl, Martha Cervantes, and they married.

While living in Acapulco, Alphonse admitted that he studied maps of Texas and pondered his future. His perusing turned serious when he ordered a soil survey book for McCulloch County, Texas. When it arrived, Alphonse marked several spots that interested him as potential vineyard sites.

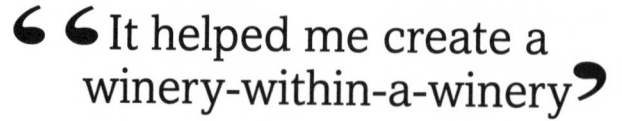

It helped me create a winery-within-a-winery

He said, "I finally got the courage to call a real estate agent and told him that I wanted between sixty to a hundred acres of McCulloch land. The agent called me back later and said he'd found three pieces of land and faxed me the information. I was amazed that the parcels he found were all on my hit list. I honestly believe that the 'Divine Individual' from above who's been watchin' over me for some time now had his hand in my search."

The story of finding the vineyard was interesting, but the story of just how Alphonse capitalized his foray into Texas Hill Country farming is another. The story involves Alphonse's son, Santana, who also played professional football, was NFL Rookie of the Year in 1992 with the Tampa Bay Buccaneers, and later played in two Super Bowls with the Green Bay Packers. When Santana became a free agent, Alphonse made the gutsy move of representing his son in contract negotiations.

When the deal was struck, he had the grubstake necessary to fund a Hill Country vineyard.

Alphonse and Martha purchased over eighty acres and scratched out their twenty-two-acre vineyard, naming it after Alphonse's grandfather, who inspired and influenced him so long ago. This property is situated on the northwest rim of the Texas Hill Country near Voca, a town of only fifty people.

After saying mañana for almost ten more years, Alphonse and Martha realized they were ready to go but still lacked the capital necessary to start a new grassroots winery in Texas. However, armed with a recent augmentation to the Texas wine laws and their newly developed "Wines of Dotson-Cervantes" moniker, Alphonse and Martha went down the road to longtime friend and business collaborator Ed Auler at Fall Creek Vineyards. Alphonse and Martha knew Ed and Susan Auler well, becoming like family from collaborating closely over the years. Ed is a big fan of their Certenberg Vineyard grapes, having used them in his Fall Creek Chardonnay and in his ultra-premium Bordeaux-style red blend, Fall Creek's Meritus.

Alphonse said, "The new thing about our winery is that it's the first in Texas to utilize recent changes in wine laws allowing 'alternating proprietorship.' It's something really new here, where winemakers can legally share common facilities. It helped me create a winery-within-a-winery;

within Ed's Fall Creek winery each of us operates separately under the same roof."

We were up to our third pour of Gotas de Oro as Alphonse continued the Dotson-Cervantes start-up story in his characteristic unhurried, methodical manner. He related that since Wines of Dotson-Cervantes was a first-of-its-kind operation in Texas, many of the regulators were unsure exactly what type of documentation was needed to comply with the new law. Alphonse described talks with state and federal regulators as being like learning how to speak a foreign language. This made the process slow and somewhat daunting, but Alphonse and Martha prevailed—though it took longer than either had planned.

"When I thought that we had everything finished," Alphonse said, "they started asking me lots of personal questions as to how I was going to fund our little winery venture. I started to get a little bothered by it, but figured that we were so close that I needed to calm down a bit."

As it turned out, Alphonse and Martha used some of the proceeds from the sale of their Las Playas villa that looked out over the Acapulco seashore. It must have been quite a decision to give that up; however, the vision of their own winery was something that they both felt deeply about.

Just when I thought the story was coming to an end, and the wine pouring would continue, Martha interjected, "When the papers were signed, Alphonse and I were happy and we thought the hard work was done. After all, we'd experience working with Ed at Fall Creek, and we had confidence that our wine would be first-rate."

I noticed a veneer of seriousness come over Alphonse's face as he related still another chapter of their story. The pair wanted their wine in a distinctive bottle and settled on a tall, slender, dark, near-black bottle. It was something suitable to contain their premium wine, which would carry a black and silver label with the same dignity that Alphonse had when he wore those colors as an Oakland Raider.

He said, "When the bottling line started, Martha and I couldn't believe what was happening. Before our eyes, the bottling equipment started knocking the bottles over and our wine started spilling all over the floor! Before the line could be stopped, we'd lost a lot of wine."

Apparently, the necks on the bottles were a bit out of kilter. To get the wine bottled, Martha and Alphonse, along with most of Ed's winery staff, had to steady every one of the thousands of bottles as they went through the bottling line. Then, the capsule and labels had to be applied by hand, too. While it's not exactly how they anticipated the final steps would be, if some wine writer at a later date decides to refer to their Gotas de Oro as a "fine hand-crafted and balanced wine," he'd be spot on the mark.

Before their departure, I asked Alphonse if he wanted to be remembered as an Oakland Raider or a Texas winemaker. He surprised me by revealing a completely different side of his personality:

his endeavors in oil painting and poetry, and his experience teaching special-needs children. I later found out that Alphonse graduated cum laude in fine arts and that he was asked by Texas Governor Rick Perry to serve on his Executive Committee of the Texas Commission on the Arts.

Alphonse said, "There are things that I've had the good fortune to do that were far more rewarding than football and even wine. On top of the list, there was the time I spent in New Orleans working with a difficult class of special-needs kids. They'd run off four teachers and the school year wasn't half over when they gave me a call to help out. The kids and I worked together. It was a sharing; they taught me and I educated them. We both came away from that experience as better, smarter people."

When I seemed surprised by the breadth of his experiences and skills, Alphonse paraphrased a favorite Chinese poet, Li Po. He said, "Listen, to understand me, you must go through what I go through as I go through it. If you don't, you only know of me. God spared me. He could have taken me away several times during my long life. I've more to do and more that I want to offer others before I leave this earth."

Alphonse laid out the vision for Wines of Dotson-Cervantes. He and Martha want to build a bricks-and-mortar winery in the style of Mexican wooden beams with tattered stucco. Alphonse described a veranda and rocking chairs, where customers sit and savor their wines, sipping them from mason jars. Alphonse said, "I can see in the future an older Alphonse Dotson tending the needs of winery-goers while finding time to savor some wine and, for sure, returning to my painting."

With a laugh he said, "When the visitors come by and take a winery tour, they're gonna see me in the barrel room messin' with wine while I'm hobbling around all the tanks and vats. I know that they'll take one look at me and pray that my sorry old ass isn't gonna end up in one of the tanks while they're visiting."

Of Wine and Memories

22

I'm always amazed how old wines bring back memories: some expected, while others just hang out in dusty mental folds, places that I seldom visit. Fine old Rieslings do it to me. Whenever I find one, it brings back memories of chance encounters, hilltop castles, fine dining, and exceptional wines shared with friends and associates in Germany over two decades ago.

In the fresh clear air of a Texas Hill Country afternoon there was just enough chill to remind me that it was winter. The sun was starting its yellow slant across the still green grass adjoining Becker Vineyards. As I arrived, Dr. Richard Becker was just finishing a tour and tasting with a group from his San Antonio–based medical practice. I tagged along until the tour was finished.

Remembering my first visit, I was amazed how cavernous the Becker winery had become. There were new rooms in old buildings and altogether new buildings already stacked to the ceiling with oak barrels of aging wine.

As the tour ended, Richard asked me to follow him. We shuffled through the winery to a small room made even smaller by racks of wine bottles on every wall, a table and chairs occupying the center, and his sizable presence commanding the space between them.

As he perused his library of aging wines, Richard left me with a glass of a new Becker wine, a medal winner, but one that I didn't expect. It was made from Barbera, commonly grown in the Piemonte region of northern Italy, but not yet widely planted in Texas. Richard explained that these grapes came from Mason County, Texas, just up the road a piece to the northwest of Fredericksburg. The surprising aspect to me was that Richard was always Francocentric, choosing to focus on French-style wines in his Texas Hill Country winery.

Richard and Bunny started the winery in 1994, and since then Richard's paid careful attention to the tried, true, and widely recognized grapes of Bordeaux and Burgundy and doing everything he can to emulate French winemaking style. As his interests moved farther south in France, he started making his wines from Malbec and a host of Rhône-style grapes, such as Syrah, Grenache, Mourvèdre, Viognier, and now Roussanne—all grown in Texas Hill Country and High Plains vineyards.

I declared that I was pleased with his Barbera and impressed with its full-bodied character, something that would possibly show a new direction in Texas winemaking. Richard, sometimes a man of few words, particularly when commenting on his own accomplishments, acknowledged my comment with a bob of his head and simple thanks. Then, as he walked back to the racks of wine, he slipped in an additional softly spoken comment: "I'm pleased, too."

We bantered a bit, then agreed that Italian grape varieties like Barbera and grapes originating from the south of France could help but take some of the load off Texas growers, since these sun-loving types of grapes just seem to want to grow here. On the other hand, Richard had proved that locally grown Chardonnay can be made into an award-winning wine. But he admits that all things have to go just right. Chardonnay is just one damn hard grape to grow here, and it's not likely to be the backbone of the Texas wine experience.

As I savored my wine, Richard continued to navigate the tiny room. He pulled bottles in a seemingly indiscriminate manner, but what later became apparent was that he had an eye for varietals and vintages that had personal meaning. I held my breath as he pulled out wine bottles from racks that came away from the wall, twisted and shook, looking like they were ready to topple around me. As I perused the racks, I heard the pop of a cork, followed by the characteristic glugging sound behind me accompanying Richard's commentary.

He said, "This is our 1998 Ballinger Cabernet. It might not be good, but let's try it. Just then, his wife and partner in life and wine, Bunny, peeked into the room and asked if we needed more glasses, but Richard was so focused on his wine-finding task that he didn't actually respond to her question. His eyes were transfixed on the racks of wine as he asked her to come in and join us.

As I swirled, Richard said, "This is a single-vineyard Cabernet from what were then twenty-three- or twenty-four-year-old vines from a vineyard in Ballinger, Texas." Although over a decade old, this wine was deep with purple extraction that some much younger wines would covet. It was made from 100 percent Texas Cabernet Sauvignon. The striking characteristic that both Richard and I proclaimed in near unison was its fine bouquet: mature notes of cedar, earth, and smoke laid over berry jam, followed by the sensual awareness of the thick, rich fluid. When I asked about the vineyard, Richard was swirling. He gazed at the wine as though it was speaking to him.

He said, "A doctor up in Ballinger, Texas, planted it." After a long, pensive look into the wine, he continued: "He got himself crosswise with local authorities. Well, actually he didn't pay his taxes for a while."

Surely, the contents of the old bottle of wine and the freshness of its taste drew out from his mental crevasse a host of memories of the vineyard's complex past in a way no other beverage could.

Richard added, "Bunny, this is good stuff. It's better than I recall. Ya know, now it's quite reminiscent of an old French Cheval Blanc that we've tasted."

We recalled our tasting experiences of old Texas reds: a 2001 Becker Reserve Cabernet Sauvignon from his recollection and, from mine, a 1998 Blue Mountain Cabernet Sauvignon from the hand of another Texas winemaker, Patrick Johnson. Richard and I reminisced that the vintages around the recent "turn of the century" were actually pretty darn good years for red wines: rich, well-extracted, and long-lived.

> " This wine was deep with purple extraction that some much younger wines would covet "

Before I knew it, we were going further back in time as Richard started to pull the cork on a bottle of his 1996 Merlot, a wine made from grapes grown on his winery's estate vineyard in Stonewall. In mid-pull, the cork came apart, but the remnant looked like it was still sealing. Richard reinserted the corkscrew with a slow, careful motion and deftly used a steady, unhurried action to coax out the remaining cork. I complimented him on his skill as a sommelier, to which he responded, "More likely my doctoring skills."

Holding the glass of the Becker 1996 Merlot

side by side with the 1998 Cabernet Sauvignon, the Cabernet was just a tad denser, but both had the purple color of far more youthful wines. Richard broke the sad news that many of the original grapevines in his estate vineyard had succumbed to Pierce's disease, an ever-present danger in the Hill Country, and the vineyard had had to be replanted. In fact, they'd lost nearly all of the white grapevines, but many of the red grapes continue to thrive in his vineyard.

He said, "For some reason, we don't know why, the only white grape that's lasted in our estate vineyard over the long haul without need for replanting is Sauvignon Blanc. Nobody's been able to tell me why."

While I was still savoring the mature elements of the Cabernet and Merlot, it was evident that Richard was now in rapid-fire mode. He opened and poured a 1996 Becker Cabernet Franc as the rack of wine bottles on the wall was again on the brink of toppling. This wine, like the Merlot, was made with his estate vineyard grapes only a year after the opening of the winery. It gave an interesting herbal note and, again, a cedarlike aromatic. This wine, in contrast to the previous two, had the look of maturity, with its purple hues having turned to garnet, but the wine was still luscious and intense.

With the three reds in front of me, my thoughts went to an old friend, Chesley Sanders, who from his days as proprietor of Lone Star Wines near the Fort Worth Stock Yards, had tasted more Texas

wine than, as he described it, "anyone else in the whole dang galaxy." He thought that the cedar quality that he and many wine drinkers found in Texas wines, especially after they'd seen a little bottle aging, was a special aspect that he referred to as "Texas terroir." Might this quality be the result of the close proximity to the Hill Country cedarlike Ashe juniper trees, just as eucalyptus is identified in many Napa Valley Cabernets where these tall trees border their vineyards?

Richard's focus on French wines includes trying to make a worthy Chardonnay from Texas-grown grapes. His long arm reached across the table for a bottle of his Becker 1999 Estate Chardonnay. At the time, I thought Richard to be a brave man. That's a Chardonnay from Texas, and it's over ten years old. Before opening the bottle, Richard sat back for a moment looking at the bottle, lost in meditation.

He opined, "There's definitely a lot of blood, sweat, and tears in this wine. It's like fingernails on the blackboard to me now when I think about what it took to make this wine. It's not been effortless." Richard left the bottle unopened and set it aside.

We recalled a previous conversation we'd had prior to a luncheon event at Becker Vineyards during a Hill Country Wine and Food Festival. Before his medical career, Richard had been an English major in college. He described the personal and emotional experiences that came from reading the works of Texas author John Graves. Graves realized that "sense of place," something akin to the French viticulteur's term "terroir," is a strong element in Texas.

The sense of place that Graves embraces goes beyond mere place and the natural elements composing it. It's the conjunction of land, nature, and man alongside man's history, culture, and influence that gives a comprehensible meaning to terroir. As Graves highlights, terroir can be associated with great wines, but it can equally apply to bucolic purposes such as raising cattle, sheep, or goats, or something as mundane as Graves's own version of "jungle juice" made from grapes grown on his patch in Texas hardscrabble country.

Richard said, "I realized from our travels that our Texas geology has more in common with what we've seen in France than it does with that in California. When French winemakers came to our winery, they took the vineyard dirt in hand, smelled it, and smiled, impressed with its minerally character. I recall that they were also quite surprised with this Cabernet Franc. I've always thought that if we are going to make comparisons of Texas wines to other regions, it should be with the Old World, and especially with France. These are the wines I drink and the wines I remember." Obviously, a worthy Cheval Blanc had made a lasting impression on Richard. His comments lingered a spell, then he said, "and that's the type of wine I've always strived for in Texas."

Captured by the aura of the unopened bottle of 1999 Becker Chardonnay, I could see that Bunny was thinking too, perusing the nooks and crannies of reminiscence. She asked, "Richard, weren't the grapes in the 1999 Chardonnay from the old Luck Vineyard?" Richard thought for a moment, then said, "I seem to remember that it was our Cabernet that we made from the Luck Vineyard that year." Bunny responded, "Anyway, I recall taking the 1999 Chardonnay to taste with sommelier Virginia Philip, many years ago. She liked it and she ended up buying our Chardonnay for Ruth's Chris Steak House."

Flashing back to John Graves, Richard said, "After the Korean War, Graves went to graduate school at Columbia and then came back to Texas. He longed for his boyhood land along the Brazos River. He wanted to reconnect with it and define its essence in prose before the Corps of Engineers dammed up the river in the name of flood control. To me, Graves's *Goodbye to a River* is the quintessential thesis on what makes Texas so special. He narrates his experiences, both physical and mental, as he traveled down the Brazos with incantations of his boyhood campsites and nearly forgotten Indian forays along Comanche raiding routes from even farther back in time."

Richard, well connected with literature from his college days, said, "I met Graves when I was a graduate student. He was on a panel at the Texas Institute of Letters in San Antonio when I was twenty-five-or-six years old, and I corresponded with him. Later, when I was a medical student, I took a canoe trip on the Brazos to follow John's path, as best I could. I took John's book in the canoe and witnessed the places and tried to gain a sense of what he described."

For several generations, Richard's family hailed from central Texas, around Brady. Like Richard, Graves also had family ties to rural Texas. Richard was inspired by Graves's body of work describing the transition from the Texas of pioneer times on the frontiers of civil society through to what are now more settled times. Richard thought that while things have changed immensely here in Texas, Texans still have the drive to take on new frontiers.

> ❝❝In my blood, I knew I wanted to go back and make something from the land❞ ❞

He said, "In my blood, I knew I wanted to go back and make something from the land, and I wanted it to be sustainable. After we bought this land, we got a better feel for making it productive, but it was even harder than Bunny or I expected. This is where I felt another bond; it was with John Graves's challenges farming on his own piece of Texas hardscrabble. We cleared the land . . . Bunny drove the tractor. In my mind, we were going to produce something real here, and it was going to be something excellent."

It was a pleasure listening to Richard talk. Thinking a while, I could only comment that the native sons and daughters of Texas are not averse to doing things that take a bit of risk, no matter what other people think. In response, Richard said,

"Other doctors have said that we took real risks here. In hindsight, the risks were perhaps bigger than we realized. When we were starting up this place, I guess that I just didn't see them."

During the winery start-up, Richard augmented his knowledge by reading, talking to consultants, and traveling. From his experience in medicine, the biochemistry of winemaking came easy. He found that tasting and memory were important winemaking attributes and compared them to something like perfect pitch, or memory in his field of medicine."

Richard said that he also had an interest in geology, another useful pursuit for growing grapes. His vision of the Texas Hill Country soil that makes up his winery's estate vineyard was something like a large swirl cake. He described it as one-hundred-million-year-old beach sand mixed with the erosion of still-older Precambrian granite. Richard heard about what the area's old peach growers called the Hensel sand, which held their best orchards, and he decided on a vineyard site that had a predominance of this soil type.

Richard seemed to get refocused on his white wines and particularly his Chardonnay. He decided that we'd work our way back, starting with the 2002 vintage. As Richard poured, he gasped. The wine came out dark amber, a sign of oxidation.

This wasn't a good start for our retrospective view into Texas Chardonnay.

Regaining the rapid-fire approach used in our red-wine tasting, Richard moved up a vintage and poured a 2003 Becker Reserve Chardonnay. It was fruit from Alphonse and Martha Dotson's Certenberg vineyard near Voca, Texas. This wine looked better than the last one, with rich, golden hues. As we sloshed it in our glasses, the viscous fluid clung and dripped with golden tears around the glass. What I found particularly interesting was its pleasant vanilla-driven and tropical fruit aromas combined with a component that I'd not expected in a Texas Chardonnay: crispness. Richard noted his reactions in punctuated comments: "Tropical! It's a dandy!"

Then, in short order, came a glass of the Becker 2000 Chardonnay. It showed even better than the previous Chardonnays, despite its elderly ten years of bottle age. As I examined the bottle, I noticed the words "For Sale in Texas Only" on the back label, indicating there weren't enough Texas grapes in this wine to garner Texas appellation. I didn't say a word to Richard. I just held up the bottle so that he could see the back label. He said, "Oh! That means that it's likely California fruit. We must've run short of Chardonnay from Texas that year. No wonder this wine is so good."

After what could have been a showstopper, Bunny and then Richard looked over at the bottle of the Becker 1999 Estate Chardonnay. By the estate designation on the label, it was clear that this Chardonnay was, beyond a doubt, Texas born and bred and ready to be Texas savored. The bottle was waiting patiently on the table throughout the tasting. It was as if Richard and Bunny were each trying to encourage the other to open the wine, now eleven years after its vintage date.

Finally, ending what seemed to be an extended silence, Richard recalled a situation that they'd experienced at the 1997 Texas Hill Country Wine and Food Festival.

He said, "Bunny and I were set up in a corner booth to pour our wines. That was the year that Robert Mondavi was the invited wine luminary. As I recall, even though we were the new kids, Robert came right over and held out his glass, awaiting a pour of our Viognier. He swirled and sniffed for a moment and said a single word that I remember to this day: "Brilliant." Then, he sniffed and swirled some more and questioned me for what seemed like a half hour. He thought that our Viognier was actually from somewhere else, and was not a Texas wine. Mondavi said to me, 'If you've made this wine, then just keep it up.'"

Richard recollected that later in the festival Mondavi showed up at the fine and rare wine auction, but sat there all night, not making a move for most of the evening. The Beckers had a double magnum of their Viognier in the auction that didn't come up for bid until eleven o'clock. Mondavi got it.

With me hanging on to that thought, Richard finally opened his 1999 Estate Chardonnay and poured it for Bunny and me. In the glass, it had the lush look of a fine old Chardonnay, with a rich amber-gold hue. When I tasted the wine, I realized that the showstopper had finally arrived.

A succession of brilliant, aged qualities ran across my palate. First were roasted-nut characteristics, followed by the zing of intense minerally notes. I immediately put down my glass and picked up the bottle and looked again to confirm the wine's vintage and its Texas appellation. Richard was right. Good and even great Chardonnay can be made in Texas when all elements come together in just the right way, and this was it! When I looked over to Richard and Bunny, they were immersed in pleasure and accomplishment, having created something great that stood the test of time.

Richard smiled, looked back at me, and said, "Ya know, I'm proud of this wine. It received gold medals at the *Dallas Morning News* and Long Beach California wine competitions. That was many years ago, but it's still all here."

We lingered on the 1999 Becker Estate Chardonnay as the afternoon grew late, with the sun taking its early winter departure. Richard and Bunny were savoring their wine, a reward for their years of hard labor on the Texas wine frontier.

After another taste, Richard said to Bunny, "It's lasted."

Part V

Southeastern Region

The Impresario of Wine

23

It was a cold, frosty-breath January morning, something that we don't see too often down here in southeastern Texas. As I drove northwest from Houston, I thought about the events that were going to unfold at the Messina Hof Winery and Resort in Bryan, Texas. Something unexpected and a bit grandiose. Texas winemaker and Messina Hof owner Paul Bonarrigo was putting his wines on the line against some of the best-selling wines in the marketplace in a blind tasting with a group of wine-savvy professionals as judges.

To take this tasting to an even higher level of play, Paul was doing the unthinkable. He wanted the tasting to be completely unfettered, with the judges launching their live comments out over the social network Twitter. I remembered the call I received from Paul that spawned this unlikely event. It happened a couple months earlier when I was hiking high in the mountains of Utah, and it went something like this . . .

Paul said, "Russ, I want to do a tasting of Messina Hof's wines. Will you help me?"

I said, "That sounds fine to me. What can I do?"

He said, "I want to do it as a Twitter tasting, like the Texas Twitter thing you did previously in Dallas. You line up the judges, people from the wine trade and media that you think are competent at rating wines and that will Twitter or blog about it."

Before I could ask anything further, Paul continued, "My idea is, instead of just doing Texas wines versus other Texas wines, I want the judges to compare my wines against some of the best-selling wines that we can find from around the world. What do you think?"

I stopped on the trail, took the cell phone from my ear, and said to myself, "Paul, do you really want me to tell you what I think? I think it's crazy!" Then, in a flash, I recalled an advertisement I once saw for an electronics store in New Jersey with the headline: *Owner Has Brain Damage!* Did Paul really want my honest opinion?

Then I considered who I was talking to; after all, this was Paul Bonarrigo, the acknowledged impresario and august showman of the Texas wine industry. Some here in Texas may think that he's a bit capricious at times or some blithe spirit, given his flamboyant wardrobe and his flair for eccentricity. Au contraire. Paul with his lovely wife, Merrill, make a splendid pairing at their Messina Hof Winery, combining his lust for winemaking and gusto for showmanship with her savvy acumen for business and marketing. I knew right off that he was serious.

My only trepidation with Paul's idea was that

I'd seen comments regarding wine on Twitter that ranged the gamut. Some were lavishly praising, others amusingly witty, but still others included some of the most gutturally rude statements imaginable.

After what was surely a very long pause, I responded, "Paul, you can count me in."

Paul and Merrill started their winery in the early seventies with little more than a single-wide house trailer on a bare plot of Brazos County land and Paul's experiences with Italian family winemaking. With that and a whole lot of personal energy, they've created one of the top-selling Texas wine brands. Paul's role in all this was first and foremost to figure out how to make good wine in Texas. He also identified starring roles for his wines, challenging the best in the industry, even if they came from renowned places in the wine world like California or France or had well-regarded names like Mondavi or Rothschild. Why would I suspect that Paul's entry into the world of Twitter would be any different?

Later, during lunch at the winery's Vintage House Restaurant, Paul told me the story of how he and Merrill started. He said, "Around 1970, while still serving on active duty in the navy, I traveled through the state, and I was impressed with the Texas hospitality that was extended to me as a serviceman. Texas was a different kind of place compared to New York, New Jersey, or, frankly, anywhere I had been before. When I later had a chance to locate my physical therapy practice, a colleague recommended Texas, and, based on my previous experience here, I ended up in Bryan, Texas."

Paul and Merrill's paired vision for starting a winery came about slowly and, after some encouragement, led to the planting of a small vineyard in 1977. The event that really got this project going occurred through Paul's physical therapy practice. One of Paul's patients was Ron Perry, a graduate student working at nearby Texas A&M University. Ron told Paul that he was doing a study on the viability of growing grapes and making wine in Texas. He asked Paul if he would consider putting in an experimental vineyard. This piqued Paul's interest, particularly since his Italian family in the Bronx had a tradition of making wine, albeit mostly small quantities in the basement of the family's house.

Paul recalled: "The first vineyard that we planted had no fruit the first year, but it started to get some in the second year. We made a small amount of wine in 1978, and in 1979 we made more wine. By 1981, we decided to enter the wine from our vineyard in a competition at the Texas state fair. We won an award and were ecstatic, but I knew that at this point we needed to make a decision. Were we going to jump into the wine business in Texas?"

I arrived a bit early to Messina Hof the afternoon before the Twitter tasting to view the venue before the other judges arrived for dinner. Then, I bundled up and walked Messina Hof's thirty-acre estate vineyard. The vines were hunkered down in their naked, dormant state, holding tight onto the trellis wires, awaiting the spring thaw.

The plan for the tasting was for the judges, including me, to be presented with a series of twelve flights of wine, each containing two unmarked glasses of wine for blind tasting and evaluation. Each judge was to evaluate the wines based on a twenty-point scale and then try to discern if the wine was from Texas or not. Only after the tasting was complete would we be allowed to know the origin of the wines and the overall results.

> **"Were we going to jump into the wine business in Texas?"**

As the judges arrived we shared a glass of wine, followed by dinner. The judges included chef and *Texas on the Plate* cookbook author Terry Thompson-Anderson, journalist and wine writer Jeff Siegel, wine marketer and former sommelier Martin Korson, beverage consultant and PBS celebrity winemaker Ross Outon, wine marketing and PR consultant Denise Fraser, wine educator and author Jane Nickles, San Antonio food and wine writer John Griffin, Brookshire Brothers wine buyers Dan Huerta and Phil Metzinger, and me—self-styled aficionado and the acknowledged Texas Wineslinger. I lingered in the Messina Hof wine bar, recalling a few of my past discussions with the Bonarrigos.

Reflecting back on our lunch, I recalled Paul

saying, "At the start, we did everything ourselves. We planted the vine stock, ten plants of each kind. Some were European vinifera, some hybrids, and some even native American varieties. Ron Perry helped us by making arrangements for the vines. I was already working two jobs, so Merrill, who was pregnant with Paul Mitchell at the time, worked on the irrigation lines and planting the vines."

When they made the decision to seriously pursue the winery business, Paul and Merrill had already learned from the experimental vineyard that they were likely going to be limited to one grape variety on the property in Bryan—Black Spanish. So, in 1984, Paul made his first trip to the Lubbock area and started to develop relationships with the grape growers there.

Paul said, "I was surprised to find out how aggressively arrogant many of the established wineries were towards growers at the time. They blamed the growers for all the negative qualities of their wines, even though in many cases the problems were of their own making. There was initially a glut of grapes and a limited number of wineries in Texas. The wineries were picking and choosing and being ruthless on the prices they would pay for grapes. When I went up there in 1984, it was easy to find growers that wanted to start a new relationship; some are still growing for us more than twenty years later."

Then I remembered to ask the duo where they got their reputation for doing what others in the Texas wine industry might consider grandiose.

Paul's first recollection went way back to the beginning. Without a blink, Paul said, "I went up to the Lubbock area to buy some Zinfandel grapes. I took the truck and trailer with a tank strapped to the bed. It looked like something from the *Beverly Hillbillies*. I made arrangements for the grapes to be picked, de-stemmed, and pressed up there. Then, I pumped the juice into the tank and started back on the road to the winery. When I got back, I realized that during the trip home the wine had started to ferment and produce alcohol. I started to count the number of dry counties I had driven across during the trip home where alcoholic beverages are illegal. I wondered how many laws I broke in the process with my 'winery-on-wheels.'

"When I got home, I went to bed, and Merrill pumped the juice into the fermenter and the wine went to completion over the next couple weeks. Later, we entered that wine in a competition up in the eastern United States and were amazed when we found out that our "Cuvée Trailer" actually won a medal."

As we gathered for the judges' dinner, I launched my first tweet, a picture of the grand cast of judges gathered around the dinner table. Seconds later it popped up on Twitter for all to see. Several others chimed in, commenting on the fine dinner that included presentations of Texas shrimp, beef, and all the fixings.

Jane Nickles tweeted, "Looking forward to the Messina Hof Twitter Taste-off tomorrow . . . they make an awesome un-oaked Chard!" Immediately, almost like a wireless flash, she had four retweets from her followers to their followers. I thought: Wow! People are actually following our wine and food frivolity at nine o'clock on a Saturday evening.

Then I thought I would explore the borderline of cute with a tweet saying, "Twitter taste-off @Messina_Hof with bestselling wine brands this weekend. Texas Shootout or Smackdown...." In seconds, I got a tweet from Mike Wangbickler, California wine PR and marketing guru, who participated in one of my previous Twitter tasting events in Dallas. His tweet said, "Unfortunately, I'm about 2,000 miles away and won't be able to join you."

After the lavish dinner and a toast to the adventure of the following morning, I lay in my bed in the Messina Hof B&B ensconced between cherub lamps. Their warm glow, highlighting the fleur-de-lis pattern on the walls, lulled me to sleep while the cold winter wind blew outside. Hours later I awoke to the smell of breakfast outside my room in the lobby of the B&B. It primed my engine and buffered my stomach for the upcoming early-morning wine tasting.

After all the anticipation, we finally assembled and began tasting through the twelve flights of wine that Paul arranged to challenge our Sunday morning palates. Like I always say, "I love the smell of Gewürztraminer in the morning!"

"Twitter tasting is like doing play-by-play sports"

The Twitter tasting was a frenetic mashup. We all worked hard just to keep pace tasting the wines, recording scores, and making the decision, Texas wine—yay or nay. All the while I was trying to periodically tweet and monitor tweets from the other judges, commingled with comments from the virtual participants throughout the blogosphere.

I recall seeing Jeff Siegel's comment early in the tasting. Jeff was a sports writer before he combined his passion for writing with his passion for wines. While sports may be in his past and wine in his present, his short remark about his Twitter tasting experience was succinct.

He said, "Twitter tasting is like doing play-by-play sports." He was right. The wine tasting and associated tweets were moving at the pace of a 6-4-3 double play.

I believe that Ross Outon, our celebrity PBS series winemaker judge, was the first to give a name to our august Twitter event. He called it the "Judgment of Bryan, Texas," alluding to Steven Spurrier's "Judgment of Paris," a tasting held in Paris in 1976. A raft of then "no-name" California Cabernets and Chardonnays had won that competition, judged against wines from some of the best-regarded châteaux of Bordeaux and domaines of Burgundy.

Several comments were launched from the judges during the tasting about how difficult it was to discern the Texas wine from the non-Texas wines. When I first read these comments, it didn't strike me as anything special. However, the more I thought about it, I started to realize that this was actually the best news possible.

About halfway through the Twitter tasting, we took a break. During this respite, I talked to Paul and Merrill. I mentioned that I had once been told about a Messina Hof event that involved somebody riding a white horse into the lobby of a big-name Houston hotel. I asked Paul, "Was that you?"

Paul laughed while shaking his head and said, "No, it wasn't me. But it did happen. It was back in 1987 during the release of our first Nouveau Red Zinfandel. We wanted to do something akin to the release of the Nouveau Beaujolais in France, but with a distinctive Texas flair. I actually don't know how we did this." Then he gave Merrill a long look.

She said, "I'm actually the one that called the Shamrock Hilton to try to arrange that event. The Shamrock was my first big hotel experience when I was growing up, and, back then, it was still a big name in Houston high society. I really didn't know if they would do it."

Merrill continued as she and Paul nearly wept with laughter while reliving what had to be one of the most memorable of Texas wine moments.

She said, "The movie *Rhinestone Cowboy* had been released back a year or so before, so I wanted a glittered-up cowboy mounted on horseback to carry a bottle of our wine into the lobby of the Shamrock Hilton where the tasting was being held. The hotel manager suggested that I call the county sheriff's office and ask if one of the off-duty sheriffs would do it, and sure enough, one said he would. I remember that he wore a spangly cowboy outfit and came down Main Street on a big white horse with a fancy saddle. He came riding on horseback right into the hotel lobby to deliver our wine. It was one of the most amazing things that I've ever seen. People stopped on the street and in the hotel to see what was happening."

After completing another session of Twitter tasting, the judges were doing a bit of basking in self-made glory. By then, they were referring to what had just transpired as simply "The Judgment." The difficulty in differentiating the Texas wines from the non-Texas was still the one element of the tasting that astounded everyone.

Later, *Houston Chronicle* wine writer Dale Robertson, who monitored the event, reported, "The Judgment of Bryan, Texas, doesn't appear to have yet rocked the wine world like Steven Spurrier's Judgment of Paris did in 1976. But it seems that the event could be remembered as at least a seminal moment in the evolution of perceptions of Texas wines."

After viewing the results from the Messina Hof tasting, the judges thought that Paul had upped his game, and they bantered on that Paul might have stacked the deck, and *not* in favor of his Texas wines. In several flights, his wines were going against far more expensive and more famous wines. The most extreme example was the Mondavi-Rothschild creation "Opus One," costing over $160, that went head-to-head against his premium Messina Hof Paulo, a similar Bordeaux blend but costing a mere $40. The remarkable result of the blind tasting was that a majority of the tasters favored the Messina Hof Paulo.

When told of this result, Dale Robertson put the following disclaimer in his column: "Don't shoot the messenger . . . unequivocally, the truth with a capital T resides in blind tastings. I've repeatedly seen 'presumed lesser' wines kick tail in my monthly *Houston Chronicle* sessions, which are always done blind."

After I reviewed the judges' scoring sheets, I found that of the twelve flights presented to us, most of the judges scored the Messina Hof wines as either higher rated or comparable to a majority of the non-Texas wines. Most of the judges correctly identified only half of the pairings according to their origin: Texas or not.

Before leaving, I stopped to say my good-byes to Paul and Merrill and thanked them for being wonderful hosts. I also asked the grand impresario how he felt about the results.

He said, "Each year, the question surfaces of how Texas wine stacks up against the world's best wines, and now I've got the 'Judgment' that proves that Texas wines are on par with big-name wines and can even offer better value."

> **❝❝I hope they're not thinking that I've stopped drinking my own!❞❞**

As I walked out the door, Paul said, "Getting ready for this tasting, my dining room looked like the pre-set for a major international wine competition. I got to thinking that the wine retailers around here are probably wondering why I've developed such a penchant for other people's high-end wines. I hope they're not thinking that I've stopped drinking my own!"

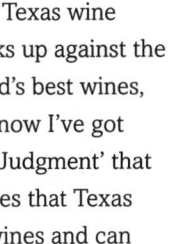

Bull Riding, Blues Guitar, and Blanc Du Bois

24

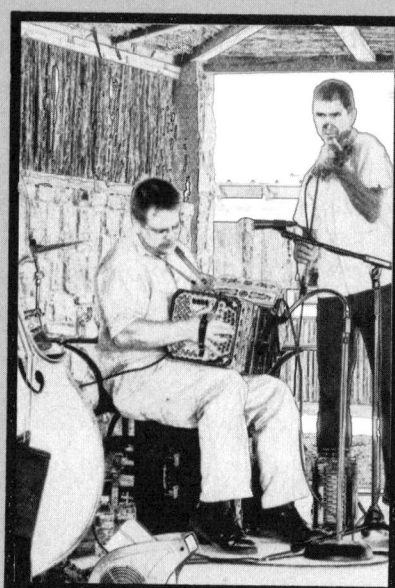

O n a sultry Saturday evening in Houston, I waited as patiently as possible for my wife to arrive. Her flight was delayed, and I knew we were going to be late for the wine tasting at Haak Vineyards as guests of Raymond and Gladys Haak on their winery's tenth anniversary.

Upon our arrival at the winery, we tried to surreptitiously make our way down the stairs into the cellar to join a congregation of guests already engaged in a retrospective tasting of wines from the Haak library. The tasting of the first wine in the set of six Cabernet Sauvignons was already in progress. A knowledgeable woman was talking about the wine's strong acidity, edgy tannins, herbal undertones, and cherry fruit when Raymond caught our movement down the stairs. Our stealthy entrance was exposed by his full-throated call to join him. Raymond's voice halted the presentation and caused a quick jerk in the crowd's attention toward the stairs.

This hearty welcome was so characteristic of the Haak hospitality. It exemplified the honest and humble traits that I've grown to love in both Raymond and Gladys. In their presence, there's no pretense or pride to get in the way of down-home Texas hospitality.

We waded through the sea of white-clothed tables to the center of the cellar, where Raymond grasped my hand and gave it a vigorous pumping and Gladys smothered us both with hugs. I then met the lady who had been making the presentation before our intrusion, Nadia Hetzel, Raymond's winemaker. I apologized for our rude interruption, but with the same warmth showed by the Haaks, she said in a simple melodic tone, "Don't worry about it."

While the first course was being served, Raymond leaned over and in a subdued voice said, "Russ, these have been great years for us and these six wines tell a lot about our beginnings. In the first two years our wines were made from Cabernet grapes that I imported from Lodi, California. Back then, it was all new to me. I didn't have any contracts for Texas fruit. All I knew was that California grew damn good grapes, and I was going to make even better wine with their grapes than they could. I look back now and realize how naïve I was when we started this operation."

Back when Raymond got out to California, he didn't really know what to talk about with the guy that was going to sell him grapes. All Raymond knew was that he sprayed a lot in his vineyard back in Texas—a nearly weekly ritual. So, Raymond asked him how often he sprayed his grapes. The man had to stop and think about it for a moment and then answered that he thought he'd sprayed once last year. Raymond felt like a greenhorn.

Raymond continued: "The Cabernet that I made from those California grapes was good. However, there was one thing that I really didn't realize back then, but I do now. When Texans go to a Texas winery, they don't want to drink California wine."

In their third vintage, Raymond looked hard within Texas to get wine grapes and started an association with Texas High Plains grower Dr. Vijay Reddy. Starting that year, the Haak Cabernet

Sauvignon was made from Vijay's grapes, and in all but one year since, the wine's label has designated the Reddys' vineyard, something growers consider an honor.

Later that evening, in a flash of Haak unpretentiousness, Raymond asked me to stand and address the crowd about my recollection of one of the first wine competitions that he entered with his Cabernet made from the California grapes.

I rose, faced the audience, and began. "I was a judge in a competition here in Houston. After that wine competition was over, I called Raymond to let him know that the judges really liked his Cabernet wine so much that we gave it a gold medal in a red-wine division. But, after the competition tasting was completed, several judges went into the back room to confirm that the label on the bottle read 'Cabernet Sauvignon.' I admitted to Raymond that we really liked his 'Cabernet,' but that it didn't taste like Cabernet." Raymond then proceeded to enlighten the crowd with the rest of the story.

He said, "Ya know, back then I bought those grapes from a guy in California. When you do that, you're at their mercy. I was still green at all this and didn't know very much. I thought I was buying Cabernet. They said that they were Cabernet grapes, and the papers they gave me said I was going to get Cabernet grapes, so I trusted them. As I think about it now, for all I knew, the grapes that showed up here could've been Barbera, Syrah, or Grenache. Back then, I didn't know any better."

Most winemakers or winery owners wouldn't have shared that story, but Raymond always tells a story straight and doesn't blink or blush even when it puts egg on his face. In this case, he just chalked it up to experience.

Gladys also has a warm, folksy manner that often comes across in her winery newsletter. She describes, in first-person accounts, winery events or personal exploits of their travels to different wine-pouring venues or worldwide trips in pursuit of wine knowledge.

My favorite Gladys commentary was when she described a trip to Washington DC to pour their wines at the President George W. Bush Black Tie & Boots Inaugural Ball.

She wrote, "Our hotel had a metro station under it with an escalator going down into the tunnel that was long and deep. We were all dressed up to go to the ball and I started down the escalator when I felt my skirt being pulled down. I grabbed it and started pulling back, but it was stuck tight in the escalator. I thought, 'well here it comes Lord. I'm fixin' to get all chewed up by this dang thing.' Finally, I got my skirt loose and the entire side was covered with black grease. There was nothing for me to do but go back to the hotel and change. All I had was my black jeans from Wal-Mart that cost $12.00 and a top borrowed from one of my Ya Ya Sisters. So that's what I wore to the ball. Anyone else would have been mortified, but these duds were so comfortable and warm."

Several months later I stopped in at the Haak winery again to talk to Raymond about his focus on Blanc Du Bois, a white grape gaining favor in Texas. In the middle of our tasting, the conversation took a detour, and, before I knew it, we were talking about the exploits of a much younger Raymond Haak.

Wine was being racked in the back of the winery, and the place was alive with activity as we eased down into the quiet of the cellar. Raymond gathered a few bottles of wine and glasses and juggled them as we descended the stairs and sat at a solitary table set with formal linens. He pulled the corks and poured the first wine, but then ran back upstairs to get some cheese and crackers. After returning, Raymond recounted his younger days.

He said, "Back then, I thought I was bigger and badder than I really was. There were things I wanted to do and I just did 'em. Gladys says that I'm still that way and that's how we ended up in this goldarned winery business."

Reflecting even further back, Raymond said, "When my mother and I moved in with my step-father here in Santa Fe, I got exposed to farming and ranching; real country living and I loved it. I had a high school friend who had horses that we raced, and we began practicing for the rodeo. We met some real rodeo cowboys who let us work their horses. It was a blast. I can still remember the rush I got riding on the bucking horses. From there, I tried my hand at bull riding, which proved even more of a rush. Gosh, those bulls were huge! I saw the hazards—cowboys with broken bones sticking out of their skin and with their ears ripped off. Thank God I finally got some sense and moved on. But, ya know, back then I always thought I was bulletproof."

We tasted a white wine Raymond had made from the Blanc Du Bois grape that was chillingly crisp and dry. It tasted more like a Sauvignon Blanc, something similar to a wine you might find in California or Sancerre in France, but it came from a hybrid grape grown right here on the Gulf Coast.

As our discussion meandered, I found out that music was also a part of Raymond's early experiences. His grandmother, a full-blood Cherokee, was an evangelist and played guitar. From his description, she was quite a character. She played guitar at spiritual revivals, was married eight times, and had thirteen children. She's the one who taught young Raymond how to play guitar.

Raymond said, "Walking on new turf and the thrill that it brings—that's what I like. The flash of excitement I got from playing and singing in a blues band was similar to the horse- and bull-riding experience. It's like the feeling I got with the pull of the bull rope up around my hand, with the bull squeezed between my legs as he made the dash out of the chute. I'd think, Oh, shit! Here it comes! Gosh, ya know, I can still feel it."

After the first white wine and our short discussion, we tasted another Haak Blanc Du Bois wine, but this one was a real fooler. Raymond called it his Reserve Blanc Du Bois, aged in oak, made in a style called *sur lie*. That's where the wine's left with the yeast cells after fermentation is complete. The lees and wine are stirred occasionally, which in combination with the oak aging creates a richer and more complex wine. When I said this wine was a fooler, I meant that if given this wine and

asked to taste it blind, I would most likely have guessed that it was a Chablis-style Chardonnay. Raymond gave credit for this wine to help from his friend and fellow Blanc Du Bois grower Jerry Watson in Cat Spring, Texas.

Interestingly, Raymond said that there's nothing in the standard winemaker's reference books about how to make Blanc Du Bois into wine, nothing on harvest parameters, yeast selection, or fermentation. When he started working on Blanc Du Bois, he took his lead from the information available for Sauvignon Blanc; but it's still different, and he had to learn with each vintage. Raymond and Jerry were the first in Texas to find the methods for making Blanc Du Bois, which they've now shared with many Texas winemakers. As we tasted, I asked Raymond when he got the bug to grow grapes.

He said, "Back in 1969, Gladys brought two vines home after I said I needed a hobby. Then, I planted thirty more vines, and later three hundred more. One day, I just came up with the idea to make wine because I thought that it was something that would be new and interesting. So, I started to make wine at home. It was like walking on new turf again; I got the feeling, the bug, and I couldn't shake it. Ya know, I made some pretty nasty-tasting wine at first, but for some reason I had a passion for it and I stuck with it, getting better little by little. In the back of my mind I'd always thought of starting a winery, but assumed that it was just a passing fancy. I said to myself, 'Raymond, get real. After all, this is Texas. Shoot, it's Galveston County! Who'd come here to a winery, anyway?'"

Our third wine was another form of Haak Blanc Du Bois, this one semisweet. As he poured this wine in my glass, Raymond reminded me that the Blanc Du Bois, while being developed and first grown commercially in Florida, now covered more acres in Texas than anywhere else in the wine world. Raymond said, "I don't think that they took it seriously, but in Texas we did, and now it's basically our own grape varietal. It came to Texas and was naturalized."

I was surprised by the rich floral quality that combined with the silky smooth mouth-feel of this pour. Whereas the previous dry Blanc Du Bois wines were lean like Sauvignon Blanc and a lightly oaked Chardonnay, this sweeter version of the wine from the same grape seemed more stylistically like a German Riesling.

As the story continued between sips of wine, Raymond told me that at a point in his career he had been laid off from an engineering job. The way he tells it, he lost his drive and was simply burned out. For a while, Raymond, Gladys, and the family

> **"I don't think that they took it seriously, but in Texas we did"**

lived off their Amigo Mart convenience store and mini-storage businesses.

Finally, Raymond and Gladys decided to sell the convenience store and retire. But, once they sold the store and the dust settled, Raymond realized that he didn't have a hobby other than growing a few grapes. He thought that he'd shaken the idea of starting a winery, but, after they sold their store, the feeling was still too strong. He admitted that they had the money from the sale of their store, and it was just sitting there burning a hole in their banker's pocket.

Then, Raymond finally decided that he could do it—start a winery. However, he's not one to put much credence in business plans. His approach was something more like . . . well, if you need an appendectomy and you want Raymond to do it, don't give him a book to read on the subject or send him to school to learn about it; just give him a knife and lie down flat on the table. I've no doubt that Raymond would find that swollen bugger and cut it out and be done with it. That's precisely how Raymond, with Gladys's help, started their winery.

He continued, "But ya know, about halfway through construction, I looked out the window of our house and stared at the big hole next door where the winery's cellar was going to be. I looked over at Gladys and said, 'What've I done?' Who am I to think that I can build a winery in the middle of nowhere, Santa Fe, Texas, of all places, and make it work?"

In a moment of Haak sincerity, Raymond said,

"I started to tear up. I nearly lost it, big time. Then, I realized that there were five million people that live within a hundred miles of this place. At two gallons of wine consumed per person in Texas every year, that's a lot of wine for us to sell. From that day, Gladys and I never looked back, and our winery's grown every year. Now, that's not to say it's been easy; it's actually been a wild ride, something like that bucking bull that put the fear of God in a much younger Raymond Haak."

Raymond said, "Just in case you didn't notice, our favorite grape here is Blanc Du Bois. It's a French-American hybrid that's resistant to Texas grape growers' worst enemy, Pierce's disease. We've become known for the wide range of wines that we make from Blanc Du Bois. I've almost lost track of the number of wines it supports."

I agreed with him, since we were already through three of his Blanc Du Bois wines and still had two more to go, all with amazingly different characteristics. Raymond started to pour a glass of his white port-style wine also made from this grape. It was fermented all the way up to 22 percent alcohol with special yeast, followed by a hefty dose of aging in new American oak. The resultant wine was again a totally different experience from what we tasted previously. It was like a fruit cocktail, yet crisp and bright with a profound undertone of vanilla. Sounding a bit like a proud parent talking about a child's accomplishment, Raymond started talking and simultaneously pouring the next wine.

"The white port that you just tasted is the starting stock for the Haak Blanc Du Bois Madeira wine. After the first period of oak aging, the barrels of wine go into our special aging oven called an estufa, where they stay at 105 degrees Fahrenheit for three months. It's really barrel aging at high temperature, where the temperature increases oxidation of the wine and caramelizes the sugars. It also speeds up the diffusion of the moisture in the wine through the barrel, resulting in a concentration of the wine."

Raymond's Madeira hit the mark. It was a light coppery color very characteristic of wines originating from the island of Madeira. The aromas were of baked pineapples and baking spices, followed by a fresh, zesty, and minerally finish.

Gladys hollered down into the cellar to locate Raymond. It was getting late, and she was trying to plan dinner for the family. Before I could start packing to depart, Raymond said, "You gotta stay and have steak with us tonight." I called to tell my wife not to expect me home for a while and then accompanied Raymond up the cellar stairs.

On our way up we ran into Harold, Raymond's eleven-year-old grandson. In a quick and animated conversation, he mentioned that he plays drums. Harold showed me a video of his band on a palm-sized player. Focusing past a very nervous looking lead singer, I noticed that Harold had that no-fear look of confidence, a trait that was characteristically Raymond.

I told Harold that I was a drummer too, and that I had been eleven when my band played its first paying job. With that he gave me a big smile and walked away watching his video, his face revealing a bright-eyed thrill as he watched himself in musical motion, a reflection of passion from within. The slack in the bull rope was tightening for Harold, just as it had for his grandfather. It was plain to see.

Ghosts of Wineries Past

25

Jerry Watson and I first spotted lanky Crockett Leyendecker as we entered the whitewashed Bernardo Farm and Ranch Supply in Cat Spring, Texas. He was standing near the back counter next to one of two long white benches that faced each other. I imagined that these benches had been used for decades, maybe longer, by bib-overalled philosophers as they gathered here and passed the time opining on current events and exchanging local gossip.

As Jerry and I approached, I overheard Crockett talking to the equally slight but much shorter Larry Ulhig, saying, "Ya know, I was fifteen years old when I started to make my own wine. I just saw some wine labels my wife made for me, and she put some propaganda on 'em that said that I'd been makin' wine since 1945. Shoot, it's true, but in the early days it weren't exactly all legal."

Jerry, a longtime Gulf Coast winegrower, set up this meeting and wasted no time interjecting, "Y'all ready to ride?"

Crockett and Larry continued their lighthearted banter and then asked Jerry when he had started making wine. Jerry responded that it was far too long ago to matter much. To this Crockett responded, "I think I still have a bottle of the first wine you made." Jerry just shook his head, took off his hat, and ran his fingers through his more salt than pepper hair for a moment. He said, "Lord have mercy! That was my Cynthiana wine. I'd recommend that you just leave it sit on the shelf. That was just terrible stuff."

"I made some berry wine one time," admitted Crockett. "It was so bad that I left it in my old smokehouse. After a while, I hauled it off, bottles and all, and just buried it. But ya know, I made some watermelon wine once. I thought that it was pretty bad, too; I couldn't drink it at first. But, I set it on a shelf and came back five years later. It turned into some pretty damn good wine."

That day in Austin County convinced me that winemaking had a unique legacy in Texas. It all started in the days of the Spanish missionaries, but was kept alive in small towns across Texas, like Cat Spring, where European immigrants brought family traditions and tried to root them in the local soil of their newly adopted homeland.

The group of men around me eventually professed that wines from the area around Cat Spring had now reached a pinnacle of achievement, the best of which they referred to as "the good stuff." They agreed that the best local grape wines made nowadays are likely from French-American hybrid grapes called Black Spanish and Blanc Du Bois: Black Spanish used for red wines often in a dessert or port-style, and Blanc Du Bois used for dry, off-dry, and sweet white wines.

Jerry headed for the door and hollered, "We can follow if you want, or y'all can ride with me." Crockett responded with his decision to drive in the lead and waved for us to follow. As we drove, Jerry clued me in that Larry came from a long-standing German family in the area, the Uhligs, going back well into the 1800s. He used to run the post office in Cat Spring, and he's become the area's de facto historian. Crockett, well . . . he's the local conversationalist.

Jerry said, "You know that this area was the 'mother colony' for Germans in Texas. Most of them came into Galveston, and this was their first stop. Some moved on to settlements in New Braunfels and Fredericksburg. Reportedly, one of the first Germans to make it to Texas was a man named Ernst, and he settled near here in a town called Industry."

We passed the time en route to our destination with Jerry's predictions for this summer's rain and temperatures and his lament of how often he was going to have to spray to control weeds and

> " "It turned into some pretty damn good wine" "

fungus. Then we talked about another of Jerry's vineyard nemeses, the deer.

Jerry, a Texas oil-field geologist for more years than he can remember, pointed out, "You'll notice we're into what the locals call the 'Rolling Hills.' It's a point where you get up to an elevation of about two hundred feet where the land has a ripple that makes for a right pretty countryside. The post oak trees predominate here, unlike the land nearer the Gulf of Mexico. We're where the Texas coast ended about two million years ago. Erosion's brought our good soil down from the hill country, and likely even as far away as the high plains near Lubbock." Jerry seemed to understand that what gave this area its special terroir also makes it a natural place to grow Black Spanish and Blanc Du Bois.

We drove down a back road that turned to a dirt road and finally came to a stop at the home of Leonard and Earline Drumm. Jerry gave me a heads-up that Earline was a descendent of John Berger, one of the old-time German settlers and likely the first major grape grower in the area. Inside their home we sat around a dining table covered by a red-checkered tablecloth, on which were scattered loose photos and letters, and even more in albums.

Earline had a magnifying glass in hand and was looking over some of the finer details in the photographs that lay before her. She was particularly pondering one photo of her great-grandfather John Berger, who originally arrived with his parents from Germany in the 1850s. The photo showed an older and mustached man. He was in a suit and tie and sported a well-worn fedora, and sat before a backdrop of hilly terrain with a banner at his feet announcing the picture's location, Santa Monica, California. I asked the group what John had been doing in California.

Earline said, "All we know is that he went to California and sent back cuttings of a grape to make white wine. From letters and winery documents, we know that the grape was called Herbemont. However, Leonard and I are amazed that he went all the way out to California."

At first John tried to grow grapes that were brought over from his homeland of Germany. He grew them, and records show that he made wine with them, but after a number of years there was a blight of some sort and all the grapevines died. Then he went out to California looking for another white grape that might grow here. Why he went out there and how he found out about those California grapes was always a mystery to Earline.

I felt I was hearing a story of a ghost winery, a winery that once resided near the Texas Gulf Coast well before the dawn of today's modern wine industry and now existing only in Earline's old photos and documents. I was also struck by something much different that I'd read many years ago that now appeared relevant to this story.

What I had read were the descriptions of how

immigrants brought grapevines with them when they came to Texas, or how they later had them shipped from their ancestral lands back in Europe. However, the results in Texas were universally bad; the story was always the same. After a period of cultivation the grapes died, and these farmers in a new land had no understanding of the likely causes and potential cures. The disease that limited cultivation of the European varietals of grapes in Texas was likely what we now know as Pierce's disease.

We also know that this disease was not limited to Texas and the southeastern states. A disease with similar traits decimated vineyards in southern California as far back as the 1800s. The name that they gave it was Anaheim disease, since it was particularly bad in the area of Anaheim, California.

This gave me a suspicion as to why John Berger made the trip to southern California and how he probably got clued in to the Herbemont grape. The group assembled around the table grew silent as I presented my theory.

I told them that Anaheim had a similar heritage to the area here in Austin County. Both settlements were originally started in the nineteenth century by immigrant colonies of German farmers and vintners. I was willing to bet that John Berger had a personal relationship or, at least, a correspondence with a German countryman in Anaheim, both with an interest in growing grapes and making wine.

This theory would also explain why he focused on Herbemont grapes in California. The Herbemont grape was one of a few hybrid white grape varieties known to be resistant to Pierce's disease, aka Anaheim disease.

I opined that it was understandable why at the time John didn't want to use the local Black Spanish grapes. They could only be used to make red wine, and Germans had a penchant for white wine. Herbemont, while having a red-brown skin, gives off a white-amber juice, something that would be highly prized by German winemakers in either Cat Spring or Anaheim.

The looks on the faces of the assembly were unanimous. Their eyes bright and faces with broad smiles indicated that they'd finally found a plausible explanation for what was previously only a conjecture on John Berger's motivations to go to faraway California.

Earline continued, "My grandfather told me that when he was a little boy he'd see the Lutheran minister come by. The minister was one of those circuit preachers that made the rounds of the nearby cities on a regular basis. He used to say how the preacher always seemed happiest after he stopped by the Berger house because he could sit around and drink wine."

Earline finally unveiled two photographs that captured a much different Texas wine industry than we see today. She said, "This was what the winery looked like in 1908." The first photo showed a three-story wooden winery looking much more like a barn than a tasting room destination in the modern sense. The second photo, dated from 1910, showed the nearby rows of grapevines trained to grow like bushes, a style still found in some old European vineyards.

Earline offered us a tour of the old Berger winery that she said was still on their nearby family land. We boarded our trucks and sailed past rolling green hills with thickets of wild grapevines so high that they hung from the tops of the post oaks and so dense they were like a knitted green wool cape that covered the ground, low bushes, and fences.

In just a short spell, we came to an open field and a locked metal gate with no sign of a winery. Once through this portal, we traversed overland to a small clearing in the trees about a hundred yards off the road. There before me lay open the book of Texas wine history; the winery from Earline's picture appeared in sun-beaten gray wood. The winery seemed supported by the outstretched limbs of an old live oak tree and was ensconced within a vast network of tendrils from an old Mustang grapevine.

As Leonard and Earline opened the door of the old winery building, I peered into its dark, dank cavern and saw a collection of old bedsteads, chairs, and rusty farm equipment. They invited me to climb up a rickety handmade ladder, telling me that John Berger made nearly everything in the winery, starting with the winery's first basket press and likely the ladder on which I was now standing.

It was obvious that the three floors were built for people of shorter stature. I tested the ladder and then the second-floor landing before letting them handle my full weight. Higher up, on the third level, wedged between the winery's roof and a wooden beam was a wine barrel containing possibly the last vestige of Berger wine. As I roamed half-hunched, unable to reach the barrel, I recalled Earline's old photo that showed a barrel being hauled up by cable and pulley to the top of the winery.

During our visit, I asked a hypothetical question, only half expecting a response: "What do y'all imagine a Berger wine tasting was like?" Crockett responded, "I remember Papa telling me that his uncle loaded up the family and they'd go over to taste wine at the Berger winery at Christmastime. The wine was probably sweet, and it must've been enjoyable because they sang 'Tannenbaum, O Tannenbaum' really loud, all the way home."

Crockett said, "We've one more stop, and it's getting late." So, we said good-bye to the Drumms and returned to our procession with Larry and Crockett. After about fifteen minutes of skirting the spring-green countryside, we were maneuvering down a winding dirt road and up to the home of Lee Roy Schuette, descendent of Frank and Louise Laake.

Lee Roy greeted us and talked about his Laake roots and lineage. Frank came to Texas from Germany and settled in Austin County. His first-generation German-Texas family grew with the addition of ten children, and they later saw it blossom with thirty-one grandchildren. With a glass of cool well water in hand, I perused his family photos and artifacts. I heard Jerry reading from a small framed document he held in his hand at about an arm's length: "This says 'wine maketh glad the heart of man.' I think that this is a quote from the Bible."

Jerry was reading from a label from the Oak Hill Vineyard established in 1878 by Laake and Sons. I later found these words in the book of Psalms, in a passage that reads, "He causeth the grass to grow for the cattle, and herb for the service of man: that he may bring forth food out of the earth; and wine that maketh glad the heart of man, and oil to make his face to shine, and bread which strengtheneth man's heart." Surely the old Germans had the right perspective on life in including a vital role for wine to sooth the complexities and hardships of early Texas.

> ❝ And wine that maketh glad the heart of man ❞

Lee Roy said, "The winery building out back used to have a sign on it that called it 'District Winery Number Four.' I guess that I should've asked more questions. All I know is that Grandpa grew grapes, farmed cotton and tobacco, and sold milk, hogs, and other stuff. He ran it as a year-round business."

From Lee Roy's photographs, it appeared that it took quite a few people back then to work the twenty-plus-acre vineyard at harvest time. After all, it was a totally manual operation. From vineyard records I'd seen, I estimated that back then a twenty-acre vineyard could produce upwards of ten to fifteen tons of grapes, based on a yield of a half ton per acre. I figured that, in its heyday, Oak Hill Vineyards produced the equivalent of about 650 to 1,000 cases of wine.

The photos also showed that the Laake vineyard operation had family, friends, and local African Americans who came out to the vineyard and worked side by side. This was not how I expected things to be in Texas back then. Crocket said, "That's not surprising to see black folk and Germans working together. In general, the German immigrants had a better relationship with the African Americans than they did with some of the Anglo Americans, who always thought the Germans were kind of different and somewhat strange."

We went out back to see the old winery building, a single-story structure that looked like a large red garage. The board with the winery sign was removed long ago and replaced with a row of birdhouses over the main entry. The inside represented a compacted history of the combined Laake and Schuette families that included an old basket press and parts from another, a music stand from a Schuette polka band, and eighty years of lumber, pails, and boxes, not to mention numerous layers of dust and dirt that seemed to cover everything.

While we tried to make some sense of the

agglomeration of history that lay before us, we listened to a narrative from Crockett on his early experience with German wine culture in Texas. He said, "I can remember when I was a boy at home with my brothers. On really cold days we still had to go out and do our chores. Mama always kept an iron kettle of sweet wine warming on the stove in the winter. It warmed me up and just tasted so good, too."

At the end of our visit, Lee Roy fetched from around back of the house two old boards that he pieced back together for us to view. They brought another momentary hush to the group. If any of us had any doubt of the legacy of German winemaking in Texas, these mere pieces of wood manifested it at a ghostly yet very personal level, something that we could see and touch.

On the wood, in large, handwritten script, were the words, "E. W. Laake, Oak Hill, Sept. 22nd, 1903." No one now knows the significance of this date or why it was recorded. From the time of year, we surmised that it might have something to do with a batch of wine or perhaps a completion date for fermentation. Regardless of the meaning, old man Laake left this artifact to commemorate his personal bit of Texas wine heritage and left us to ponder his legacy long after his last batch of wine.

VI

In Reflection

A Winegrower's Prayer

26

It was a sunny spring afternoon with a bracing north wind when Neal Newsom came for me in his large white pickup truck that seemed to be in proportion to the vast Texas High Plains themselves. My plan was to meet with several of the High Plains winegrowers at the Newsom B&B near Plains, Texas, just a hop and skip from the New Mexico border in Yoakum County. As originally conceived, the arrangement was to give us some time to kick back with steaks and a little wine.

Stopping to let his large white truck's horses guzzle some diesel, Neal looked pensively to the west. He directed my attention to the haze, diffuse and gray, building on the horizon.

We discussed the grim forecast that boiled down to just two possibilities—cold, dry, and windy, or cold, wet, and snowy. According to Neal, the night's forecast for subfreezing temperature was already a given. The weatherman's most recent forecast didn't cut him any slack; it was for strong winds and mostly dry conditions . . . a worst-case scenario. The only remaining questions were how low the subfreezing temperatures might dip and for how long they'd persist. These two variables would determine the extent of the crop loss in his vineyard.

One of the first to start growing wine grapes twenty-five years ago, Neal has seen it all as he built up his vineyard year after year. In the process, he developed a reputation for growing the best darn grapes Texas had to offer, particularly Cabernet Sauvignon, something that's not easy in this state. Several years ago, Neal decided to cast most of his agricultural future, something like a high-stakes roll of the dice, with his hundred or so acres of wine grapes and lease his cotton fields to be cropped by others. Since then, Mother Nature has sent late-spring freezes and damaging hail to Neal and his winegrowing brethren across the state, creating a string of what they simply call "off-years" that have reduced grape harvests to less than half of a normal-sized crop.

As the growers started gathering at Neal's B&B for our dinner, the weather was obviously on their minds, evidenced by wrinkled brows and frequent stares from the patio to the gray clouds still building in the west. Their anxiety was heightened by the nearly two weeks of unseasonably warm spring weather that had preceded the coming incursion of this late-spring cold front. Each grower seemed keenly aware of the extent of new growth. As we passed Neal's rows of vines on our way in,

he showed me some vines that were barely in bud, but others reached out with two- or three-foot-long tendrils of new growth.

You might expect these types of problems in Texas given its neophyte status among wine-producing regions, but it was just a few years back that California's premier wine regions experienced one of their worst spring cold spells on record. Even in the Rhône valley of France, spring frost can damage the buds, thus reducing the overall yields. The Texas "blue norther" is just our version of what the winegrowers in southern France call "le mistral."

In Texas, the weather is dominated by two major influences, the cold north wind from Canada that gets channeled unimpeded down the Great Plains by the Rocky Mountains to the west, and the southern wind, moist and warm, pushing northward into the state from the Gulf of Mexico. Springtime in Texas sets the stage for a continual overhead clash of winds that culminates in perhaps the most difficult of times for grape growers. Most folks think of Texas as a warm-growing region and cite the heat as being the greatest hurdle to a successful grape crop, but most grape growers that I've talked to seem to allocate more worry to the late-spring freeze.

I'd volunteered my services as a cook for the gathered ensemble and arrived with a suitcase packed full of essentials that included two bottles of the best non-Texas wine from my cellar to share with growers. They were wines made from the grapes they were now growing, but from notable vineyards sites in Italy and France. My selections were an Italian Brunello di Montalcino, made from a special variety of Sangiovese in central Italy, and a Bandol AOC, a red wine based on the Mourvèdre grape from southern France.

In my suitcase, I'd also stashed three bottles of seasonings, two tubes of anchovy paste, a package of demi-glace, a bottle of marinated South African Peppadew peppers, a bottle of virgin olive oil, and a heavily spiced Italian salami that gave my clothes a new aromatic quality. As I unpacked, one of the growers said from behind me, "I bet the contents of your bag drew a long gander by Homeland Security before it flew to Lubbock."

I popped the corks on my wine, then readied the kitchen while Nolan Newsom, Neal's son and heir apparent, prepared and grilled the steaks. My job was to sauté mushrooms and chopped garlic in thick green olive oil and to convert the demi-glace into a red-wine reduction sauce to accompany the steaks.

During a short lull in the food preparation, I looked around for my Brunello and Bandol wines. They were being passed around and poured in judicious amounts so that everyone could have a sample. There was no doubt that the assembled growers felt that grapes like these from Italy, southern France, and Spain are destined for greatness here in Texas. They'll make the base ingredients for dark, red wines and even dry rosés, the plentiful summer mainstays consumed around the warmer Mediterranean regions of Europe.

While cooking, I asked the assembled growers to speculate on what would be the top five varieties of wine grapes grown in the Texas High Plains appellation fifteen years from now. The answers started to come back fast. The first two were nearly unanimous; multiple voices offered up Tempranillo, a grape of Spanish heritage, as the red, and Viognier, originating from the French Rhône River valley, as the white. When someone voiced a concern about Viognier and its propensity for early budding, other votes came in for Roussanne, another white grape from southern France that buds later than Viognier, then Vermentino, a white grape from Sardinia. These were followed in quick succession by other voices that nominated red Italian grapes: Dolcetto and Aglianico.

I sure hope that the wine drinkers across the state have their lexicon of Mediterranean wines updated, because if these grower predictions are correct, Texas is heading down a disparate route from the standard California offerings of Cabernet,

> **"I bet the contents of your bag drew a long gander by Homeland Security before it flew to Lubbock"**

Merlot, and Chardonnay. It'll be a different kind of wine country than California, by a long shot.

We sampled some of the Texas wines that the growers brought to share, some still in shiny, label-less bottles and some sporting duct tape with vineyard and grape names scrawled in Sharpie marker.

I talked with a particularly nervous Jet Wilmeth that night. He recalled his recent experiences with hail and freezes in his High Plains vineyard in Tokio, Texas. Jet said, "I'm optimistic if the temperatures tonight hang around twenty-eight or twenty-nine. However, I expect that we are going to be in a world of hurt if the temperatures drop much farther. We've simply had too much early warm weather this year."

It was apparent that Jet knows adversity. He continued, "There was a year when there were five hailstorms on the High Plains. The first hail sheared the leaves off my vines. The following week, another hail got a good deal of my grapes and caused some vine damage, too. I'm thankful that my grapevines survived the ordeal and are still relatively healthy. This year, I just finished pruning my vines, having postponed it as long as possible to delay bud break. I'm dreading another late freeze."

With the steaks on the grill nearing completion and dinner in the offing, Jet gathered the growers, their family members, and guests and asked everyone to join hands in prayer. Our line of thankful souls stretched from the kitchen into the dining room and back. Quite mindful of the impending weather, we obliged and joined hands.

Jet offered a simple winegrower's prayer, and said, "Dear Lord, thank you for this day, and thank you for this gathering of our families and friends. Bless us all. We could use a little rain, but most of all, please keep the frost away. In Jesus' name, we pray, Amen."

As only a farmer's silent inner strength can convey, there was no doubt that the fate of this year's harvest was in the hands of a greater being.

Later that evening after others had left the Newsom B&B, Neal's wife, Janice, made sure that I had everything needed to bunk down for the night. Then, Neal and I slipped out back of the house and took a moment to listen to the wind, glance at the night sky, and stand in silent communion with the spirits of the land.

We took in what appeared as a billion points of light between fingers of foreboding gray clouds. The Milky Way's river of stars was the dominant feature. Neal pointed out the Orion constellation and the fuzzy spot, the middle "star" in Orion's sword that's actually a nebula. From there his gaze lingered on the Pleiades, the star grouping represented in Western astrology as "coping with sorrow." This cluster, dominated by hot youthful stars, was formed within the last one hundred million years, about the time when the place called Texas was born.

We said our good nights, and as he walked to his truck, I wished Neal well for what I realized would be a very troubled night's sleep.

Wineries Participating in TDA's GO TEXAN Program

Western Region

The 501 Winery
204 Commerce Street, Childress, Texas, 79201
www.501winery.com

Bar Z Wines
19290 FM 1541, Canyon, TX 79015
www.barzwines.com

CapRock Winery at Lubbock
408 East Woodrow Road, Lubbock, TX 79423
www.caprockwinery.com

Christoval Vineyards
5000A Cralle Road, Christoval, TX 76935
www.christovalvineyards.com

Delaney Vineyards at Lamesa
One mile north of Lamesa on Highway 137, Lamesa, TX 79331
www.delaneyvineyards.com

La Diosa Cellars
901 17th Street, Lubbock, TX 79401
www.ladiosacellars.com

For current listings, see www.gotexanwine.org

Llano Estacado Winery
PO Box 3487, Lubbock, TX 79452
www.llanowine.com

McPherson Cellars
1615 Texas Avenue, Lubbock, TX 79401
www.mcphersoncellars.com

Pheasant Ridge Winery
3507 East County Road 5700, Lubbock, TX 79403
www.pheasantridgewinery.com

Seifert Cellars
15051 Lake Ivie Drive, Millersview, TX 76862
www.seifertcellars.com

Star Canyon Winery
2601 North Stanton Street, El Paso, TX 79902
www.starcanyonwinery.com

Ste. Genevieve, Peregrine Hill Wines
PO Box 130, Fort Stockton, TX 79735

Val Verde Winery
100 Qualia Drive, Del Rio, TX 78840
www.valverdewinery.com

Zin Valle Vineyards
7315 Highway 28, Canutillo, TX 79835
www.zinvalle.com

Northern Region

Arché
228 Wagner Road, Saint Jo, TX 76265
www.archewines.com

Barking Rocks Winery & Vineyard
1919 Allen Court, Granbury, TX 76048
www.barkingrockswine.com

The Blue Armadillo Winery
2702 Lee Street, Greenville, TX 75401
www.bluearmadillowinery.com

The Blue Rooster Winery
606 West Pine Street (US Hwy 80), Edgewood, TX 75117

Bluff Dale Vineyards
5222 County Road 148, Bluff Dale, TX 76433
www.bluffdalevineyards.com

Brushy Creek Vineyards and Winery
572 County Road 2798, Alvord, TX 76225
www.brushycreekvineyards.com

CALAIS Winery
3000 Commerce Street, Dallas, TX 75226
www.calaiswinery.com

Collin Oaks Winery
6874 County Road 398, Princeton, TX 75407
www.collinoakswinery.com

CrossRoads Winery
15222 King Road #301, Frisco, TX 75034
www.friscowinery.com

Cross Timbers Winery
805 North Main Street, Grapevine, TX 76051
www.crosstimberswinery.com

Crump Valley Vineyards
127 Crump Lane, Sulphur Springs, TX 75482

Delaney Vineyards at Grapevine
2000 Champagne Boulevard, Grapevine, TX 76051
www.delaneyvineyards.com

Enoch's Stomp Vineyard and Winery
870 Ferguson Road (FM 4312), Harleton, TX 75651
www.enochsstomp.com

Fairhaven Vineyards
5340 South FM 2869 Hawkins, TX 75765
www.fairhavenvineyards.com

Fuqua Winery
3737 Atwell Street, Suite #203, Dallas, TX 75209
www.fuquawinery.com

Grayson Hills Winery
2815 Ball Road, Whitewright, TX 75491
www.graysonhillswinery.com

Homestead Winery at Denison
220 West Main Street, Denison, TX 75020
www.homesteadwinery.com

Homestead Winery at Grapevine
211 East Worth, Grapevine, TX 76051
www.homesteadwinery.com

Homestead Winery at Ivanhoe
PO Box 35, Ivanhoe, TX 75447
www.homesteadwinery.com

Inwood Estate Vineyards at Dallas
1350 Manufacturing Street #209, Dallas, TX 75207
www.inwoodwines.com

KE Cellars
4574 South Broadway, Tyler, TX 75703
www.kecellars.com

Kiepersol Estates Vineyards
3933 FM 344 East, Tyler, TX 75703
www.kiepersol.com

La Bodega Winery
Dallas/Fort Worth International Airport, Terminal A, Gate A15, Terminal D, Gate D14, DFW Airport, TX 75261
www.labodegawinery.com

La Buena Vida Vineyards at Grapevine
416 East College Street, Grapevine, TX 76051
www.labuenavida.com

La Buena Vida Vineyards at Springtown
650 Vineyard Lane, Springtown, TX 76082

Landon Winery
101 North Kentucky Street, McKinney, TX 75069
www.landonwinery.com

LightCatcher Winery
6925 Confederate Park Road/FM1886, Fort Worth, TX 76108
www.lightcatcher.com

Lone Oak Winery
2116 FM 731, Burleson, TX 76028
www.loneoakwinery.com

Lone Star Wine Cellars
103 East Virginia Street, Suite 104, McKinney, TX 75069
www.lonestarwinecellars.com

Los Pinos Ranch Vineyards
658 County Road 1334, Pittsburg, TX 75686
www.lospinosranchvineyards.com

Maydelle Country Wines
175 CR 2108, Rusk, TX 75785
www.maydellewines.com

Paris Vineyards
545 County Road 43500, Paris, TX 75462
www.parisvineyards.com

Paris Vineyards Winery on the Square
2 Clarksville Street, Paris, TX 75460
www.parisvineyards.com

Red Caboose Winery
1147 CR 1110, Meridian, TX 76665
www.redcaboosewinery.com

Red Caboose Winery at Clifton
903 South Avenue G, Clifton, TX 76634
www.redcaboosewinery.com

Red Road Vineyard and Winery
105 South Front Street, Naples, TX 75568
www.redroadvineyard.com

San Martiño Winery and Vineyard
12512 Hwy 205 North, Rockwall, TX 75087
www.sanmartinowinery.com

Savannah Winery & Bistro
574 East Highway 64, Canton, TX 75103
www.savannahwinerytx.com

St. Rose Vineyard & Winery
2170 County Road 4110, Pittsburg, TX 75686
www.strosewinery.com

Sugar Ridge Winery
353 Sugar Ridge Road, Bristol, TX
Mailing address: Ennis, TX 75119
www.sugarridgewinery.com

Sunset Winery
1535 South Burleson Boulevard, Burleson, TX 76028
www.sunsetwinery.com

Sweet Dreams Winery
2549 Anderson County Road 441, Palestine, TX 75803
www.sweetdreamswinery.com

Tara Vineyard & Winery
8603 County Road 3914, Athens, TX 75752
www.tarawinery.com

Texas Roads Winery
1455 Trade Days Blvd. (Hwy 19), Canton, TX 75103

Texas Vineyard and Smokehaus
2442 Anderson County Road 2133, Palestine, TX 75801
www.texasvineyard.org

Texoma Winery
9 Judge Carr Road, Whitewright, TX 75491
www.texomawinery.com

Times Ten Cellars
6324 Prospect Avenue, Dallas, TX 75214
www.timestencellars.com

Triple "R" Ranch & Winery
2276 County Road 125, Whitesboro, TX 76243
www.thetriplerranch.com

Valley Mills Vineyards Winery
8532 Hwy 6 North, Waco, TX 76712
www.valleymillsvineyards.com

Wales Manor
4488 County Road 408, McKinney, TX 75069
www.walesmanor.com

Weinhof Winery–Forestburg
16678 FM 455, Forestburg, TX 76239
www.weinhofwinery.com

Weinhof Winery–Muenster
123 West Division Street (Hwy 82), Box 217,
Muenster, TX 76252
www.weinhofwinery.com

Wichita Falls Vineyards & Winery
3399 Peterson Road South, Iowa Park, TX 76367
www.wichitafallsvineyardsandwinery.com

Central Region

Alamosa Wine Cellars
677 County Road 430, Bend, TX 76824
www.alamosawinecellars.com

Becker Vineyards
464 Becker Farms Road, Stonewall, TX 78671
www.beckervineyards.com

Bell Mountain Vineyards
463 Bell Mountain Road, Fredericksburg, TX 78624
www.bellmountainwine.com

Bell Springs Winery
3700 Bell Springs Road, Dripping Springs, TX 78620
www.bellspringswinery.com

The Bella Vista Ranch
3101 Mount Sharp Road, Wimberley, TX 78676
www.texasoliveoil.com

Bending Branch Winery
142 Lindner Branch Trail, Comfort, TX 78013
www.bendingbranchwinery.com

Brennan Vineyards
802 South Austin Street, PO Box 399, Comanche, TX 76442
www.brennanvineyards.com

Chisholm Trail Winery
2367 Usener Road, Fredericksburg, TX 78624
www.chisholmtrailwinery.com

Comfort Cellars Winery
723 Front Street, Comfort, TX 78013
http://www.comfortcellars.com/

Driftwood Estate Winery
4001 Elder Hill Road, Driftwood, TX 78619
www.driftwoodvineyards.com

Dry Comal Creek Vineyards
1741 Herbelin Road, New Braunfels, TX 78132
www.drycomalcreek.com

Duchman Family Winery
13308 FM 150 West, Driftwood, TX 78619
www.duchmanfamilywinery.com

Fall Creek Vineyards
1820 County Road 222, Tow, TX 78672
www.fcv.com

Fawn Crest Vineyards
1370 Westside Circle, Canyon Lake, TX 78133
www.fawncrest.com

Fiesta Vineyard and Winery
18727 West FM 580, Lometa, TX 76853
www.fiestawinery.com

Flat Creek Estate
24912 Singleton Bend East, Marble Falls, TX 78654
www.flatcreekestate.com

Fredericksburg Winery
247 West Main Street, Fredericksburg, TX 78624
www.fbgwinery.com

Georgetown Winery
715 South Main Street, Georgetown, TX 78626
www.georgetownwinery.com

Grape Creek Vineyards
10587 East Hwy 290, Fredericksburg, TX 78624
www.grapecreek.com

Inwood Estates Vineyards–The Vineyard at Florence
8711 West FM 487 Via Francesco, Florence, TX 76527
www.inwoodwines.com

Kerrville Hills Winery
3600 Fredericksburg Road, Kerrville, TX 78028
www.kerrvillehillswinery.com

La Cruz de Comal Wines, Ltd.
7405 FM 2722, Startzville, TX 78133
www.lacruzdecomalwines.com

Lost Creek Vineyard
1129 Ranch Road 2233, Sunrise Beach, TX 78643
www.lostcreekvineyard.com

McReynolds Wines
706 Shovel Mountain Road, Cypress Mill, TX 78663
www.mcreynoldswines.com

Pedernales Cellars
2916 Upper Albert Road, Stonewall, TX 78761
www.pedernalescellars.com

Perissos Vineyards and Winery
7214 Park Road 4 W, Burnet, TX 78611
www.perissosvineyards.com

Pillar Bluff Vineyards
300 County Road 111, Lampasas, TX 76550
www.pillarbluff.com

Poteet Country Winery
400 Tank Hollow Road, Poteet, TX 78065
www.poteetwine.com

Rancho Ponte Vineyard
315 Ranch Road 1376, Fredericksburg, TX 78624
www.ranchoponte.com

Rising Star Vineyards
1001 County Road 290, Rising Star, TX 76471
www.risingstarvineyards.com

Rising Star Vineyards–Salado
110 North Main, Salado, TX 76571
www.risingstarvineyards.com

Salado Creek Winery
371 South Main Street, Salado, TX 76571
www.saladoswirlandsip.com

Sandstone Cellars Winery
211 San Antonio Street, Mason, TX 76856
www.sandstonecellarswinery.com

Singing Water Vineyards
316 Mill Dam Road, Comfort, TX 78013
www.singingwatervineyards.com

Sister Creek Vineyards
1142 Sisterdale Road, Sisterdale, TX 78006
www.sistercreekvineyards.com

Solaro Estate Winery
13111 Silver Creek Road, Dripping Springs, TX 78620
www.solaroestate.com

Spicewood Vineyards
1419 County Road 409, Spicewood, TX 78669
www.spicewoodvineyards.com

Stone House Vineyard
24350 Haynie Flat Road, Spicewood, TX 78669
www.stonehousevineyard.com

Texas Hills Vineyard
878 Ranch Road 2766, Johnson City, TX 78636
www.texashillsvineyard.com

Texas Legato
2935 FM 1478, PO Box 1238, Lampasas, TX 76550
www.texaslegato.com

Three Dudes Winery
125 Old Martindale Road, San Marcos, TX 78666
www.threedudeswinery.com

Torre di Pietra Winery
10915 East Hwy 290, Fredericksburg, TX 78624
www.texashillcountrywine.com

The Vineyard at Florence
8711 FM 487, Florence, TX 76527
www.thevineyardatflorence.com

William Chris Vineyards
10352 US Hwy 290, Hye, TX 78635
www.williamchriswines.com

Wimberley Valley Winery at Driftwood
2825 Lone Man Mountain Road, Driftwood, TX 78619
www.wimberleyvalleywinery.com

Woodrose Winery
662 Woodrose Lane, Stonewall, TX 78671
www.woodrosewinery.com

Southeastern Region

Bernhardt Winery
9043 County Road 204, Plantersville, TX 77363
www.bernhardtwinery.com

Braman Winery
424 FM 774 Refugio, TX 78377
www.bramanwine.com

Bruno & George Winery
400 Messina Road, Sour Lake, TX 77659
www.brunoandgeorge.com

Circle S Vineyards
9920 Highway 90A #B-268, Sugar Land, TX 77478
www.circlesvineyards.com

Colony Cellars
35955 Richard Frey Road, Waller, TX 77484
www.colonycellars.com

Cork This! Winery
21123 Eva Street, Suite 100
www.corkthiswinery.com

Haak Vineyards & Winery Inc.
6310 Avenue T, Santa Fe, TX 77510
www.haakwine.com

Messina Hof Winery & Resort
4545 Old Reliance Road, Bryan, TX 77808
www.messinahof.com

Piney Woods Country Wines
3408 Willow Drive, Orange, TX 77632
www.pineywoodswines.com

Pleasant Hill Winery
1441 Salem Road, Brenham, TX 77833
www.pleasanthillwinery.com/

Retreat Hill Cellars
14343 Liberty Street, Montgomery, Texas 77356
www.retreathill.com

Retreat Hill Winery and Vineyard
15551 FM 362 Road, Navasota, TX 77868
www.retreathill.com

Rohan Meadery
6002 FM 2981, La Grange, TX 78945
www.rohanmeadery.com

Rosemary's Vineyard & Winery
5521 Hwy 71 East, La Grange, TX 78945
www.wines-made-in-texas.com

Saddlehorn Winery
958 FM 1948, Burton, Texas 77835
www.saddlehornwinery.com

Tehuacana Creek Vineyards & Winery
6826 East Hwy 6, Waco, TX 76705
www.wacowinery.com

Texas SouthWind Vineyard & Winery
16375 Hwy 183 South, Refugio, Texas 78377
www.texassouthwind.com

White House Winery
308 North Main Street, Conroe, TX 77301
www.whitehousewinery.com

Wimberley Valley Winery at Old Town Spring
206 Main Street, Old Town Spring, TX 77373
www.wimberleyvalleywines.com

Windy Winery
4232 Clover Road, Brenham, TX 77833
www.windywinery.net

Yepez Vineyards
12739 FM 2354, Baytown, TX 77520
www.yepezvineyard.com

Bibliography

Adams, Leon. *The Wines of America*. New York: McGraw-Hill, 1990.

Alvarez, Elizabeth Cruce, and Robert Plocheck, eds. *Texas Almanac 2008–2009*. Dallas: Dallas Morning News, 2008.

Andre, H. *A Guide to the Cultivation of the Grape-vine in Texas, and Instructions for Wine-making*. Dallas: Texas Farm and Ranch, 1889.

Blackwell, Danny Craig. "Economic Analysis of Wine Grape Production in the Texas High Plains." MA thesis, Texas Tech University, 1993.

Booz, Allen, Hamilton, Inc. "Study of the Commercial Feasibility of Grape and Wine Production on University of Texas Lands." McLean, VA, 1982.

Carlson, Paul H. *Deep Time and the Texas High Plains: History and Geology*. Lubbock: Texas Tech University Press, 2005.

Clarke, Oz. *Wine Atlas: Wine Regions of the World*. Boston: Little, Brown, 1995.

Dobson, Betty. *Fruit of the Vine*. San Francisco: Lexicos, 1988.

Doughty, Robin W. *Wildlife and Man in Texas: Environmental Change and Conservation*. College Station: Texas A&M University Press, 1983.

English, Sarah Jane. *The Wines of Texas: A Guide and History*. Austin, TX: Eakin Press, 1989.

Firstenfeld, Jane. "Merlot Made in a Goatskin?" *Wines and Vines,* December 28, 2009. www.winesandvines.com/template.cfm?section=news&content=70115.

Francaviglia, Richard V. *The Cast Iron Forest: A Natural History and Cultural History of the North American Cross Timbers.* Austin: University of Texas Press, 2000.

Giordano, Frank. *Texas Wines and Wineries.* Austin: Texas Monthly Press, 1984.

Graves, John. *From a Limestone Ledge: Some Essays and Other Ruminations about Country Life in Texas.* Houston: Gulf, 1980.

———. *Goodbye to a River: A Narrative.* New York: Vintage, 2002.

Holmes, Lucia. *The Lucia Holmes Diary, 1875–1876: The Hoo Doo War Years.* Mason, TX: Mason County Historical Commission, 2003.

Hushmann, George. *American Grape Growing and Wine Making.* New York: Orange Judd, 1883.

Johnson, Hugh, and James Halliday. *The Vintner's Art.* New York: Simon & Schuster, 1992.

Jordan, Terry G. *German Seed in Texas Soils: Immigrant Farmers in Nineteenth-Century Texas.* Austin: University of Texas Press, 1994.

Lynch, Kermit. *Adventures on the Wine Route.* New York: North Point Press, 1988.

Maguire, Jack. *Texas: Amazing but True.* Austin, TX: Eakin Press, 1984.

Marshall, Wes. *The Wine Roads of Texas.* San Antonio, TX: Maverick, 2007.

Mayle, Peter. *A Year in Provence.* New York: Vintage, 1991.

McEachern, George Ray. "A Texas Grape and Wine History." *Proceedings of the 10th Annual Oktober Gartenfest.* Texas Cooperative Extension, Winedale, Texas, 2003.

McEachern, George Ray, and Larry A. Stein. *Growing Grapes in Texas.* TAEX Bulletin 1425. College Station: Texas Agricultural Extension Service and State Employment and Training Council of Texas, 1982.

McKinney, Charles O., and John E. Crosby. "Vineyards in Texas—Past and Present." *Wines and Vines,* June 1990. http://findarticles.com/p/articles/mi_m3488/is_n6_v71/ai_9137681/.

McLeRoy, Sherrie S., and Roy E. Renfro. *Grape Man of Texas: Thomas Volney Munson and the Origins of American Viticulture.* San Francisco: Wine Appreciation Guild, 2008.

Mills, William W. *Forty Years at El Paso, 1858–1898: Recollections of War, Politics, Adventure, Events, Narratives, Sketches, etc.* Book 190 (digital file). Denton: University of North Texas Libraries, Portal to Texas History.

MKF Research. "The Economic Impact of Wine and Grapes on the State of Texas 2007." San Francisco: Division of Frank, Rimerman and Company, LLP. Updated August 2008.

———. "The Economic Impact of Wine and Grapes on the State of Texas 2009." San Francisco: Division of Frank, Rimerman and Company, LLP. Updated January 2011.

Mortensen, John A. *Blanc Du Bois: A Florida Bunch Grape for White Wine.* Circular S-340. Gainesville: Agricultural Experiment Station, Institute of Food and Agricultural Sciences, University of Florida, 1987.

Munson, Thomas V. *Foundations of American Grape Culture.* Denison, TX: T. V. Munson & Sons, 1909.

Osborne, Lawrence. *The Accidental Connoisseur.* New York: North Point Press, 2004.

Overfelt, Robert C. *The Val Verde Winery: Its Role in Texas Viticulture and Enology.* Monograph no. 75. El Paso: Texas Western Press, 1985.

Perry, Ronald L., and Hollis W. Bowen. "Feasibility Study for Grape Production in Texas." MA thesis, Texas A&M University, 1974.

Pierce, Kim. "Neal Newsom's Grapes Are Coveted by the Top Texas Wineries." *Dallas Morning News,* May 6, 2008.

Pinney, Thomas. *A History of Wine in America from the Beginnings to Prohibition.* Berkeley: University of California Press, 1989.

———. *A History of Wine in America from Prohibition to the Present.* Berkeley: University of California Press, 2005.

Pirtle, Caleb, III. *Deep Roots: A Celebration of Texas Agriculture and a People's Love of the Land.* Dallas: Dockery House, 2007.

Rose, Peter R., and Charles M. Woodruff, Jr. *Geology, Frontier History, and Selected Wineries of the Hill Country Appellation, Central Texas.* Guidebook 25. Austin, TX: Austin Geological Society, 2005

Sanchez, Eric D. "Forked Tendrils: Llano Estacado Winery and the Rise of the Modern Texas Wine Industry." MA thesis, Texas Tech University, 1996.

Sommers, Brian J. *The Geography of Wine: How Landscapes, Cultures, Terroir, and the Weather Make a Good Drop.* New York: Plume, 2008.

Spearing, Darwin. *Roadside Geology of Texas.* Missoula, MO: Mountain Press, 2005.

Stephens, A. Ray, and William M. Holmes. *Historical Atlas of Texas.* Norman: University of Oklahoma Press, 1989.

Taber, George M. *Judgment of Paris: California vs. France and the Historic 1976 Paris Tasting That Revolutionized Wine.* New York: Scribner, 2005.

Thompson-Anderson, Terry. *Texas on the Plate.* Fredericksburg, TX: Shearer, 2002.

Timmons, Wilbert H. *El Paso: A Borderlands History.* El Paso: Texas Western Press, 1990.

Wilbarger, J. W. *Indian Depredations in Texas.* Austin, TX: Eakin Press, 1985. First published 1870.

Wilson, James E. *Terroir: The Role of Geology, Climate, and Culture in the Making of French Wines.* Berkeley: University of California Press, 1998.

Winters, Ronald L. "Origin and History of the Black Spanish Grape." Hawkins, TX: Fairhaven Vineyards, 2009. www.fairhavenvineyards.com/information/research.html.

Woodruff, Charles M., Jr., Peter R. Rose, and James W. Sansom, Jr. *The Hill Country Appellation: A Geologic Tour of Selected Vineyards and Wineries of Central Texas.* Guidebook 18. Austin, TX: Austin Geological Society, 1998.

Illustrations

Index

About the Author

Russell D. Kane divides his time between Houston and Fredericksburg, Texas. A technical writer whose research spans three decades and has garnered two awards for writing excellence, he has covered Texas wines and cuisine since 1998 and now blogs on the subject of Texas wine at VintageTexas.com.